e ever wondered about the sound of one hand clapping (or if you~~~~~~~~~~~~~~the *concept* of Hanoi Rocks), this book will make you ext~~~~~~~~~~~~

:k Klosterman, author of *Killing Yourself to Li~~~~~~~~~~~~~~~ Puffs*

rn-man has revivified the practice of air guitar ~~~~~~~ orating than suppressing the sheer schmuckiness of the whole art jörn is a madman, of course, best known for his cacad-arpeggios, but he is not in denial. He lays bare le artist-as-schmuck/schmuck-as-artist bi-at Greil Marcus has devoted so many pages nstructing. He is the past of air guitar future. My man!"
Hickey, author of *Air Guitar:*
s on Art & Democracy

"At long last, after years
of neglect, the
noble art of air
guitar has its
own what-
ever-the-best-book-of-
all-time-about-painting is."
—David Rees, author of
Get Your War On

"Few men can mix the tragic nature of the male episode with
that extraordinary super-antidote to the pedestrian that is
air guitar. Björn, however, is such a man.
Read this book. Understand."
—Zac "The Magnet" Monro,
Air Guitar World Champion 2001, 2002

If I may paraphrase Elvis Costello—
writing about air guitar is like
choreography about blueprints.
—Björn Türoque

TO AIR IS

One Man's Quest to Beco

HÜMAN

e World's Greatest Air Guitarist

BTÖRN TÜROQUE

with Dan Crane

RIVERHEAD BOOKS
NEW YORK

THE BERKLEY PUBLISHING GROUP
Published by the Penguin Group
Penguin Group (USA) Inc.
375 Hudson Street, New York, New York 10014, USA
Penguin Group (Canada), 90 Eglinton Avenue East, Suite 700, Toronto, Ontario
M4P 2Y3, Canada (a division of Pearson Penguin Canada Inc.)
Penguin Books Ltd., 80 Strand, London WC2R 0RL, England
Penguin Group Ireland, 25 St. Stephen's Green, Dublin 2, Ireland
(a division of Penguin Books Ltd.)
Penguin Group (Australia), 250 Camberwell Road, Camberwell, Victoria 3124, Australia
(a division of Pearson Australia Group Pty. Ltd.)
Penguin Books India Pvt. Ltd., 11 Community Centre, Panchsheel Park, New
Delhi—110 017, India
Penguin Group (NZ), cnr Airborne and Rosedale Roads, Albany, Auckland 1310, New
Zealand (a division of Pearson New Zealand Ltd.)
Penguin Books (South Africa) (Pty.) Ltd., 24 Sturdee Avenue, Rosebank, Johannesburg
2196, South Africa

Penguin Books Ltd., Registered Offices: 80 Strand, London WC2R 0RL, England

Copyright © 2006 by Dan Crane
Cover and stepback design by Benjamin Gibson
Cover and stepback author photos by Susannah Sayler
Page 305 constitutes an extension of this copyright page.
Book design and interior illustrations by Benjamin Gibson

First Riverhead trade paperback edition: August 2006

Library of Congress Cataloging-in-Publication Data

Türoque, Björn.
    To air is human : one man's quest to become the world's greatest air guitarist /
Björn Türoque ; with Dan Crane.
       p. cm.
    ISBN 1-59448-210-1
    1. Türoque, Björn. 2. Rock musicians—United States—Biography. 3. Air guitar.
4. Rock music—Humor. I. Title.

ML419.T88T6 2006
787.87092—dc22
[B]   2006044040

PRINTED IN THE UNITED STATES OF AMERICA

10 9 8 7 6 5 4 3 2 1

For Jane Air

MARSHALL STACKS

TUNING PEGS

NUT

FRETBOARD

BRIDGE

STRINGS

PLECTRUM

STRAP

TONE/VOLUME KNOBS

1/4" CABLE INPUT

PICKUP TOGGLE SWITCH

PICKUPS

PICK GUARD

Figure A: Air Guitar Anatomy

CONTENTS

Part 3: Carry On My Wayward Son

Author's Note:

I didn't do all this so that I could write
a book about it. Hell, the book wasn't even
my idea. No, I wanted to conquer air guitar
for the same reason George Leigh Mallory
sought to climb Mount Everest in 1924:
"It was there."

—*BJ*

Prologue

For art to exist, for any sort of aesthetic activity or perception to exist, a certain physiological precondition is indispensable: intoxication.

—Friedrich Nietzsche

OULU, FINLAND August 29, 2003. I am at the after-party in a large old house in the middle of the forest, crawling around on a table, drunk. I'm not sure how I got here, though I vaguely recall sharing a rapidly diminishing bottle of whiskey with Zac as we stumbled through the woods. Underneath my sweater, the words "Make Air, Not War" are writ large on my bare chest in indelible marker. I am half singing, half mumbling, "Get your hands off of my woman, mutherfu . . ." when a guy who looks blurrily familiar taps me on the head several times. After a few seconds of tapping, I finally look up at him. He is upside down. Actually, there are two of him, upside down, telling me, "Mr. Monro is about to throw up. We need to go."

I roll off the table onto the floor and stumble outside. No sign of Mr. Monro.

The next thing I know, I am inside the Grilleriina, a foul-smelling, fluorescently lit all-night Finnish hamburger stand. The walls are white and bare, and everyone is smoking. The air is a thick, juicy grease-alcohol-and-smoke sandwich. Zac Monro is there. He doesn't appear to have just thrown up—in fact, he looks just fine. He's devouring a plate of fries lathered in what might be Thousand Island dressing. Or throw-up. It's hard to tell.

Hanoi Rocks' lead guitarist, Andy McCoy, and his wife, Angela (who, earlier in the evening in her role as air guitar judge, gave me a 5.9 out of a possible 6), are also there grabbing a late-night snack. They look like they just crawled out of a limo after chasing a lethal dose of heroin with a bottle of grain alcohol. Andy—a gristly, raisin-faced shell of a man wearing a red cowboy hat and a black scarf with white skulls on it—is draped on Angela's shoulder, clinging to her like a slice of cheese melting over a burger. Angela, wearing large dark sunglasses covering most of her face, looks slightly less undead than her husband.

Angela chats it up with the patrons as I attempt to order some fries from the colossal, surly Finnish woman behind the counter.

"Fun stuff tonight," slurs Angela. "Former air champ right here. He's awesome. I haven't seen him, but I've heard."

"I am quite good," says Zac.

They hug.

"You gotta show me. I was impressed tonight, but I was not floored."

"That's because I wasn't playing," says Zac.

Then she recognizes me. "You were . . ." she burbles. "You're . . . you—you were . . . air guitar . . ." Angela is rapidly losing the ability to speak in complete sentences. "You . . . you were really sexy! I *liked* you. You were . . ." She is wobbling right and left as Andy, who has apparently just awoken from a momentary coma, chimes in.

"Yeah, great. Really good," he bobs, attempting to focus, then grabs me by the back of the head and pulls me to within inches of his wizened, leathery visage.

"Hey!" he shouts at me. He is a dragon, exhaling fiery toxins of alcohol and narcotics in my face. He pauses to slowly look me over, and then asks in a frail, gravelly voice, "Are you . . . gypsy?"

Angela interrupts. "I tried, I voted for you, but that Asian guy . . . he was—" She is suddenly distracted by a plate of food.

Andy steadies himself by wrapping his left arm around me, and then repeats, his hand pointing at me accusatorily, *"Are you a gypsy?"*

I am scrambling to figure out the right answer. Is he speaking in code? If I *am* a gypsy (which, to my knowledge, I'm not), is that good or bad? His face is sagging, his voice agitated. He's got a little puddle of drool hanging from the left side of his lower lip. His eyes are vacant black holes of drug-addled madness.

" 'Cause *I'm* gypsy," he says, flopping his right hand against his chest for emphasis. He pauses and looks deep into my eyes—past my eyes, into my soul—as if he is about to impart his last words, some nugget of dying rock star wisdom.

"We were just in LA, y'know," he continues. "The Foo Fighters . . . those guys . . . those are *nice* guys." He shakes his head back and forth, recalling what nice guys the Foo Fighters were. And then he drives it home: "*Really* nice guys."

Why Andy McCoy, lead guitarist from Hanoi Rocks, is telling me about what nice guys the Foo Fighters are, I have no idea. And who cares? It's four thirty in the morning and I'm drunk, hanging out in a hamburger shack in northern Finland after the Air Guitar World Championships with an *actual* guitarist from a legendary eighties hair metal band.

Sure, he's drooling on me, but in my own way, I am living the dream.

One Man's Quest
to Become the World's
Greatest Air Guitarist

Part 1:

Welcome

to the

Jungle

Chapter One: Björn Is Born

In music, as in everything, the disappearing moment of experience is the firmest reality.
—Benjamin Boretz, *Perspectives on Musical Aesthetics*

first heard about the Air Guitar World Championships in 2002, after an Irish friend of mine named Cedric Devitt returned to New York City from Finland. He had traveled thousands of miles to a city just below the Arctic Circle, called Oulu (pronounced *oh-LU*), to find out what the battle for the title of Greatest Air Guitarist in the World was all about. He's never been the same since. In Finland, he acquired the stage name Aer Lingus and entered the competition, playing to a Sebadoh song titled "Brand New Love." He came in fourth place. That's fourth place *in the world*. And he had never even played the air guitar. I had hardly imagined that a world of competitive air guitar even existed, but once I heard about it, I instantly understood its brilliance.

Upon his return, Lingus (as we referred to him for weeks afterwards) regaled us with tales of jam-packed bars and outdoor stadiums full of fans, mystical training rituals, late nights of inebriated iniquity—and it sounded a lot like the rock star Shangri-la in which I had always imagined myself living. I envied Aer Lingus, as anyone would.

Lingus told me that he and a friend (Kriston Rucker, aka DJ Teddy Ruckspin) had gone to Finland not only to compete but also to license "air rights" from the Finns in order to launch competitions in the United States. Why the Finns had the exclusive on competitive air guitar was difficult to understand. Later, I found out the Finns also had the monopoly on the international sauna,[1] wife carrying, and mobile phone tossing competitions as well.

What little history is known of the annual air guitar event is as follows: competitions began happening in Oulu in 1996, based around the Oulu Music Video Festival, and the concept for an air guitar competition grew out of a fictional Finnish civil war that required "air guitar forces" to mend the wounds of the divided country. The competition, from its inception, adopted the core principle that if one is busy playing the air guitar, he or she cannot simultaneously hold a gun, and therefore air guitar will inevitably lead to world peace.

Keep in mind the average annual temperature of Oulu, Finland, is thirty-six degrees Fahrenheit.

In just a couple of years after its inauguration, the Air Guitar

---

[1]The International Sauna Competitions began in 1999 in Heinola, Finland, with the following rules: The sauna temperature starts at 230 degrees Fahrenheit and a half liter of water is poured on the stove every 30 seconds; to prove they are still among the living, competitors must regularly provide thumbs-up signals to the judges; and the last one to run from the oven wins. In 2002, 10,000 spectators are reported to have witnessed the event. The men's winner was Leo Pusa, lasting just over 12 minutes—it was his third consecutive victory. The women's champ was Annikka Peltonen, who roasted for an inhuman 13:32.

World Championships rapidly generated tons of international press and spawned national "feeder" competitions in countries like Belgium, Australia, and Germany—proof positive that the phenomenon of air guitar is universal, an inherent atavistic response to hearing music, as natural as dancing, singing along, having sex, or, for advanced listeners, air drumming. But after seven years of international competitions, only one American had ever entered, and lost.

Though Lingus and Ruckspin firmly believed, as I do, that air guitar was actually *invented* in the United States,[2] they weren't really sure if anyone would show up for a competition, but they thought it would be amusing, and might make for a good TV show or documentary. So they plunked down a hefty sum of their own money in order to bring competitive air guitar to our shores and change the lives of many Americans, including myself, forever.[3]

It was announced that the First Annual East Coast Regional Air Guitar Championship was to be held at a rock club above a strip bar called the Pussycat Lounge in downtown New York City. The winner of the East Coast semifinals would be flown to Los Angeles

---

[2]A young Jimi Hendrix, so poor he couldn't afford a guitar, is reported to have practiced on a broom for nearly two years until he could afford an electric guitar. So we can surmise that air guitar is likely as old as rock 'n' roll itself—perhaps older.

[3]According to Ruckspin: "The Air Guitar World Championships (AGWC) in Finland has established itself as the undisputed international governing body of air guitar over the past decade. In order for any national championship to be recognized by them (meaning they will accept your winner as a contestant for the world title), a national event team must secure a contract with the AGWC. As such, US Air Guitar (USAG) has agreed to pay a not insignificant rights fee to the AGWC every year, has agreed to abide by their rules, has agreed to pay for our champion to travel to Finland to compete, and has agreed to respect the ideology of air guitar as defined by the AGWC."

to battle against the winner of the West Coast semifinals, and that victor would be flown to Finland to vie for the international crown. I've played guitar and bass in bands all my life, and now here was a chance to play what would likely be a crowded gig, get some free drinks, and be judged on my merits as a rock star—all without having to carry any gear to or from the venue.

On the US Air Guitar Web site, I learned the rules of a standard air guitar competition, as handed down by the officiating air guitar body in Oulu. I needed a stage name, a sixty-second song clip, and an air guitar. I already had one out of three. No props were allowed, though I could use a plectrum (or pick). No backup band was allowed, but I could have an air roadie. There would be two rounds, each consisting of a sixty-second performance. In round one, each contestant plays a song of his or her own choosing. Performances are scored on a 4.0—6.0 scale, like Olympic figure skating. Scores are based on technical ability, stage presence and Airness—a term defined by USAG as "the extent to which a performance transcends the imitation of a real guitar and becomes an art form in and of itself." The five best air guitarists of round one, as determined by the judges' scores, move forward to round two: the compulsory round. During this round, each of the five competitors must wow the judges with their own interpretation of a "surprise" track preselected by the competition organizers.

For several weeks after I had made the decision to enter the competition, two things held my brain's attention and fueled my chronic insomnia: my song and my stage name. I seriously considered doing Kermit the Frog's rendition of "The Rainbow Connection," which is, technically, played on a banjo. My plan was to wear a giant googly-eyed frog's-head mask that I just happened to have in my closet and begin the song in earnest—starting off slow, then switching into a seizure of rocked-out hysteria, as if Iron Maiden were playing the song instead of a Muppet. This concept was mocked as "probably lame" and "a little stupid" by my girlfriend and other friends. The other top song contender was Blur's 1997 hit, "Song 2." With its potent mix of quiet verses (played on what sounds like a ukulele) and raucous choruses (drenched in distorted power chords), all topped with the internationally crowd-pleasing lyric "Woo hoo!" how could I lose? I settled on "Song 2."

With my song decided, it was time to come up with a stage name. One day while instant-messaging with my girlfriend (whom I will call Jane Air) about the competition, she suggested the name Bjorn Turock. It immediately resonated. There was the obvious pun, and I am a sucker for puns; but more than that, the name Bjorn conjured Swedish tennis pro Bjorn Borg, and a tennis racquet often serves as one's first air guitar. Borg's Swedish descent was another perfect association since (in my mind) Sweden was practically Finland. I already had an alter ego of sorts at the time—his name was Jean-Luc Retard, my nom de guerre as bassist and occasional singer for a fake French band I played in called Les Sans Culottes. I decided that as a nod to Jean-Luc, Bjorn should be of both Swedish *and* French descent, so I embellished the last name, making it Bjorn *Turoque*. My nom d'air.

Then, as any metal band worth its weight in cocaine would, I added the double umlauts.[4]

And thus Björn Türoque was born.

I began to wonder who this alternate me—who Björn—would be, exactly. In a traditionally Freudian analysis, I imagined Björn as pure id: uncut aggression mixed with the urge for instant gratification in the forms of sex, drugs, and rock and roll. In Björn's eyes, I would function as the Freudian superego: knowing right from wrong, having decent morals and whatnot, but overall a little dull. The air guitar, in turn, would act as the ego: an intermediary between Björn and me. It would allow Björn (the id) to "rock out with his cock out" (Freud called this "cathexsis"), and notify me (the superego) when it was time to leave the groupies behind, behave myself, and go home.

I looked forward to getting to know this Türoque guy.

As plans for the competition heated up, I found out that a few of my friends had also decided to enter. Friends competing against each other didn't seem like it would be a problem until another expatriate Irishman (one who fully lived up to his cultural stereotype) started insisting on several drunken occasions that he'd *invented* air guitar and that I had zero chance of win-

[4]Blue Öyster Cult is said to have been the first band to use the *gratuitous umlaut*, or "röck döt" (gratuitous since the umlauts did not function to alter the pronunciation, and were grammatically incorrect), doing so at the suggestion of an influential rock critic named Richard Meltzer, who also wrote the lyrics to BÖC's "Burnin' for You." After that, gratuitous umlauts became *dë rigueür*, mostly in the metal realm, with bands like Motörhead, Mötley Crüe, and Queensrÿche. The practice was ultimately parodied in the title of the fake rockumentary *This Is Spïnal Tap*, which cleverly placed the umlaut over the consonant *ñ* instead of over a vowel.

ning. He sparked a fierce rivalry between us, and, though I was the one who should have been out for *his* blood because of an incident several months prior involving him, some Vicodin, and a broken lamp in my apartment, he was relentless. He came up with his all-too-apt stage name, Air-Do-Well, and vowed to destroy Björn Türoque—by any means necessary.

NEW YORK CITY June 6, 2003. It's the day of the competition. I am hard at work as an educational software producer. Lately my job consists primarily of e-mailing and instant-messaging friends, and occasionally (after a cup or two of free mediocre coffee) making sure things are running smoothly on the Web site that administers my company's software. For the past several months I have somehow managed to convey to my overlords that I am really busy, and they continue to overpay me. It's as good as an office job gets.

I had done a little Web research on past air guitar events, but it isn't until today that I decide to look at a video of last year's winner of the World Championships. It turns out that two-time world champion Zac "The Magnet" Monro had ascended to air guitar fame by playing none other than Blur's "Song 2"—the very song I had spent at least twenty grueling minutes practicing, and that I'm planning to play tonight.

In a panic, I leave work early and bike home to troll through my CD collection hoping to find a replacement song. I have irrationally come to the conclusion that if I play Zac Monro's winning song, the judges—who obviously have the same access to the Internet as I do, and must have, I reason, looked at past winning performances—will surely subtract points for the lack of originality in my song choice.

I am probably overthinking this.

Should I return to "The Rainbow Connection"? I open up the closet and stare at the giant googly-eyed frog's head on the floor. The googly eyes stare back. Our staring contest continues for what seems like minutes until I abruptly shut the door.

In my drawer of CDs, among the Led Zeppelin, the whiny indie rock, and Jane Air's *Best of George Michael* (double album), I find Hüsker Dü's seminal late-era punk masterpiece, *Warehouse: Songs and Stories.* I went through a big Hüsker Dü phase during my first year of college, a time when everything I was feeling seemed entirely in sync with the lyrics of their once-suicidal front man, Bob Mould. I imagine I'd be seeing a lot of metal tonight, so why not go for an obscure eighties punk song? Plus, Hüsker Dü = dual röck döts![5]

I load the CD in my computer and scan through the tracks, finally arriving on what seems like a song with the right fervor and ferocity. Also, there's a cool pick slide sound in it that I can envision myself doing onstage. I begin practicing.

Jane Air gets home from work, and I play her Hüsker Dü's "Ice Cold Ice." She's not impressed. Then again, she thinks Pantera is a shampoo. She thinks I should stick with the Blur song, but I am adamant that it's a huge mistake. She helps me pull together an ap-

[5]Even Hüsker Dü's umlauts were gratuitous. They named themselves after a Danish game called Husker Du, which means "Do you remember?" but added metal umlauts to make it look edgier.

propriate post-punk costume consisting of a black-and-white checkered shirt, a thin white leather zipper tie (recently acquired on eBay), and a white headband on which I write with thick black permanent marker "Björn Türoque."

"To me it says Ric Ocasek, not Hüsker Dü," I grumble to Jane Air. But my time is up. I am due at the club in half an hour. I throw the clothes into a brown paper grocery bag and hop into a cab to battle traffic as a hot summer's day sweats its way towards a hot summer evening in New York City. Jane Air will meet me there later, closer to showtime.

The Pussycat Lounge sits two blocks south of where the World Trade Center used to be. As the cab careens down Manhattan's West Side Highway towards the club, I think about the last time I trekked southward along the West Side for a performance. My fake French band, Les Sans Culottes, used to play regular gigs at Windows on the World, the bar on top of the World Trade Center. I always loved playing there. To look out onto a crowd of people dancing to your music, and then look through the windows beyond to see Manhattan's nighttime skyline from more than a hundred stories up was as close to "the top" as our band would likely ever get. I had watched the towers fall from the roof of my building on Twenty-fourth street, about forty blocks north. As they stood burning and then each collapsed, I thought, those are *my* buildings. This is *my* city. I have memories in there.

I've never been to the Pussycat Lounge. There were conflicting reports that the venue was either *above* a strip club or in fact *was* a strip club. It turns out there are two venues connected via a dark staircase: a small, dingy music space upstairs and a seedy strip club on the ground floor. It seems almost too perfect, in a way, that while quintessentially male rock star fantasies will be enacted on a stage above, strippers will be making their living exploiting men's sexual fantasies below.

I arrive on time, but nothing is really happening yet. I drop my stuff off in the dressing room and then take a look around. There's a tiny stage, a slightly larger area for the audience, and a narrow bar along one wall. The room doesn't appear at all big enough to hold the crowd I am imagining will show up. Satellite news trucks are parked outside, and guys with video cameras the size of Volkswagen Beetles on their shoulders are wandering in looking for a spot to set up. Apparently that morning Howard Stern announced he was coming down to check it out. CNN is reportedly "in the house." The lurid smell of a media orgy is in the air. Speaking of lurid, the strip club downstairs is already open for business. I grab my friend Ralph (who will be competing tonight under the stage name Rufus Sewer), and we head downstairs to have a beer while things get cooking.

The music is loud, and the strippers are anything but a turn-on. They stroll along the bar talking nonchalantly to the club's low-life patrons, exuding about as much sexuality as a bowl of stale bar snacks. This is not a strip joint for high-rolling Wall Streeters—it's your average dive bar, with the added bonus of naked ladies. Ralph and I try to make conversation, but the bar is too loud and the strippers all look like they're living on a steady diet of cheap vodka and crack. It's distracting. We each take a few sips of our beers and then decide to head back upstairs.

I poke my head outside. There's already a line halfway down the block, and I am starting to get a sense of just how packed this place is going to get. As I walk back upstairs, I pass a sign posted on the wall:

ABSOLUTELY NO GUITARS
PERMITTED BEYOND
THIS POINT

Upstairs, in the dressing room area, cameras are everywhere. You can't move three feet without walking into a lens. Other contestants start showing up. One girl, a skinny blond chick wearing a sweatshirt with cutoff sleeves, knee-high argyle socks, and a tennis skirt stands in the corner as her friend paints something on her forehead.

"Does this look like a vagina?" she asks. Nobody answers. Having just seen some *live* vaginas downstairs, I can say definitively no. It looks to me more like the scar from a botched lobotomy, or the imprint of a melting Choco Taco. Her stage name? Snatchface. Another girl is wearing a skintight silver bodysuit that's cut very low in the chest area, with a high collar in the back and a matching cape. She fills it out well in all the right places, and the whole ensemble exudes eroticism. It worries me. Sex could easily play well tonight.

In the corner, a guy sits, looking mysterious, with signature white iPod earbuds plugged into his ears, practicing along.

I go into the bathroom to change into my Björn outfit. Like Dr. David Banner becoming the Hulk (minus the green makeup and the lacerated clothing), I transform into Björn. When I return, metamorphosed into a rock-god-to-be, the room is packed with enough reporters to cover a Floridian hurricane.

Cans of warm Rheingold beer are provided to get the air circulating. Björn is on his third when Jeanne Moos from CNN approaches him for an interview. "You're Candy Crowley, right?" he asks.

"No, that's another CNN reporter." She seems slightly annoyed. (A few days later, watching CNN, I realize that Candy Crowley is their *other* heavyset female reporter.)

Türoque and Moos do a short interview where he answers some FAQAGs (Frequently Asked Questions about Air Guitar) like:

CNN: How long have you been playing the air guitar?

Björn: All my life. Maybe longer. My father was an air guitarist, so I think his sperm—wait, can I say sperm on CNN?

CNN: Do you actually know how to play the guitar?

Björn: Yes; in fact, I've been playing guitar for over twenty years. I suspect this might hurt my chances of winning— like, I may know *too much*.

CNN: How do you train for such an event?

Björn: Air guitar training really begins and ends with a lot of drinking. [Björn takes a sip of his beer.] As you can see, I'm still training even at the last minute.

Björn speaks to reporters from CBS and Howard Stern's show, a guy from Japan, another from Germany, and some lady from a newspaper in Texas. He is already a media slut, and he's only just begun.

Air-Do-Well, Björn's self-proclaimed nemesis, shows up late and looks like he hasn't slept in two days. Turns out he hasn't. He's been up all night partying. His eyes are vacant and bloodshot. It's totally rock-and-roll—but he can hardly stand up, and thus he is mentally eliminated from Björn's list of competitors. Ralph, now Rufus Sewer, dons a long scarf and a black Gaultier jacket that he *stole* from Mick Jagger's closet at a party a few years back.[6] He does a mean Jagger impersonation at karaoke—wielding the scarf in a mock-Mick chicken dance—and although Mick did play guitar, he was never known for his wailing leads, so Björn doesn't consider Rufus, his scarf, or his jacket worth worrying about.

A guy known as Air Raid claims he is going to light his kerosene-soaked arm on fire midperformance. *Kerosene?* It's only been a few months since ninety-six people were trampled and burned to death at the Great White concert in Rhode Island, so it's safe to assume he's making an ironic reference to that incident, and that he's joking.

The silent guy from the corner has changed into a red kimono. He's all business.

Björn is tossing back Rheingolds like Gatorade when Jane Air arrives.

Jane seems embarrassed for me. She starts flirting with one of the judges—the keyboardist from the band Dopo Yume—whom it

---

[6] I've been sworn to secrecy as to the details of this story.

turns out she knows and once discussed taking "violin lessons" from. I can only hope she's buttering him up.

Lance "The Shred" Kasten boasts that despite his old age (he's forty-one and refers to himself as "the Geritol competitor"), he stays in shape by playing air guitar every day. He claims to have been the undefeated air guitar champion of his home state of Maryland in the eighties. I am not sure I believe him (and even if I did, who gives a shit about Maryland?), but the more I hear, the more the thrill of victory seems suddenly, urgently desirable. International press, cute girls in tight outfits, and free beer—I realize this is better than any gig I've ever played. I could get used to this.

We are all instructed to line up backstage in the order predetermined by the organizers. The show is running late, and the more-than-sold-out crowd (more than three hundred people were reportedly turned away), sandwiched into the claustrophobic club, is getting rowdy. They are chanting, *"Start the fucking show,"* until finally the emcee, a comedian named Christian Finnegan, attempts to calm them down.

"The show is going to start in about ten minutes," he says.

The audience instantly pummels him with boos and taunts of "You suck." They are now out for blood. As I stand crammed against the wall on the side of the room, I can see someone hanging up a US Air Guitar banner onstage. This is all very last-minute.

Finally the emcee gets back on stage and says, "I just have one question. . . ."

"Start the fucking show!" someone shouts.

"Are you ready for some serious rock?"

The hungry audience roars, and the first air guitarist is served

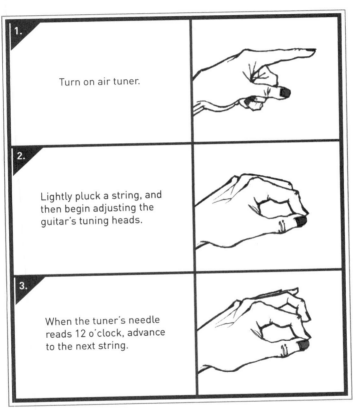

1. Turn on air tuner.

2. Lightly pluck a string, and then begin adjusting the guitar's tuning heads.

3. When the tuner's needle reads 12 o'clock, advance to the next string.

Figure 1. How to achieve proper air guitar tuning

Note: If air guitaring to a song from the punk rock genre, ignore steps 1-3.

up for their consumption. "He's a financial analyst by day and a wacky lunatic by night. Please welcome your first contestant, Mr. Pauly Legs." Legs has a mustache and a receding hairline, and looks as if he might even be older than geriatric "The Shred." As he gets onstage in his AC/DC shirt and jeans, he is instantly booed. He tunes up and then his song, "Shoot to Thrill," starts playing, and he begins jogging in place, nervously gripping his fists like he's holding handfuls of loose change. I can tell this is probably the most exciting and terrifying moment of Pauly Legs' life. With a high kick, Pauly Legs quickly wins the crowd over, as they are eager to see something—anything—interesting happen. He finishes with a healthy round of applause and cheers, and is followed by The Goober.

The Goober—a guy shaped like a former frat boy who still drinks as much as he did in college but has since stopped playing football—wears a black wig and a blue T-shirt, and has a cigar butt in his mouth. He looks like an escapee from *Heavy Metal Parking Lot* who only moments ago finished tokin' up in his Camaro.[7] His song is Zepp's "Good Times Bad Times," and in the pause right before Page's raging solo, The Goober stomps on his air distortion pedal, sending his wig flying off as he continues jamming as hard as he possibly can. He's intense. I like The Goober.

One of the reporters who interviewed me earlier backstage is up next. She's from CBS's *The Early Show*, and her name is Melinda Murphy. She has no stage name. She plays to Avril Lavigne's "Sk8er

---

[7] *Heavy Metal Parking Lot* is a fifteen-minute video shot in the parking lot of a stadium prior to a 1986 Judas Priest concert in Maryland. It features numerous mulleted dudes and their frizzy-haired ladies drinking, playing air guitar, and screaming the mantra "Priest fuckin' rules!" It is perhaps the finest historical document of the heavy metal era.

Boi," and it's painfully obvious she's been asked by her producers to cover the event and, consequently, to compete. Wearing a zebra top and leather pants that are tight in all the *wrong* places, she fails miserably. The vengeful crowd loudly derides her, and her air guitar gradually shrinks until by the end of the song it looks as if she is playing a miniature air mandolin. Murphy's sixty seconds culminate with her covering her face in shame and cowering offstage.

A few more people go up, and they too get booed. The crowd is merciless. Air Raid, the guy who earlier boasted of planning to light his arm on fire, *really does try* to light his arm on fire. There's a spark and a brief plume of smoke, but thankfully his arm quickly extinguishes itself.

Snatchface takes the stage in her skimpy outfit and bounces like a perky cheerleader to Hole's "Rock Star." The way Snatchface moves her hands, I envision her less playing guitar than kneading air bread or giving someone an air back rub. She prances around the stage smiling, full of enthusiasm, but she's falling on her ass. She too gets a shitstorm of boos, to which the emcee responds, "Come on, now, this woman painted a vagina on her face—that's worth the price of admission!"

My friend Ralph—now Rufus Sewer—goes next, totally living up to the title of the song he is playing: Iggy Pop's "Loose." He twirls his long white scarf in his right hand and does a lot of high kicks with his left foot, bringing, as the emcee announces after Rufus' performance, "some much-needed sexuality to the floor tonight." He's also the first onstage tonight to conjure an actual rock star rather than just a fan.

Rufus is followed by Super Julie, she of the skintight silver bodysuit and ample chest. Super Julie has chosen to play "Fame"—not the song by David Bowie, but the discoed-out theme from the musical and film of the same name. Super Julie stands in all her spangled glory with her eyes closed, halfheartedly playing along and barely moving onstage. When the solo arrives,[8] she seductively kneels on the floor, dangling her breasts like forbidden fruit over those in the front row. Despite all that, she is still getting booed. When the chorus chimes back in, I am tempted to shout, "Lame!" over "Fame," but I stop myself. I'll be up there getting ridiculed momentarily.

Then Air-Do-Well lurches onto the stage. "Debaser" by the Pixies starts playing, and despite his lack of sleep, Air-Do-Well musters the enthusiasm. It's just that he appears to be playing a different song from what everyone is hearing. At one point, he looks as if he's repeatedly trying to pull-start a lawnmower with a great deal of frustration. Then he changes his approach and looks like he is sawing a large tree trunk in an air lumberjacking competition. He's incredibly focused—most likely on remaining standing—but I can tell he knows he's bombing. Even so, the crowd lauds his effort, and he is sent offstage with effusive applause.

Now my time has come to rawk. "His mother is a personal friend of one of the members of Styx.[9] Please say *domo arigato* to Mr. Björn Türoque!" announces the emcee, and I hit the stage like a young welterweight entering the ring, but my song volume is way too low. I can barely hear it. The audience doesn't seem to hear it at all. Ap-

[8]Yes, the theme from *Fame* has a solo. It's actually not bad.

[9]I am ashamed to say this is true.

parently when I edited "Ice Cold Ice" down to sixty seconds, I exported it with a low volume, and now the live rock and roll simulation is all too real: just like I've seen so many guitarists do at shows, I keep gesturing towards the soundman to turn up the monitors, but all I get is a shrug in return. My pick slide punctuated by a high kick is solid, and because I do know how to play guitar, my accuracy is for the most part dead-on, but I strum as hard as I can and it's basically all fury—very little sound. The crowd is somewhat enthusiastic, but I walk off the stage feeling shame upon the House of Türoque. It's over, I am sure.

I squeeze through the crowd, and Jane Air gives me a hug. She attempts to console me, and I attempt to get to the bar for another beer. Then I look up as the emcee announces, "Ladies and gentlemen, he's trained in the Suzuki Method and is a master of the Asian Fury technique. Mr. C-Diddy!" The mysterious one with the red kimono takes the stage. He opens his robe to reveal a Hello Kitty breastplate fastened to his chest with binder clips, and a set of tight red leggings with dragons on them. He looks serious. Deadly serious. Someone in the audience shouts, "Awwww shit!" and I turn and raise both eyebrows at Jane.

C-Diddy then tears into the most explosive performance of the evening by far. The crowd goes completely haywire. This is what they have been waiting for—speed, precision, ferocity—and that's just his tongue. His hands are moving like twin Tasmanian Devils, nearly imperceptible to the human eye. His arms snap to punctuate every symphonic note of Extreme's "Play with Me"—a song that sounds like Mozart wrote it, if Mozart had played guitar in a hair metal band in 1989. C-Diddy strums the guitar with one hand and puts his other hand to his ear, listening for the cheers of his adoring fans—and this goads the audience into cheering even louder. He builds the song to a spiraling climax, pulling at his air guitar strings like musical taffy—extruding every possible note until there is simply nothing left. He ends by whipping his left hand into the air in the form of the classic rock music devil horns. The audience is unhinged. Awe has been inspired.

In the unenviable position of having to follow C-Diddy, another guy named Dan (without a stage name) plays to a Foo Fighters song and fares well, particularly considering what's preceded him. Then The Shred takes his turn to kick some ass. Brushing the rust off the moves in his ancient arsenal, Shred goes behind the neck, plays with his teeth, and indeed shreds with a degree of technical prowess heretofore unseen this evening. I've all but given up at this point, but Jane Air and I wait as the first-round scores are tallied. I feel certain that my brief air guitar career has already come and gone. Then the top scorers of round one are announced: Rufus Sewer, The Goober, Super Julie, The Shred, Björn Türoque, and C-Diddy will advance to round two. I am shocked—not only that I made it, but that Super Julie did as well. I'm also excited for a second chance to prove I've got the chops.

Our preselected compulsory song is "Bullet with Butterfly Wings" by Smashing Pumpkins. The Goober is nowhere to be found, and we later discover he already went home. So the five of us are called to the stage to hear the song one time through. Then, in ascending score order from the first round, we return one by one to perform. I stand at the side of the stage as the aggressive audience boos Rufus, Super Julie, and The Shred. It's a lion's den. They don't want any of us—they just want to see the Hello Kitty guy again. I leap onto the stage, and when the song moves from the slow quiet section and explodes into the raucous chorus, I rip open my shirt, buttons spraying the audience like urine at an Alice Cooper show. I try to hold in my beer gut as much as possible, but inevitably I feel it flapping above my pants. The audience cheers, and I score well, but they are just biding their time—waiting, drooling, for C-Diddy to get back onstage. They need him—and he does not disappoint.

C-Diddy begins the quiet part of the song looking like a toy marionette just waiting to break loose from his strings, which he quickly does upon the first distorted chord of Billy Corgan's guitar. C-Diddy then works the crowd into a furious lather. He chews a piece of gum as he plays, mashing it down with his teeth in time to the song. He is a rock deity in full control of a stadium of adoring lighter-wielding fans.

In the end, I am awarded second place, and C-Diddy is unanimously crowned victorious. He is brought up onstage and handed a strange triangular statuette as the emcee announces, "Welcome the Chink Daddy[10] himself, Mr. C-Diddy—the winner of the first East Coast Regional Air Guitar Championship! C-Diddy, tell us how you pulled it through."

"Asian Fury! How'd you like it?" C-Diddy would later explain to me that "Asian Fury" is the "parody of the emasculation of the Asian

---

[10]C-Diddy actually stands for "Chink Daddy," according to David Jung, aka C-Diddy. Why he modeled his name after hip-hop impresario Sean (aka P. Diddy, Puff Daddy, and just plain Diddy) Combs is unclear. It certainly doesn't scream air guitar.

male." In other words, the stereotype of the meek Asian man can be seen as Dr. Jekyll, and Asian Fury is the untethered Mr. Hyde.

Shouts of "Encore!" "Free Bird!" and "Asian invasion!" are heard.

The emcee asks if the crowd wants more, and they do, so C-Diddy and I are asked to perform a duet to a mystery song.

"They have no idea what the song is," says the emcee, and he's not lying. "But they are going to do it for you because they love you."

I get back up onstage, my shirt still ripped open, and C-Diddy and I lean together, back to back, and begin an impromptu air duet to what couldn't have been a better surprise song choice. It's C-Diddy and Björn Türoque, trading licks and sharing kicks over Goober's track—Led Zeppelin's "Good Times Bad Times." I strum his gut and he strums mine. We're more than John Paul Jones and Jimmy Page, more than the sum of our parts. C-Diddy is Ace Frehley and I am Paul Stanley—he's got the Gibson Les Paul and I've got the Explorer. We are the Scorpions' Schenker brothers playing twin Flying Vs. We bang our heads in alternating synchronicity and we are true rock stars, he and I, transposed from insignificance into supernatural supershredding superheroes.

Afterwards, a sea of cameras swallows C-Diddy. He will fly to Los Angeles for the national championship—and he might just go all the way to Finland. He autographs a blond girl's left breast. I stand nearby, still playing air guitar, alone, unnoticed, to Joan Jett's "I Love Rock 'n' Roll." I'll go back to being Dan Crane, and I imagine I might try again next year.

*You don't choose air guitar,
air guitar chooses you.*

—C-Diddy

When I was growing up in the banal suburbs of Denver, my primary goal in life was to be a rock star. I started playing guitar in third grade, beginning with the obligatory Zeppelin, Floyd, Bowie, and Beatles songs. I was an impassioned album collector, poster worshipper, and lyric ponderer. I recall learning the word "obligatory" from the Pink Floyd song "Nobody Home," off their 1979 epic prog-rock opera, *The Wall* (though I'm still not sure what "pinhole burns" are or why they are "inevitable"). My rock heroes were larger than life. They were from another world, and their music provided me an escape hatch through which I could travel seamlessly from my average, monotonous life into their rock-and-roll fantasy.

My first rock persona was born, according to my mother, during living room concerts for my family when I was around age two. I'd pick up a tennis racquet and strum and sing along to Elton John songs. At the time I had no idea that I was playing a primitive form of air guitar, nor that most of the music I was playing along with originated on a piano. I also had no idea how fat and pathetically uncool Elton John would become later in his career.

In fifth grade I started my first band and called it Flower Child. I was the only member of the band, which practiced exclusively in my prepubescent brain. A year later, I started playing music with other guys from school. We'd practice "Back in Black" incessantly in my friend Brody LaRock's basement until the lights would flicker on and off, and then eventually Brody's father would resort to using the circuit breaker to cut our power.[1] In high school, I had a band with no name that played covers of Clapton's "Cocaine," Zeppelin's "All My Love" (our keyboardist loved playing that keyboard solo), and Edie Brickell's inescapably irritating hit, "What I Am." We never played in public, but obviously veered dangerously close to breaking some intense musical ground.

There were other cover bands in college: first the party-friendly Sesame Freak, and then the rougher-edged Ziploc Child. They pretty much sucked as well (though I felt Ziploc Child did do justice to Jane's Addiction's "Mountain Song").

Postcollege, the drummer from Ziploc Child and I finally formed a "real" (noncover) band in San Francisco, called Connie Comfort, after our college thesis advisor of the same name. We wrote songs like "Big Feet"—about fraternal competition ("My feet make yours look so small")—and angry, Kurt Cobain—esque screamers with choruses that quoted Elmer Fudd/Daffy Duck car-

[1] I did not make up Brody LaRock's last name. He was the drummer and now teaches the subject at a high school near Seattle.

toons: "Shoot me now / or wait till we get home?" Just when we were getting good (okay, maybe "Coffee Shit" wasn't a potential chart-topper, but some of the songs actually rocked), the drummer moved to Seattle, not to pursue grunge but rather a woman, and Connie Comfort—the band—was dead.

In 1996, I moved to New York and joined a band that would eventually be called Calamine, named after the soothing balm. Our biggest success was doing the theme song for an animated cult cable hit called *Sealab 2021*. While I was playing in Calamine, an old friend of mine from high school named Matt asked if I wanted to play in a Hawaiian band with him. He had become obsessed with vintage Hawaiian music after a weeklong heroin binge during college, when he locked himself in his mountain bungalow and listened to nothing but the swaying sounds of the Hawaiian Islands. He never did heroin again, but he vowed to start a band that would capture, if not the sound, then at least the mood. Unfortunately he couldn't really play any instruments.

We teamed up with an eccentric animation director named Mike, who played ukulele. We called ourselves the Easy Leis and rehearsed in Mike's apartment in downtown Brooklyn. Mike would later move to an illegal loft space in another section of Brooklyn, and use a five-gallon bucket, filled with kitty litter and topped with a toilet seat, as his bathroom. He called it the "human litter." During the first Easy Leis practice, Mike asked if I wanted to join his other band, a fake French sixties pop tribute band called Les Sans Culottes. Being in three bands at once seemed like a good idea at the time, so I did.

While the Easy Leis only played the occasional loft luau or Mermaid Parade party, Les Sans Culottes eventually had a modicum of success. We were never true rock stars, but it was a start. Playing in LSC allowed me to meet Jane Air and many amazing and insane people, make some money, lose more money, permanently damage my hearing, record five albums, and even get sued in federal court; but more important, playing in a mostly ridiculous fake French band allowed me to enjoy some of the trappings of the rock star life I fantasized about (drinking, drugs, assorted occasional groupies) without having to be earnest—without having to invest myself or commit to taking any of it seriously.

It was a little bit like air guitar.

There is no truth. There is only perception.
—Gustave Flaubert

"That's one of the dumbest things I've ever seen. *Air guitar?*" Thus Jack Cafferty contemptuously closes the two-minute segment covering the 2003 New York regional competition. (Jack, by the way, is the balding anchor who had been relegated to the job of reading viewer mail on CNN's *American Morning* until 2005, when he got bumped to the three-p.m. snoozer *The Situation Room*.) All the journalists who covered the event have churned out their stories, and so for days following the event, air guitar is everywhere. People send me newspaper clips and links to articles online and ask me to demonstrate my techniques in bars and restaurants, and my whole life is now literally *up in the air*. In some ways, I didn't mind not winning—it felt cooler to be drinking in a bar and be able to say, "Check it out—I'm the *second-best* air guitarist on the East Coast," and for several days following the competition, I say that *a lot*.

As for C-Diddy, two days after the competition he ended up on the *Howard Stern Show*. While the notion of someone playing air guitar on the radio might be considered akin to a Braille driving-instruction school, it actually worked. C-Diddy's interview was hilarious, and the funniest part of it all was how seriously Stern—usually prone to giving his guests no end of shit—took it all.

But why did the press go so gaga for air guitar? What is it about a bunch of dorks imitating rock stars that they found so compelling? There's an obvious absurdity in watching people strum along to rock music with invisible instruments, but it's also because air guitar is so universal—we've all done it, or thought about doing it, or laughed at a friend we've caught making a drunken attempt at doing it. Further, air guitar is, primarily, a private act—a personal experience. Shoving it into the spotlight of the competitive arena offers a novel reason to be intrigued, but is there any more to it than that?

Dave Hickey, a professor of art criticism and theory at the University of Nevada, Las Vegas, wrote a book titled *Air Guitar*, which has almost nothing to do with air guitar and is more concerned with art criticism. He mentions air guitar only briefly towards the end of his book, likening art criticism to "the written equivalent of air guitar—flurries of silent, sympathetic gestures with nothing at their heart but the memory of the music. . . . It's a loser's game and everybody knows it." Perhaps Hickey is just a self-hating critic, though probably not—his dismissal of air guitar as an empty gesture (which sounds a lot like CNN's Cafferty calling air guitar the dumbest thing he's ever seen) is just a way of being provocative: Hickey is suggesting that writing about art will never be *as good* as the art itself, in the same way that an air guitar performance will never live up to the music from which it draws its inspiration. Ultimately, however, Hickey suggests that writing about art can be its own form of artistic expression—just as an awe-inspiring air guitar performance can transcend mere mockery to become something we observe and celebrate on its own terms.

NEW YORK CITY June 9, 2003. On Monday I return to work, spitting distance from having been a regional champion. My computer-geek officemates, desperate for news from a fabled "Outside World," gather around the watercooler (yes, we really did gather around the watercooler) to hear about the competition. "It was that Asian dude who won, right? I saw him on the news—he looked amazing!"

Yes . . . it was the Asian dude. . . .

"Oh yeah," chimes in another, "I totally saw that dude on TV—he had that Hello Kitty breastplate? That was hilarious!"

Yeah, yeah, he was hilarious. I quickly begin to tire of talking about C-Diddy and how amazing he was. I head back to my desk and put on my wrist guards. While I work, due to frequent bouts of carpal tunnel syndrome and severe tendinitis in my arms and hands from typing and playing bass, I have to wear large black Velcro-fastened wrist guards that begin below my elbows and wrap around my hands like Rollerblading gloves. They tend to get really hot and sweaty after a full day of sitting at my computer, so I keep a small dispenser of Dr. Scholl's shoe deodorizer in my desk drawer to periodically dust the insides and keep them from smelling like rotting plaster casts. Every time I get up from my computer, I rip open the Velcro and take them off. They make my forearms look like Darth Vader's, and I frequently feel upon returning to my desk that I am getting back into my chair at the command post of the Death Star.

I remove the wrist guards and head out, alone, for lunch. In the elevator, I look up at the Reuters TV that provides daily weather, business, and news updates, and I am startled by what I see: C-Diddy is there, air guitaring on the television in my elevator. He's mocking me. Taunting me in his Hello Kitty armor. (*Maybe I needed armor of my own? Should I have worn my wrist guards onstage?*) I let out a loud sigh of disgust, and the woman next to me, a stranger, looks at me, confused. I glance up again to try to explain that the portly guy with the kimono on the TV had edged me out of fame and fortune, but he has already been replaced with a four-day forecast, forcing me to look on the bright side—the next few days, according to the TV in the elevator, will be sunny.

Later that day, back at my desk, I get a call from Aer Lingus. "Is this *Björn Türoque*?" he asks, amused with himself.

"Aye, Lingus. Björn here," I reply.

"So I just got a call from our buddies over at Fox News. Looks like they want you and C-Diddy to make an appearance on some show called *Fox & Friends* next week." Lingus laughs heartily.

Fox News? I immediately imagine entering "The No Spin Zone" only to have Bill O'Reilly yell at me as I try to explain the art of air guitar.

"Sounds genius," I say, and we firm up the details.

NEW YORK CITY June 16, 2003. Unfortunately *Fox & Friends* is an early morning show. Not an ideal time for air guitar. I wake up at some ludicrous hour. It's still dark out. I chug two cups of coffee and, wearing a red sleeveless T-shirt, sunglasses, my skinny leather tie, and a headband, hail a cab to Midtown. The cabbie is unfazed. I'm sure he's seen far stranger sights. At 6:15 a.m. I meet Aer Lingus and C-Diddy outside the Fox Studios on the corner of Sixth Avenue and Forty-eighth Street in Manhattan. It's the first time I've come face-to-face with C-Diddy since the competition. Our greeting, a quick man-hug, evokes in me a potent blend of bitterness and respect. I am sure C-Diddy wonders what the fuck I am doing there. So do I.

Lingus takes out a video camera and starts getting footage for a documentary that will cover the competition. They've been shooting every air guitar move any of us has made thus far, in addition to filming lengthy interviews with everyone on the night of the competition. It's my first taste of what being a reality-TV star must feel like. This early in the morning, the taste is not so sweet. We enter the Fox building and are immediately yelled at by the security guard. "Nope! No filming! Can't film in here," he shouts at Lingus, who plays dumb.

"What? We're just doing a documentary—it's cool, man."

The security guard is behaving as if Michael Moore just waddled in with an entire crew.

"I said you *cannot* film in here. I will confiscate your camera and your tape. . . ." he continues.

"These guys are goin' to . . ."

"I don't care who these guys are, *you cannot. film. in. here.*"

Finally Lingus relents and puts the camera away. Fox takes our pictures, and they laminate them onto temporary ID cards. Lingus strikes a pugilistic pose and I jam out in mine.

We're ushered upstairs to the greenroom, where we sit around trying out our rock star personas on the Fox News interns. They are singularly unimpressed.

C-Diddy is wearing a blue bandanna around his head (gangster style), a white T-shirt, and baggy jeans. He is without his kimono and Hello Kitty breastplate, and he doesn't look like he's all that happy to be there. Maybe C-Diddy isn't cut out for the fame that comes with being a nationally ranked air guitarist?

"This guy is the second-best air guitarist on the East Coast," says Lingus to one of the less underage-looking girls, pointing at me.

"Hmmmph," she replies. "Would you like any coffee or a bagel?"

"Um, no, thanks," I reply.

Someone wearing one of those fancy headsets escorts C-Diddy and me into the studio. I am planning on playing a sixty-second segment of Boston's "More Than a Feeling," and C-Diddy brought "Fight for Your Right," by the Beastie Boys. (*Not a good air guitar song at all*, I think to myself. *Maybe C-Diddy is just a one-hit wonder?*) We also plan a reenactment of our crowd-pleasing "Good Times Bad Times" duet.

Steve Doocy, one of the smarmy cohosts of *Fox & Friends*, has already decided that we are blights on his high-caliber show.

"So, let me get this straight. You guys are professional *air guitarists*?" asks Doocy, with predictable condescension.

"Completely. Completely professional," I respond.

The Fox production team then pipes in a sound effect of a crowd sighing with disgust. *"Awww . . ."* I look around, confused—there is no audience in *Fox & Friends'* tiny studio.

"So this is *your job.* You just listen to music and pretend you're playing the music?"

"It's more of a . . . passion," says C-Diddy.

"Really?"

"Yes, it's not quite at the stage where an income can be earned from this. . . ."

"So you still gotta have another job, but you still like to pretend you're somebody else?" he asks.

"Exactly," says C-Diddy, begrudgingly.

Doocy asks me to be the first to demonstrate. "More Than a Feeling" comes on in the studio, and I start playing. To their credit, they do add some sound effects of people cheering during my short-lived performance. But before my solo even kicks in, Doocy interrupts with, "Okay, that's good—I get the idea. Thank you, son." (Nothing sounds more patronizing than this guy, who is *so* not my father, calling me "son.") Then he runs his hand across his throat—making the international sign for *enough already*—and makes fart sounds with his tongue, signifying his displeasure with my work.

"Hit the music, please—let's make this go *faster*?" whines Doocy, getting C-Diddy's performance under way. C-Diddy is not giving it up for Fox; he seems completely uninterested in offering a championworthy performance. Doocy asks us to move on quickly to our duet.

"*Ohhhh* . . . kay. Fascinating stuff," he sneers as we rock out to "Good Times Bad Times."

As they do with most guests who don't fit their agenda, the fine folks at *Fox & Friends* cut into our airtime. But they can't really stop us. During our duet, I almost high-kick Steve Doocy in the head as he tries to cut us off. Meanwhile C-Diddy bounces against the windows where fans of the show are cheering outside.

Narrowly escaping with what's left of our integrity, we get the hell out of there. We then find the group of people who had been cheering at us through the windows still huddled outside the Fox News building. Lingus takes out his video camera, and C-Diddy and I decide to give these folks an impromptu lesson in air guitar. Within moments, C-Diddy and I are leading about twenty overweight tourists in lesson one in the Art of Air Guitar (including Headbanging). Moms, kids, grandmothers all join in. They are having the time of their lives. So am I.

Fuck *Fox & Friends. This*, I think, is what air guitar is all about.

Figure 2. The High Kick

* Minimum five viewings recommended.

Chapter Four: Björn Reborn

*A casual stroll through the lunatic asylum
shows that faith does not prove anything.*

—Friedrich Nietzsche

NEW YORK CITY June 20, 2003. It's a balmy summer night in Brooklyn, and I'm sitting outside in the backyard lounge of Pete's Candy Store, a tiny, homey bar where musicians with varying degrees of recognition play to audiences of about forty people, max. I've played some solo shows at Pete's, but it's been a while. With all the time I am putting into the French band, my solo career is not getting much attention. I'm there to support my friend Brooke, who's gotten her act together to play a set. I am jealous.

I'm downing my third pint of self-pity soother and boasting with friends about the air guitar competition when I feel my ass vibrating. It's my cell phone ringing—Aer Lingus again.

"Are you sitting down, Björn?" he says.

I am.

I plug my left ear with my index finger in order to fully block out the noise of the outdoor drinkers. "Yeah, dude. What's up?"

"So, the guys from the Carson Daly show just called. Apparently they wanted C-Diddy, but C-Diddy's already booked on Kimmel. So they said, 'Okay then, we'll take the number two guy,' " he tells me.

"Interesting . . ." I say.

"Number two—that's you, Björn." Lingus laughs. He's eating it up. "So, what'aya think?" (Raised in Dublin, Lingus actually does have a thick brogue. The ladies dig it.)

"Yeah, man. I'm into it," I tell him, and he says he'll call me with the details tomorrow.

The next day, I call my mom in California to tell her, and like any mother—particularly a Jewish mother—she freaks out. She goes on and on about how "crazy" it is that I am now becoming more famous as Björn Türoque, the "fake" guitarist, than I ever was as the bassist in a fake French band, or as Dan Crane the musician. I'm not sure I find it quite as amusing as she does.

I can't say that I'd ever watched *Last Call with Carson Daly*. In fact, I had no idea that Carson Daly even had a show. I remembered Carson as the slightly carb-faced guy from MTV's *Total Request Live* (*TRL*), but couldn't really fathom why they'd given him a job hosting a national network talk show. Then I found out that his show airs at 1:30 a.m., after Conan O'Brien. Okay, so it's a national network television show for insomniacs.

I have one day to prepare. My first order of business is to go to the dry cleaner down the street from my apartment to see if they can sew the buttons back onto my black-and-white checkered shirt that I had torn in the compulsory round of the New York competition, and I wanted to repeat on TV what I had decided was a Björn Türoque signature move. For five dollars, the lady at the dry cleaning place says she can sew my buttons back on, but I have to sweeten the deal with an extra five to have it done by tomorrow morning.

Next I need to determine my song. The Hüsker Dü song was hardly a crowd-pleaser at the competition, and will likely be way too obscure. I decide I should go with "Song 2," the Blur track I had already edited down to sixty seconds. If it's good enough to be used in Intel, Mercedes, and Nissan commercials, *and* in the trailer for *Starship Troopers*, it's good enough for Carson Daly.

NEW YORK CITY June 24, 2003 4:30 p.m. My phone rings to announce that a large black Chevy SUV has pulled up in front of my building. I grab my bag containing a bottle of Willie Nelson's Old Whiskey River–brand bourbon (complete with "autographed" plectrum attached to the bottleneck), the resuscitated black-and-white checkered shirt, my skinny leather zip-up tie, the headband with "Björn Türoque" written on it, an electric guitar case, and the CD with my sixty-second Blur clip, and head outside. With my guitar case slung over my shoulder, I walk in slow motion like a badass rock star as I approach the giant vehicle. And then I laugh to myself. This is truly insane.

It's a typical New York summer day, which means that the minute I am outside, I begin to rain sweat. I climb into the mammoth black SUV, and my sweat is instantly frozen by the air conditioning on full blast.

"How ya doin'?" asks the driver, who, if I were to guess, hails from somewhere deep within Queens. He's got the requisite limo driver hat and dark sunglasses, and with his three-inch ponytail, he looks like a cross between John Travolta in *Pulp Fiction* and Steven Seagal in any movie. I might as well set Björn loose on him.

Engulfed in the oversized leather seats, I reply, nodding my head, "Not bad, man. Not bad at all."

The driver turns his head to look back at me. I exude coolness. I am Björn.

"NBC studios, right?" he asks.

"Yup—Rockefeller Center."

We pull away from my apartment on Twenty-fourth Street and head uptown. He's cranking bad house music.

"Do you have a CD player in this thing?" I ask after we drive a few blocks.

" 'Course I do. Whadda ya got? You wanna' hear somethin'?" he shouts over the four-on-the-floor house beats.

I lean forward to hand him the freshly burned CD with the Blur clip on it.

"This your CD? I saw your guitar—you're in a band, right?" He asks.

"Well, yeah, I *am* in a band," I say. "But this isn't my band. I'm going to be playing air guitar to this song on the show tonight."

"Air guitar? Hmmmm. I see," he says. Though I don't think he sees at all.

"So what's that for?" he asks, pointing to my guitar case.

"My air guitar is in there," I explain.

"Hmmm . . . I get it," he claims, again—though now I really

don't think he gets it. "That's cool, man," and with that, he cranks up "Song 2" as we crawl up Sixth Avenue through afternoon traffic.

"I've picked up tons of musicians, man," he shouts while I do warm-up windmills in the freezing car. "One time I picked up Stevie Wonder—that was fuckin' cool. He's really blind, y'know?" I nod my head in agreement. "And Tony Danza—he can really sing, that guy. He was the nicest guy I've ever met. He rode up front here with me."

The driver is bouncing his head to the beat, trying to remember the name of a "totally hot chick" he once gave a ride to. I'm still practicing my moves in back as we pull up to Rockefeller Center.

The folks at NBC are a little more relaxed than the utterly aggro staff at Fox News, and they don't seem to care that Lingus is trailing me with a camera. We find Lindsay, our contact, a girl with perfectly trimmed, very clean blond hair that bounces with every step as she escorts us down the hallway, clipboard in hand. We get into the elevator and head up to the studio where *Last Call with Carson Daly* shoots.

As we ascend, I pull out my bottle of whiskey, deep into my role as a depraved rock god. "Is whiskey forbidden in the greenroom?" I ask.

"I didn't see it," says Lindsay, who stares straight ahead as I take a long swig.

We're swiftly escorted down a long hall lined with hundreds of framed eight-by-ten glossy photos of film, television, and music stars. These must be photos of guests from *Saturday Night Live*, which Lindsay tells me shoots on the same floor. I pause for a second to take a look at one of the photos, and the first one I lock in on is Tony Danza. *Nice guy and a good singer,* I think to myself.

We are escorted into the dressing room, which is stocked with a basket of fruit, a few bottles of water, and a fridge full of Cokes and Diet Cokes.

In the corner of the drab but well-lit room, a television monitor with an image of the *Last Call with Carson Daly* logo emblazoned on the screen is mounted. A mirror covers one wall, and in the corner there's a cheap vinyl La-Z-Boy recliner that looks like it's been stolen from the waiting room of a brothel. I wonder if "real" guests get better dressing rooms.

After I've downed a couple of healthy whiskey-and-Cokes, the knock comes on the door for Björn to head into makeup. I'm escorted down the hall into the incandescent room, and I plop down into a barber chair. "It's not rock and roll until you've got mascara on," I say to the makeup lady, requesting a full-on David Bowie glam rock treatment. But she goes easy on me, applying a little powder to keep me from getting too shiny.

The hair lady calls me Dave several times, apparently (claims the makeup lady) because Dave Navarro was on the show yesterday. Björn Türoque is obviously so similar to Dave Navarro that it's hard to tell the difference. I tell her she can call me Dave, or Dan, or Björn, or "The Best Air Guitarist in the World" if she wants, and she gets a real kick out of that. I, in turn, am pretty high on the idea that twenty-four hours earlier, a guy whose songs I've played on both air and nonair guitar was sitting in the same chair getting made up to go on the same show.

"I already lost a button," I say as I look down at my black-and-white checkered shirt. I'll be demanding my ten dollars back from the lady at the dry cleaner.

"It's right here," says the hair lady, pointing to my thigh, where the button has fallen.

"Do you have anybody that can fix this?" I plead.

"Yeah, Wardrobe," jokes the makeup lady.

I look around and shout, "Wardrobe!" as if a hunchbacked old lady with a needle and thread will magically appear to fix my shirt.

"They don't come when you call 'em," says the makeup lady in her thick Jersey accent.

"*Wardrobe!* We've got a situation!" I shout again. Nobody appears.

With the button gone, my beer gut rolls out of my shirt like pizza dough. "My belly must have busted the button," I say. "Can you slim that?" I ask, grabbing my gut with both hands.

"She can shade it," says the hair lady. Then the makeup lady begins to brush some face powder on the vast expanse that is my belly.[1]

Moments later, in walks actor Jamie Kennedy, who sits down in the chair next to mine to get his hair done. You may or may not remember Jamie Kennedy from his role as film-buff dork Randy Meeks in *Screams 1, 2,* and *3,* or from his *Punk'd*-meets–Ali G–style show, *The Jamie Kennedy Experiment.* Kennedy is polite, but for the most part uninterested in the world of Björn Türoque. After a few moments in the chair, Kennedy asks the hair lady if she can do anything with his bald spot.

---

[1] I've always been a "fat skinny guy." Most of my body is rail-like except the middle, which bulges out over my pants like a cupcake over its wrapper. I've had a beer gut since I started drinking at age fourteen, and occasionally describe myself as "Chris Farley's gut on Mick Jagger's frame."

The hair lady pulls out a can of what looks like spray paint and painstakingly applies a matching shade of artificial brown hair to the top of Kennedy's head.

Air Hair.

All made up and ready to roll, I am brusquely led to the stage by a guy with a headset on. We do a rehearsal, and the tech crew is really excited because they get to break out their bitchin' fog machine. I've got a healthy buzz going from the Whiskey River—and-Cokes that Lingus keeps pouring, so it's nice to get my blood flowing. My practice performance is definitely enhanced by the fog, which looks seriously stadium-rock.

We then shoot a short segment of me tuning my air guitar in the greenroom—it will be featured in cutaways during Carson's opening monologue. I head back to the dressing room to take another dip in the Whiskey River, and wait for the knock.

"I'm sure you all know that the late-night booking wars can be cutthroat," Carson Daly begins his introduction. "They can be brutal—and I don't want to brag, but tonight, on *this* show, we've got the guy who came in *number two* in the Eastern Regional Air Guitar Championship. I mean, come on, that's a big booking. Eat your heart out, Leno!" Thanks for the mad props, dude.

"He's here. Steve, do you have a shot of him back there? His name is Björn Türoque." Cut to me tuning up. "There he is backstage—that's the guy that's *number two*." (Carson really milks the whole "number two" thing—there's even a whiff of double entendre with "number two" as a bathroom euphemism.) "He's apparently, uh, air tuning his air guitar," says Carson, oozing sarcasm. "He looks like a sushi chef, doesn't he?"

Ah, yes, to be the butt of Carson Daly's jokes means one has really made it in this world.

I sit in the dressing room, looking at the monitor. Jamie Kennedy, the show's first guest, comes out and blathers on, and I can only think about his bald spot and how, as a television viewer, you can't even see the top of his head anyway. Was it really necessary? Does it wash out with shampoo? Will he keep wearing it the rest of the day? Then a knock on the door awakens me from my reverie.

"My next guest was the number two air guitarist in the Eastern Regional semifinals," says Carson Daly with another ironic wink to the audience. "That's right, I said *air guitar*. Now performing to 'Song 2,' give it up for Björn Türoque!"

I walk out onstage and the studio audience of roughly one hundred claps politely as the guitar-riff intro to "Purple Haze" serves as my processional. I lift the guitar case from over my shoulder, unzip it, and gingerly pull out my air guitar. I look out over the audience and shoot them a thousand-yard stare.

A single, lonely puff of fog ejaculates from the front of the stage.

Blur's "Song 2" starts playing. At the designated points in the song, I switch from air ukulele to air guitar and back again. That single plume of fog is all I'm going to get, and I realize I am having my first official *Spinal Tap*-ian "Stonehenge Moment." The second chorus hits with a crushing blow of guitar—distortion pedals on maximum gain, vocals emphasizing the dynamic shift on the second word "woo hoo"—as I rip open my shirt and jump into the studio audience, running along the front row like Eddie Van Halen on top of the library desks in the "Hot for Teacher" video.

I return to the totally fogless stage, and with the final chord of the song, my air guitar and I collapse into a heap on the floor.

Carson Daly and Jamie Kennedy walk out to help me up. I am completely winded. When I agreed to do the interview following my performance, I didn't factor in the enormity of the television studio's stage, how incredibly out of shape I was, or that I would be, at that point, hammered.

"Wow! Björn Türoque, everybody!" The studio audience cheers.

"I don't know about you, Jamie, but I've got a lot of questions," Daly says. "First of all, have you thought about getting an air bassist and an air drummer and starting an air band?"

"I've thought about that," I say, trying desperately to catch my breath. "But the air groupies are not as hot as I'd like them to be."

"Are there really air groupies?" he asks.

"Well, there are—but they're invisible."

It takes Carson Daly a second to get the joke. Jamie Kennedy chimes in, "You seem like you're out of air." Then Kennedy reaches over and grabs my beer gut and gives it a test squeeze. "Maybe you should do a couple of air sit-ups." The audience and Carson Daly laugh enthusiastically.

"So, what can we do for you to get you to number one?" asks Daly, cutting to the chase. I was told backstage beforehand that Carson is considering sending me to LA for a rematch, so I figure I might as well go for it.

"I'm hoping that you—*you* will send me to LA, to compete again, to take back what is rightfully mine, what was stolen from me, which is the East Coast crown. . . ."

"I thought maybe they stole your brain."

"Well . . ."

"Alright, we've got a hookup at JetBlue. If they'll fly you out there for free, I'll send you to LA."

"You'll send me?"

"If you promise to win the damn thing, all right? Björn Türoque, everybody! We'll be right back after this. . . ."

Backstage, Lingus congratulates me on my performance, and we hang out with the producer for a few minutes.

"So, how many people usually watch this show?" I ask.

"Oh, over a million. Depends on the night."

"A million people watched me play air guitar," I revel. "Now, that's pretty fucking funny."

"Yeah—a million people watched Jamie Kennedy squeeze your dick-do,"[2] jokes Lingus.

I grab my stuff (including everything salvageable from the snack tray in the dressing room), and we walk out of the studio. In the lobby I run into a friend of mine, Andrew, getting into the elevator. We're both confused about why the other is there.

"What are you doing here?" I ask.

---

[2] A *dick-do* is what my mother calls a beer gut—as in, "When your stomach hangs out farther than your dick do." I once told Lingus this, and he immediately absorbed it into his vocabulary. He's got a sizable dick-do himself, you see.

"Meeting a friend for lunch . . . What are you doing here?" he asks.

"Playing air guitar."

I hold up my hand to wave just as the elevator door closes on my friend's bewildered face.

Chapter Five: Air-Conditioning:
How to Convince Your Girlfriend That This Is a Good Idea

*Power is not revealed by striking hard or
often, but by striking true.*

—Honoré de Balzac

Jane Air and I had been dating almost one year. In fact, our anniversary would fall on the weekend of the championships in LA. Once Carson Daly had agreed to send me, and JetBlue had agreed to the free flight, there was no turning back—but I had to sell the idea to Jane, who wanted to do something special for our anniversary. And for her, "something special" did not include me competing in an air guitar competition in Los Angeles.

So I booked a room at the Chateau Marmont hotel in LA and said we would celebrate there. It was reportedly the coolest hotel in the city, was close to the venue where the competition was being held, and it certainly wasn't lacking in rock and roll history.

In the early seventies, a drunk Jim Morrison fell off a balcony onto one of the cottages below, breaking two of his ribs. Led Zeppelin reportedly threw orgies in their Chateau bungalow. John and Yoko stayed at the Chateau for weeks, meditating and writing music. Mick most definitely got laid there. And John Belushi overdosed on cocaine and heroine and died in bungalow three. Oh—and it was romantic too.

I opted for a double room, sans balcony.

Jane and I met under somewhat rock and roll circumstances, making a weekend at the Chateau seem all the more appropriate. Jane wrote for a weekly New York magazine and had proposed doing some investigative journalism for their 2002 Bastille Day theme issue. She offered herself up as guinea pig in a test to determine whether Frenchmen were better French kissers, and if so, why? So she began assembling a panel of Frenchmen, all strangers. Someone at the magazine who had heard of my fake French band suggested that one of the Frenchmen be faux—a decoy, or "control," for the experiment. When I got the phone call asking if I wanted to be a research test subject, the only requirements being that I French-kiss a young female editor from the magazine, I could only say, *"Oui, but of course!"*

Naturally I asked around to see if the girl with whom I was going to be sharing spit was attractive or not. The reports were very encouraging. *But, then, what if I'm a terrible kisser, and she writes about it, and then everyone in New York City finds out?* I decided to risk it anyway.

Around five in the afternoon, we all showed up at a swanky French restaurant on the Upper East Side. I talked to a few of the Frenchmen there, and everyone was tense. One guy was afraid his wife would be angry with him—he'd just gotten married a few months ago. (Why he agreed to do this was another matter.) When Jane Air arrived, I was relieved, to say the least. She was incredibly hot. She wore tight jeans, a pink shirt, and ass-kicking white boots, and had a sexy mane of brown hair. I was, I admit, very much looking forward to kissing her.

I could tell she was the most nervous of us all. I suggested that we start with a shot of whiskey to get us "in the mood," which helped, but the pressure was thick. I went into the bathroom, changed into my concert outfit (striped vintage pants and a colorfully striped vintage polyester shirt) and returned speaking with a fake French accent. I was now Jean-Luc Retard. The accent put a few of the Frenchmen off, but what did I care. I had a contest to win.

When it was my turn (I got sloppy thirds), I went back to the banquette where she had stationed herself, and sat down. We eyed each other timidly, but there was an instant and undeniable chemistry.

"So, what is your name?" she asked.

"My name is, eh, Jean-Luc Retard," I answered in a thick Gallic accent, and then kissed her hand.

"And what part of France are you from?"

"I am from the lower Faux region, actually. It is a lesser-known area, but quite beautiful."

"And what is your idea of the perfect kiss?"

"Well," I began. "Ze kiss, it is about intimacy and warmth—it is like a hot summer day. This is cliché, yes, but it is true."

She laughed, and I felt the heaviness lifting. Then she told me it was time to kiss.

Our kiss went on forever. It was like a French Big Red (*Grand Rouge*) commercial. She was a great kisser, and I was working hard to give it my all until one of the restaurant staff made us both start laughing by inexplicably repeating, "Chicken salad? Chicken *salad*?!" to a coworker.

"So that's it? It is over?" I asked.

"For now . . ." she said coyly.

The next day I e-mailed her to ask if she meant what she said about the kiss being over "for now," and I suggested she come over one night to my place for some *moules frites*.

A week or so later the magazine came out.

"Defying his spastic name," she wrote, "Monsieur Retard proves to be in full command of his oral faculties. Upper-lip dominant, smooth-tongued, and unafraid to go for it, he proffers a long-lasting smooch with operatic crescendo. Lipstick definitely needs to be reapplied."

Luckily, this was one contest in which I didn't take second place.

LA is really "LA" here. They got the fake tits, the fake smiles, and they've even got fake air guitars.

—Björn Türoque, in *Air Guitar Nation*

Until the mighty hand of Carson Daly reached down, plucked me from oblivion, and sent me to the City of Angels in order to claim the crown, Los Angeles was a city I always used to hate. The denizens of this sprawling suburbopolis—plastic people infatuated with fame and ignorant of culture—were, to me, everything I wanted not to be. I was happy to catch a free ride to LA, and maybe it wouldn't be so bad after all. Maybe I could beat C-Diddy this time. Maybe I would return to New York as the greatest air guitarist in America. At the very least, I'd get some much-needed sun on the old dick-do.

As the birthplace of Van Halen and eighties hair metal, LA seemed the perfect place for the Air Guitar finals—and the Roxy, where the competition was being held, was an ideal venue. Guns N' Roses, Neil Young, the Boss, Nirvana, and hundreds of other bands have rocked the Roxy since it opened on the Sunset Strip in 1972. But would a bunch of aspiring air guitarists playing no instruments at all be accepted in a club with such a lofty history?

NEW YORK CITY June 26, 2003. The day before we are to leave for LA, I finally get around to editing my Led Medley. There were lots of competing song ideas, like Metallica's "Master of Puppets" and Whitesnake's "Here I Go Again." I even considered writing and recording my own song, but a Led Zeppelin power medley seemed the strongest. I researched the rules on the Web site, and there was nothing declaring that one's sixty-second clip could not be an amalgam of several songs, so I decided to go for it. Opening my drawer full of CDs, I realize that over the years, a large portion of my Zepp collection had been pilfered or lost. I hastily ride my bike up to Tower Records and pick up the CDs I need, bring them home, and get to work. I figure it will take an hour or two.

The concept: take as many recognizable licks and a few bitchin' solos from as many Zepp tunes as possible, and edit them down to a mind-altering, thundering sixty seconds of getting the Led out. I narrow down which tracks I want, but then midway through digitizing disc one of *Physical Graffiti* my computer freaks out and completely freezes. Apparently the disk has some kind of psychotic copy protection on it. Upon restart, I see the brain-curdling image of a disk with a blinking question mark. My computer is dead. It seems like an extreme punishment for trying to make some MP3s.

I spend a few hours trying to restore the hard drive, but our flight is early tomorrow morning—it's obvious that there's no way I am getting this thing edited before we leave. I take a sleeping pill and try to get some rest.

The next morning we board our JetBlue flight, and I spend most of the plane ride anxiously worrying about who in LA I can find with a computer that has the necessary music editing software. The rest of the time I hone my stage identity. Who is Björn Türoque? More important, *why* is Björn Türoque? What does he stand for? What compels him to rock so hard? After the onslaught of press at the New York competition, I realized I needed to have a firmer grip on the life of Björn and his backstory. Talking to the press required quick quips on subjects ranging from my influences and song selection to costuming and air groupies. I didn't want to memorize answers, but I wanted to know what Björn would say. I had to get inside Björn's head.

Me: What was your father like?

Björn: My father? His name was Imus Türoque. He was a nihilist.

Me: Imus Türoque—ha. I get it. Are you a nihilist as well?

Björn: Absolutely.

Me: So, like, you believe in nothing?

Björn: No, you tool. That's the classic mistake about nihilists—that we believe in nothing. We believe in the *nonexistence of truth*. Conversely, air guitar, because it does not "exist," is therefore the *truest* art form.

Me: But if truth does not exist, then your statement is
paradoxically untrue, because in order for truth to not
exist, your statement must be incorrect.
Björn: You annoy me.

We both doze off for an hour or so before landing.

LOS ANGELES June 26, 2003. It's a beautifully warm, perfect,
cloudless Southern California day. It looks as if even the sky has
had plastic surgery. We pull our rental car up the driveway of the
Chateau Marmont, and I try not to think too much about the
twenty-five-dollar-per-day parking fee.

In 1939, Harry Cohn, the head of Columbia Pictures, fa-
mously told actors William Holden and Glenn Ford, "If you must
get in trouble, do it at the Chateau Marmont." The advice seems
as solid today as it was then. We check in to our room, and, if you
ignore the DVD player, television, and stereo, it's as if we've entered a time warp to the days when Holden and Ford were getting into trouble. There's an art deco kitchen with a vintage
stove and a refrigerator fully loaded with drinks. The bed is beyond plush. On the desk there's a note from the hotel that reads,
"Mr. Crane, a pleasure to see you again. Please enjoy your stay,"
though I've never stayed here before. It's by far the nicest hotel
I've ever been in, and truly fit for Björn Türoque. I am so impressed with the room that I immediately strip down to my box-
ers and start practicing my air guitar moves on the bed. The bed

has a lot of spring to it, and I think, *I wonder if Jim Morrison was doing this just before he fell off his balcony.*[1]

After a shower, I call my friend Mike (he of the human kitty litter), who has been living in LA for a while, to see if he knows anyone with music editing gear. He suggests a friend of his who, I am told as an added incentive, lives across the street from the *actual* apartment complex featured on the nineties TV show *Melrose Place*. Wow. I leave Jane Air by the pool and head over there. It takes about three hours to edit the Led Medley, but when it's finally completed, I know it's a sixty-second masterwork.

I head back to the hotel, listening to the Led Med burned onto CD. The stereo is cranked and the windows are down as I careen down palm tree–lined Sunset Boulevard, steering the rental car with my thighs, freeing me to air guitar ad nauseam. I wail away, making rock faces at passing cars. At a stoplight, my right foot lightly taps out the bass drumbeat on the gas pedal. "Oh, *so good*," Robert Plant sexily rants at the end of "The Ocean," the final clip of the medley. And it is.

I find Jane Air lounging by the pool with two friends of hers who are in town from New York. We enjoy a few Bloody Marys as the sun goes down over the Chateau. We all dry off, and Jane's friends come up to our suite to watch me practice my song. They agree unanimously that it's perfect.

---

[1]Years later in 2006, a sixteen-year-old Chinese business student in Singapore would fall out of his third-floor window and die from air guitar–related injuries. A court would rule the accident "death by misadventure" and say that evidence "points to the deceased unintentionally falling out of the window to his death when he was hyped up with exhilaration, jumping up and down on the bed placed against an open window, while mimicking a rock guitarist." (Reuters, 2006)

Jane and I get dressed and head out to a fancy restaurant nearby that she has chosen for our first anniversary dinner. Considering that during the few years prior to meeting Jane Air I had nurtured and then severed countless three-month relationships in a typically male, wild oats–sowing fashion, the mere idea of making it to one year with *anyone* seems just shy of a miracle; and considering how much Jane and I tend to fight, our one-year marker is all the more worthy of celebration. At the heart of all our fights is essentially the same issue: what Jane calls my "one-foot-out-the-door syndrome." I continually ask myself: if this is the right relationship, why do we fight so much? She senses my ambivalence, and that makes her insecure. This leads to fighting, which fuels my ambivalence. And so on . . .

My commitment issues didn't stop at my relationship with Jane Air, though. After all, I had been playing for more than five years in a fake French band rather than devoting time to playing my own music—which would be more challenging, more personal, and, dare I say, more *intimate*. And now I had flown across the country to compete in an air guitar competition, something that indeed required some measure of commitment, but was, as far as I could tell, a joke. I could commit, I could even get obsessed; but it was much easier to give in to something I had less personal stake in—a fake French band, air guitar, getting laid.

At dinner, Jane and I drink too much wine, fight about my not being attentive enough ("What are you thinking about?" she asks. "Um, air guitar?" I reply sheepishly—*why do I tell the truth when she asks this?*), have an expensive shitty meal, and go back to the hotel in silence. There is neither rocking nor rolling our first night at the Chateau, but we do somehow, at least, resolve the fight. Jane refuses to go to bed angry, which is probably a good thing.

Breakfast in bed magically makes everything better, and then it's off to find a Zeppelin-worthy outfit. I've brought some bitchin' Jimmy Page–looking striped pants—like the ones I was wearing when I first met Jane Air—but I need a shirt to complete the ensemble. And I only have a few hours: the *Carson Daly* camera crew that's been hired to trail me around will be showing up around three p.m. Jane and I stop at an overpriced thrift store in the heart of Hollywood that a friend has recommended. I pick up a few T-shirts that I can rip open onstage during the compulsory round (presuming I make it that far) and a tan polyester shirt with dark brown polka dots that Jane thinks will look very seventies rock.

We head back to the hotel. I try on the outfit and concur with Jane's assessment: the combo is more than roadworthy. Then there's a knock on the door. I open it up, and three guys are standing there with what looks like enough gear to shoot a feature film. Jane is terrified and runs into the bathroom to get ready. I am nervous as well. We quickly get hooked up with wireless microphones, and they shoot me getting dressed, practicing on the bed, and trying on different costume choices (even though I've already decided what to wear). As I stand shirtless in front of the camera, I wonder if my gut will become a running joke with Carson Daly. They capture Jane etching "Björn" and "Türoque" down my left and right biceps, respectively, in thick black marker, signaling my rockamorphosis. The videotaping feels contrived, and I feel extremely sober. No wonder everyone's always drunk on those reality-TV shows—it's the only way to deal with cameras following you around wherever you go.

Gathering our stuff, we head downstairs in the elevator. Everyone in the lobby seems famous, but suddenly I am the one being trailed by cameras. Jane and I are directed to climb into a taxi, but they don't get the shot right, so we have to reshoot it several times— the cab leaving the driveway and then reversing back up repeatedly. I hope they're going to tip the driver well. The crew finally gets what they need, and we all head west on Sunset towards the Roxy.

Upon our arrival, I see my best friend from childhood, Dan Kapelovitz, standing outside the club. He and I met in Denver and were friends up until about fourth grade, when we had a big fight (about what, I can't remember—maybe who was better, Cheap Trick or Styx?[2]) and never saw each other again until the first day of college, when we realized we had both enrolled at the same school. He tells me he's also competing and that his stage name is "The Airtight Messiah." I should have suspected that Kapelovitz would be here. He's the kind of guy who, when I mention that I grew up with him, eight out of ten people will say, "I've heard of that guy. He's a freak." He's most famous, perhaps, as the high priest of the Partridge Family Temple—a small cult he leads, founded around TV's *The Partridge Family.* I've never been sure what the cult does besides hang out and listen to Partridge Family records, but, then, I've never attended a meeting. Growing up, I always knew Kapelovitz was a little weird—his favorite foods were Wonder Bread balls and

---

[2]At the time, I probably argued for Styx. What was I thinking?

fried bologna. He refused to eat almost any kind of sauce (ketchup, mustard, salad dressing), and when we went to McDonald's, he had to get specially ordered cheeseburgers with nothing on them. Around his house we used to chant his food mantra to the tune of a popular song of the day, "My Sharona." It went, "Fa-fa-fa-fried bologna . . ."

After a few quick pleasantries, we begin dissecting each other.

"What's your song? Are you doing 'Fried Bologna'?" I ask.

"No, dude, I'm doing 'Crazy Horses' by the Osmonds, so *get ready*!" he shouts at me. I'm thinking, *Hmmm . . . not sure I know that one*. The Osmonds? Did they ever rock out? I know Donny was "a little bit rock and roll," but I suspect The Airtight Messiah is just approaching it all ironically. Either way, I cannot let him win. This is an age-old feud.

"What song are you doing?" he asks.

"I'm doing every Led Zeppelin song ever made, combined into sixty seconds of face-melting fury," I tell him, hoping to strike a chord of fear in his soul.

"Oh my God, man," he says with a dramatic pause. "That's actually what *I'm* doing!" he exclaims. He's joking. He's nervous. I suspect my scare tactic has worked.

Then C-Diddy shows up. We greet each other cordially, but it is clear he is not happy I am in LA competing again. He checks out my personal television crew and shakes his head disapprovingly, then disappears. Our rivalry is getting serious. The *Carson Daly* crew splits to get some food and tell me they will be back before the competition to shoot more footage.

Backstage, I hang out with The Airtight Messiah and his platinum

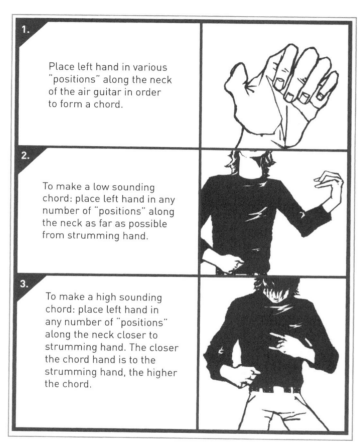

Figure 3. How to play chords

Note: You may elect to ignore chords altogether in favor of solos.

blond female air roadie. (Everyone competing in LA seems to have brought an air roadie, and I call Jane Air to ask if she'll come be mine. She reluctantly agrees.) The Messiah is wearing blue and green patterned spandex, pink sunglasses, and a pink beaded necklace. He guzzles Red Bull. His air roadie sports thigh-high red vinyl boots and a lime green shirt. They define psychedelic.

I also talk briefly on the couch with a guy wearing tight black spandex leggings, a black and red striped shirt, a short-cropped black wig, and a studded belt buckle held together with handcuffs. His name is Gordon Hintz, and he tells me he works as a budget analyst for the City of Long Beach, but tonight he is Krye Tuff.[3] He'll be playing "Talk Dirty to Me" by Poison, he tells me. I think his hair should be bigger if he's going to attempt playing Poison, but that's just me.

In my striped pants, polka-dotted shirt, and yellow scarf, I now fully embody Björn Türoque.

Björn begins conversing with and instilling fear in his fellow competitors—dudes like Scott Blossom, a guy with an all-too-real-looking mullet and large dark glasses that are usually favored by the elderly or nearly blind.

Björn: You think you got what it takes, man?

Scott Blossom: I don't know, it's pretty intense.

Björn: It's hugely intense.

Blossom: My fingerwork is intermediate at best. But my long strums are pretty fuckin' tight.

---

[3] A play on "Cry Tough," the first song on Poison's first album, *Look What the Cat Dragged In*, and the band Tuff, from Gordon Hintz's hometown of Oshkosh, Wisconsin.

Björn: That's cool. Tight long strums are what it's about.

Blossom: A lot of it is, like, Eddie Van Halen and Ing-a-Way Mom-stein? [That's how he pronounces the name of speed-demon Yngwie Malmsteen.] Their fingerwork is so blinding, you know? My fingerwork . . . [diffidently] My fingerwork isn't blinding.

Björn: Why are you wearing those glasses, then?

Blossom: Good point, good point. What about you—are you ready?

Björn: Dude, I was born ready. I was Björn Tü-*roque*, actually. [Björn shows Blossom his "tattooed" arms with "Björn" and "Türoque" running vertically down them.]

Blossom: Oh my god. Wow. Are you from Finland?

Björn: No, I'm from Sweden—well, Denver, originally, but I spent some time in a Swedish prison . . .

Björn and Blossom could go on like this for hours, but it's not long before the press descends upon everyone. Björn is waxing philosophical and, when you get down to it, just plain lying to journalists holding notepads and to camera crews from who-knows-where. If there's anything to be learned from Bob Dylan's treatment of the press, it's that one should tell the legend of the rock star he wants to be—in all likelihood, they'll probably print the legend.

"I originally hail from Sweden," Björn begins one of the interviews. "I'm the spiritual reincarnation of Jimi Hendrix, so when people ask me how long I've been playing air guitar, I tell 'em I have been playing my whole life, *plus* Jimi Hendrix's life."

"What makes you different from other air guitarists?" inquires a female reporter.

"Broadly speaking, I am a nihilist. I'm into Nietzsche. I read a lot on the plane over here just to get into the vibe of the whole thing. I enjoy the work of Richard Serra; he's a minimalist sculptor. He literally makes giant steel sculptures *filled with air*."

"Why do you do this?" interrupts another reporter. Björn is bombarded. It's as if he is holding a White House press conference.

"Ultimately, I see air guitar as taking nothingness" *[Björn's hands wave in the air in front of him, demonstrating "nothingness"]* "and making it into something." *[He pulls the air in close and shapes it into an air guitar.]*

"How do you reconcile being a nihilist with wanting to be the US champion and wanting to go to Finland?" the first reporter cleverly follows up.

"Excellent question," answers Björn. "Well, some might see that as a conflict, sure. Being a nihilist might not *jive* with my burning desire to take the world crown, but if you really get into the literature, there's this whole superman thing. . . . See, I am kind of taking the role of the Nietzschean superman. The Air Guitar Übermensch . . ." Björn is obviously out on a limb. Luckily she cuts him off.

"I see. Thanks," she says, and walks away. Apparently Björn has blown her mind.

Then my mother shows up.

Beaming with excitement, wearing a pink leather blazer, a white lace bodysuit top, jeans, and white sneakers, she is the anticamouflage—a shiny beacon of momness. It is blindingly obvious that she is someone's mother, mine, and I feel any cool points I may have accrued with anyone here receding into the abyss. Like that scene in *The Karate Kid* where Daniel (played by Ralph Macchio) is mortified when his mother pulls up to the family fun center in her behemoth brown station wagon to retrieve him and his love interest (Elisabeth Shue). Moms are just inherently embarrassing. It's not their fault. They mean well. It doesn't help when they wear pink leather jackets, but, again, they mean well.

My mother, while I'm on the subject, eats every meal with chopsticks,[4] and no, she is not Asian—though if she were, it would probably help my air guitar career immeasurably. She speaks in neologisms and *quirky* catchphrases I can never quite decipher, like, "I'll be up at o'dark thirty," "Come by the hotel and we'll have a shooter," and, "Give me a holler when you get vertical, and we'll see what's whoopin'." By her side is the guy she's been dating lately, Lynn, who has a far-off look in his eyes. He seems to be imagining

[4]Yes, even steak and pasta. My mother carries chopsticks with her in a little chopstick coffin wherever she goes, and exhumes them for any food that is normally consumed with a fork. To eat a steak, for example, she will put the chopsticks in her left hand to poke the meat down while slicing into it with a knife held in her right hand; then she'll switch the chopsticks to the right hand to pick up the bite of meat. "Why the chopsticks, Mom?" I ask. "Why the air guitar, son?" she replies. Touché.

himself elsewhere, far, far away from all this, playing golf or watching competitive bull riding on ESPN.

A reporter from the *Los Angeles Times* approaches us and is very amused that a contestant's mother is here. I decide that evasive action is my only option, so I tell them both I need to go backstage to get ready. (Later that night, my mom tells me she spent most of the competition talking to the reporter. I just can't wait to see what he prints.)[5]

Amid the chaos, Jane Air shows up, and we head to a restaurant around the corner to grab a beer and discuss her duties as my air roadie for the evening. "So, you should come out behind me carrying my air guitar," I begin. "I'll be wearing my Mexican wrestling mask and my robe. When I stop, you'll get on your knees and . . ."

"On my knees?" she says, cringing. (Kissing five strange Frenchmen is fine, but getting on her knees onstage is somehow unacceptable?)

"Yeah. Yeah—it'll be great. You get on your knees and hand me the air guitar, like you're handing me a sword before I go into battle or something. Then remove my robe and walk offstage." We practice this a couple of times, toast our beers together, and I give her a quick kiss and head backstage.

On my way, I catch The Airtight Messiah ranting to a camera crew. He's now wearing a skintight, Pepto-Bismol—pink bodysuit that covers every inch of his flesh, including his head and face. "I've been playing guitar all my life and even before that—since the

---

[5]It turns out the *Los Angeles Times* writer doesn't quote or mention my mother, but he does cite me as saying, "There's nothing funny about air guitar. . . . It's about nihilism, existentialism, showmanism, and a lot of other isms."

beginning of time!" he shouts. "I think my chances are between mediocre and *for sure*. I'm doing a song by the Osmonds called 'Crazy Horses.' It's a cosmic Mormon epistemological anthem for the masses, about the apocalyptic horseman from the book of Revelations. It's probably the hardest song ever recorded. . . ." The Messiah keeps on preaching, and I run away, with a growing concern for his Mormon anthem. Plus, I need to pee.

The time comes for us to gather in the room by the stage to listen to the air guitar rules as explained by Aer Lingus. This is my first real chance to gauge the competition. One guy wearing a long, black, stringy wig carts himself out in a wheelchair that has a giant mirrored crucifix attached to the back of it. He's got "God Rocks" written on his shirt in what looks like Beavis' (or Butt-Head's) scrawl. Another guy looks like Captain America, with a leather vest covered in red, white, and blue stars. There are a few female contestants: one with a bright red wig, a short skirt, and a dauntless look on her face; and another, somewhat older woman with a long blond mullet, who has apparently driven all the way from Arizona for tonight's event. The Airtight Messiah has returned in yet another outfit: pastel polka-dotted pajamas and a shiny red cape. His headband is cool—it has lots of plastic googly eyes glued onto it.

Aer Lingus offers us all a healthy pep talk. "Lookin' at the getups, reading the bios, I see we have an incredibly talented crowd here. Each and every one of you could go all the way." We erupt in a group "Woo!"

"This is the first time we have an officially sanctioned air guitar contest for the US. The winner is going to go to Finland, and hopefully, *hopefully* bring the crown to America." Another extended group "Woo!" "I think you'll all agree that America is the true home of air guitar!" And with that, a patriotic *"Wooooo!"*

Lingus finishes by announcing, "Beer is on its way!"

Moments before the competition begins, I meet up again with the *Carson Daly* crew, and they resume trailing me. It's utter mayhem backstage, with numerous competing camera crews, contestants, air roadies, and random blond chicks that look like strippers all running around. Most everyone is drunk, or on their way. We are told the order of our appearances onstage—chosen at random prior to the event—and that we need to get ready to go on. First will be the LA regional heat, and the winner of that will face the East Coast champ, C-Diddy, in the finals. I head downstairs to watch the opening ceremonies. Comedian Greg Behrendt (who went on to *slightly* better gigs after cowriting the bestselling breakup primer *He's Just Not That Into You*) is the evening's host and emcee. He begins the show by introducing the judges: the senior editor from *Hits* magazine, Roy Trakin; the former lead singer of Veruca Salt, Nina Gordon;[6] and one judge with true cred: the guitarist from Rage Against the Machine and Audioslave, Tom Morello.

The show begins, and it's an entirely different scene from what I saw in New York. For starters, the audience is much kinder and less prone to booing and yelling, *"Go the fuck home."* The costumes are far more elaborate, and the sexual energy is exponentially higher: at least four sets of naked female breasts—one or more of which may have been real—are seen onstage during the night. One guy called Dick Maynard inspires the entire crowd to chant,

[6]Whatever happened to Veruca Salt? I guess now we know. I wonder if judging air guitar competitions will eventually function like *Hollywood Squares* once did for out-of-work actors.

"Dick! Dick! Dick!" for what seems like an eternity following his performance.

The "God Rules" guy in the wheelchair (which I discover is electric when he maneuvers it across the stage unaided) is fucking spectacular—his entire act to the Christian metal band Stryper's "To Hell with the Devil" is done in the wheelchair, which he spins around and controls with his right hand while he fingers his air guitar with his left. At the end of the song, he falls out of the chair and onto the stage, and then dramatically rises up—as if miraculously healed by Air Guitar's divine power. This culminates with him standing fully erect, doing a front kick, making the rock-and-roll devil horns with both hands, and then jumping onto the floor to do the worm. *Amen!*

Starting with his ass to the audience, Krye Tuff embarks on "Talk Dirty to Me." A pink feather swings from his back pocket as he taps the beat with his foot. Then right out of the gate, Tuff launches into the air with a high David Lee Rothian spread-eagle kick, and that gets the already rowdy crowd thoroughly hot and bothered. His knee pads come in handy during several well-controlled knee slides, and he has a smile across his face the whole time that says, "I love my shit—and so best you." He ends in a muscleman pose as a tattooed woman leaps out of the audience to wrap herself around his thighs and nuzzle his crotch. I find out later he has never met this woman in his life.

Jane Air stands next to me on the side of the stage, and we shake our heads with concern—either the miracle cripple or Krye Tuff could have this thing in the bag.

I'm next. I put on my Mexican wrestling mask and large flowing robe, and make my way onto the stage, trailed by Jane. We do our little roadie act, which I decide as I am doing it is totally stupid and superfluous to my air performance. Jane removes my wrestling mask and my robe, and takes them offstage with her. Then I hear someone from the audience yell, "Go Kramer!" presumably referencing my tall, curly hair.

I give the soundman the cue to start the music, and when the medley reaches its first edit (from the opening chord hits of "Good Times Bad Times" into the unforgettable 8/8, 7/8 lick of "The Ocean"), the crowd cheers, but then quickly grows lukewarm. So much can happen in those sixty seconds. It's like the infamous eight seconds of a bull ride—it all goes by in slow motion. Then the solo section of "Whole Lotta Love" arrives with a *bumph bumph*: two syncopated power chords on top of massive Bonham bass drum hits, and then *doodee doodley-doodley-doodley-doodley*—Page's wailing solo filling every millimeter of space that the break in the song allows—but wait. *Where's the fucking doodley-doodley?* Apparently the Roxy is running in mono, and there is no right channel—the channel on which Page laid down his masterful licks. So, rather than being filled with the tight, fast arpeggios of Page's Les Paul, the spaces are filled with . . . silence. I am air guitaring *to air.* This temporarily throws me off, but I quickly recover, and four bars later we are into "Kashmir." I get out my air violin bow. Somewhere between the bars of innumerable triplets in "Stairway to Heaven" that declare the end of the solo (right before Plant shrieks, "And as we wind on down the road . . .") and the exploding guitar sound that introduces the solo of "In the Evening,"[7] I jump up on the monitor at the front of the stage—nearly losing my balance—but remain perched long enough to make my point. Though they cut off the song in the middle of Plant wailing, "Oh, so good" at the end of "The Ocean" (they really stick to the sixty-second rule here), the audience digs the violin bow and the use of the monitor, and seems happy with my performance overall.

"Björn Türoque, everyone!" shouts the emcee over the crowd as I depart from the stage. "The Swedes love a medley! America swells up with pride! Our first medley and our first monitor perch of the evening. We might see more of that."

Several other contestants take their shots, but nobody is nearly as interesting or bizarre as the last contestant, my childhood friend, The Airtight Messiah. Now caped in a flag that clearly once flew from the pole of a local McDonald's, and wearing his googly-eyed headband and fluorescent-framed sunglasses, The Messiah initiates his act by expelling massive amounts of fake blood from his mouth. The Osmonds' "Crazy Horses" shrieks like a tortured animal over the PA, and The Messiah leaps into a handspring, getting horribly tangled in his McDonald's flag cape. Then he runs to the back of the stage, climbs on top of the seven-foot-high rear monitors, and stands bleeding and air guitaring from there. At his song clip's completion, he runs to the front of the stage, leaps off the monitor into the crowd, and falls smack onto the floor. I feel both honored and disturbed to have spent several of my formative years being friends with the guy.

[7]This is my favorite guitar sound ever, with second place going to the *chicka . . . chicka* that ushers in the chorus of Radiohead's "Creep."

We wait backstage for the announcement, and then the top five contenders from round one are asked to return to the stage in order from lowest to highest score: Dick Maynard, The Airtight Messiah, Björn Türoque, Benjamin Walkin (the wheelchair dude), and in first place, Krye Tuff. I am relieved but not totally surprised to find I've advanced to the next round—I am, after all, no rookie.

The five of us stand onstage in anticipation, awaiting the first notes of the compulsory track. What will it be? Then, with a bludgeoning blow from the era of the New Wave of British Heavy Metal, we are dealt the "Ace of Spades" by Motörhead. Krye Tuff nearly jumps out of his spandex and starts singing and playing along. At first I think he is confused—that he thinks we are all supposed to be performing now—but then I realize he just loves that fucking song. It's as if he had selected it personally. He knows every lick, every note, every lyric, and he is overjoyed that this is the compulsory selection. I, on the other hand, obviously know the track (it's fuckin' Motörhead!), but I must admit it's been a few years since Lemmy and I last partied down.

Dick Maynard is up first, and the crowd can't get enough Dick—they just love chanting his stage name. The judges like him too, but not enough to give him very high scores. As Nina Gordon says following Maynard's performance, "I like Dick! I give him a 5.4." He gets another 5.4 and a 5.7.

His face indiscernible under his pink full bodysuit, The Airtight Messiah forgoes his air guitar and just runs around the stage like an escapee from a mental institution. He does an incredibly painful-looking front flip, landing on his back, then jumps up and begins to climb one of the large black curtains on the side of the stage until it starts to rip. Some of the audience members boo him; the rest are just confused. His scores: 5.3, 5.2, and 5.4.

It's my turn to play "Ace of Spades," and I fall flat. I rip open my T-shirt, but the bottom of it gets caught around my dick-do, and I finally have to lift what's left of it over my head in an uncoordinated act of desperation. It's as if my true physical reality has gotten in Björn's way—making him fumble, and ultimately forsake me. *Is Björn resentful? I knew I should have done more sit-ups.* I raise my air guitar up to my mouth and play a little with my teeth, but Björn has vanished entirely. I am without innovative ideas. I feel lost. I flew all this way—why didn't I plan anything for the second round?

Benjamin Walkin, the wheelchair dude, rolls out wearing nothing but a green Speedo and combat boots, spinning his electric chair around in circles. Then he stands up behind the chair, grabs the handles, puts his head down, and flips his body over the thing, landing sloppily on the stage. He then picks up an American flag off the stage and air guitars with that. Technically he should be disqualified for using a prop, but his performance, like mine, is irrelevant. Krye Tuff has the Ace up his sleeve.

Tuff's crowning move is a perfectly timed guitar toss into the air, which he catches right at the opening riff of the guitar solo. He gets two 5.9s and a 5.6, and will go on to battle C-Diddy in the final round—a match I know should have been my rematch. My air guitar dreams are trampled—I come in second place for the second time, tied with the wheelchair guy.

The coin toss is everything. C-Diddy wins it and wisely chooses to go second in the final round. He and Krye Tuff will each play a song of their own choosing, and then another compulsory track.

Krye Tuff enjoys the home turf advantage and has the audience clapping along with him on David Lee Roth's "Yankee Rose," and then C-Diddy comes out to repeat his New York performance of "Play with Me." It's incendiary once again. The LA audience initially boos the East Coast rival, but he instantly turns them around with a quick flap of his lengthy tongue. They belong to C-Diddy now. He easily trounces Krye Tuff in the compulsory round and is crowned the first US Air Guitar Champion.

We all join together for a group rendition of "Rockin' in the Free World," which I find out is the traditional Finnish way to end an official air guitar competition,[8] and I enjoy my last moments onstage with C-Diddy and the new LA champ, Krye Tuff.

The *Carson Daly* crew has abandoned me. As quickly as my star rose, it has fallen into obscurity.

I say good-bye to my mom, who is adamant that I was better than everyone else, and Jane Air and I exit the Roxy and head back to the hotel in a cab. Saturday night traffic on Sunset is moving about as slowly as Ozzy's synapses. It takes us forty-five minutes to drive one mile back to the Chateau, where we find the reason for all the traffic: a lady has been struck by a car in the intersection in front of the hotel. She's not injured, but was apparently intoxicated and sort of *fell into* a slowly passing car. At least that's how a member of LA's finest explains it to us.

Upstairs we order room service, since I never really had time to eat dinner. Forty-five minutes and eighty-four dollars later, it arrives. My fries are cold, mocking my failure. I try not to feel too de-

---

[8]Given the overall sense of anarchy at the first competition in New York, it's not surprising they forgot about the "Rockin' in the Free World" tradition.

jected, but I had wanted one more shot at C-Diddy. It's clear the dude has a gift. He may possibly be the best ever, but I just have this strange feeling that he'll fail in Finland. Jane tries to cheer me up, and we fall asleep watching *I Love the 80s* on VH1.

The next morning, I get up to go to the bathroom, and I hear laughter coming from the bed. I turn around and see Jane pointing at the mattress. Apparently, I've left a reverse tattoo of my Björn tattoo on the sheet. The Shroud of Björn. Great—I'm sure they'll charge me for that as well.

Chapter Seven: They Keep Pullin' Me Back In

If the fool would persist in his folly,
he would become wise.

—William Blake, "Proverbs of Hell"

(As quoted in *The True Adventures of*
the Rolling Stones, by Stanley Booth)

C-Diddy's staple song in both the New York and LA competitions was "Play with Me," by Extreme—a band most notable for its 1990 reverb-laden number-one hit power ballad about unrequited love, "More Than Words." If you can get past your memory of their hair and the video, the song is pretty good. With its tight harmonies and lilting falsettos, the Beatles or the Everly Brothers might as well have written it. The song's lyrics describe how saying "I love you" doesn't really mean anything until you *show* the person that your love is real. It's cheesy, but deal with it—the song sold millions of records. And, not that I want to make too much of Extreme's lyrics, but unrequited love is a subject with which I am familiar.

In 1993, I moved to San Francisco after breaking up with my

girlfriend two weeks prior to graduating from college. I had planned to move into her place in Fort Greene, Brooklyn (she was two years older than I was), just after graduation, but decided instead that I wanted to remain young forever, and the easiest way to do that would be to take loads of drugs and have sex with a frizzy blond sophomore, then tell my girlfriend about it. Despite my efforts, my youth faded anyway. And my New York plans, along with my two-year relationship with a really great girl who deserved far better, disintegrated.

I ended up in San Francisco in a four-bedroom railroad apartment with several friends from college. We got jobs, drank too much, smoked pot, drew pictures on the walls, and had the diner across the street deliver us curly fries on *90210* and *Melrose Place* nights. On one of those very nights, a friend of one of my housemates came over with a friend of hers. The minute she walked in, it was over. She had sad green eyes. Her hair was dark red and a little greasy. She wore a black leather jacket and looked like she could kick my ass. (She would, in her way.) She looked sort of like Claire Danes on *My So-Called Life* crossed with Ally Sheedy in *The Breakfast Club*. I was instantly in love with her and she wanted nothing to do with me.

Over time, through my persistence, we became friends. I foolishly got her a job at the small CD-ROM development company where I worked, in Oakland. I would pick her up in my car every day, and we'd drive east over the Bay Bridge, listening and screaming along together to the Breeders, Liz Phair, PJ Harvey, and other chick rock of the day. We became great friends. I learned about how depressed and socially phobic she was. How she had chronic migraines and many days simply could not get out of bed. How she went from prescription to prescription, looking for the magic cocktail to right her. Some days she'd get in the car and it would instantly reek of Tiger Balm. "Migraine?" I would ask. She would just nod her head, her hands covering her eyes.

I could cure her, if she would only let me, I thought.

I bought a motorcycle, in part to impress her. It didn't work, though sometimes she would ride on the back, and I would go crazy when she'd hang on tighter.

It was a quiet ride to work one Tuesday morning. We had been getting along great, hanging out all the time. We had just passed the shipping yards where the giant steel hoists that inspired George Lucas' design for the four-legged Imperial walkers from *The Empire Strikes Back* stood, lifeless and apathetic. I gripped the steering wheel hard and looked straight ahead. I turned the music down. "I have to confess something," I told her. "I think I am completely . . . um, in love with you." It wasn't so hard. It had been two years. She must have known. She knew.

"Wow. Well . . . I have to say . . . um . . . I've actually been feeling similarly lately."

I knew it. I could not be that stupid. Clearly we were in love—we just needed to rip each other's clothes off and rid ourselves of the sexual tension that had plagued us since the day we met.

"Okay . . . well, let's just take it slow, then. No rush. That's great. Okay." I was awkward. How could I not be?

A couple of days passed. I tried to pretend everything was normal. I figured maybe we could rent a movie Friday night, nothing serious. Not even a date, really. Upon this suggestion, she said, "You know, I've been thinking about this . . . and . . . I just don't think it's a good idea."

"Okay, we could go see some music, then," I suggested.

"No, no. I don't think it's a good idea for us to, like, get . . . involved," she said.

It was like getting hit in the face with a snowball. And that was about as much explanation as I ever got. We remained friends and car pool companions, and still went together on occasional motorcycle rides that were pure torment for me. After a while, I started to think I was losing my mind. I just didn't get it, and she wouldn't explain it. Why had she said she felt the same way, and then abruptly changed her mind? I too decided to take antidepressants—until they worsened my insomnia and made me lose both my appetite and my ability to, shall we say, release my inner tension. I wrote several songs about her and played them in my band, Connie Comfort. Even the drummer wrote songs about her from my point of view. The chorus of one of these songs went: "Torture fame / I guess that counts for something somewhere / but that won't change the pain / from fire to fuck."

Oh, the horror.

Of course I played the practice tapes for her in the car. It was my way of getting back at her. It didn't work.

Then one day her roommate asked me for a guitar lesson. The two of us started dating, fell in love, and moved to New York together. We dated for more than three years. The insane thing is, all of us are still friends.

Arriving back home in New York following my defeat in Los Angeles reminded me of the repeated sense of loss I would get after dropping off my unrequited love every day. I'd felt inches away from going to Finland, but then I just couldn't seal the deal. Why does wanting something we can't have exacerbate our desire for it?

I couldn't get past feeling that there was just something wrong with C-Diddy winning. Though audiences and judges in New York and LA loved him unanimously, and even I was astounded by his skills, I thought there was something fake about him. Behind that Hello Kitty breastplate, there seemed to be nothing but an actor playing the role of an air guitarist—a comedian with a costume. Though it was still a nascent art form in the US, I felt I understood what the Finns were looking for—that a truly good air guitar performance should offer something real and honest. Competitive air guitar required a certain amount of ironic self-awareness, sure, and I knew that I shouldn't care this much about losing an air guitar competition. But when you get so close to having something and it's just as quickly taken away, it can make you go a little . . . insane.

NEW YORK CITY July 1, 2003. Back at work, head low and spirits sour, I sit down at my desk, plug myself into my dorky anti–carpal tunnel syndrome wrist guards, and try to pretend I never went to Los Angeles. Various coworkers come up to my desk to find out how it went. I hold up two fingers indicating my secondary ranking.

When they ask about it, I reply, shaking my head, "LA . . . whatever. C-Diddy's going to Finland."

Bored by the tedious list of things I have to catch up on, I check out the Air Guitar World Championships Web site. From what I gather about the competition in Finland, they take air guitar very seriously. They seem earnest in their belief that air guitar could inspire world peace. After all, when was the last time Finland was involved in any kind of global conflict? The more I read, the more I come to believe that C-Diddy will get to Finland and embarrass the United States. I am convinced he will appear to the Finns as a buffoon, mocking the art form. He'll be laughed off the stage and sent home with his Hello Kitty tail between his legs.

I also think, *fuck—it would be really fun to go to Finland*.

Carefully scouring the rules and regulations of the international Air Guitar governing body, I discover that one need not win his or her nation's competition in order to proceed to the world finals. Apparently anyone can go to Finland and compete the night before the championship in a qualifying "dark horse" round, during which five winners are chosen to move on to the world finals.

I start checking airline prices to Oulu, Finland. The lowest fare I can find is $1,695 and it's on Uzbekistan Airways via Stockholm, Sweden. It seems like a lot of money and a scary airline (no offense, Uzbekistan), and what if I didn't qualify? Would it be worth it to trek to Finland in order to play just sixty seconds of air guitar? That's $28.25 per second.

I wonder if maybe I can get Finnair to sponsor me. Surely they want to root for the underdog? I contact them and tell them my story. As it turns out, they don't want to root for the underdog. And though they refuse to be my sponsor, they do point me to a Finnair flight for twelve hundred dollars. It's cheaper than Uzbekistan Airways, but still a lot of money.

Wasting yet more time at work, I do a search on eBay for "air guitar," and I'm shocked to find several for sale. Most are described as being in "like-new" or mint condition, and some even come with air amps. They all offer free shipping. I wonder if people really bid on these things. Then it dawns on me that I could help finance my trip by setting up a Web site and getting people to donate to my cause: help send me to Finland to defeat C-Diddy and defend America's honor in her first official foray onto the world stage. It seems like anyone can raise money on the Internet these days—why not Björn Türoque?

I build a makeshift Web site with a video clip of my appearance on *Last Call with Carson Daly* and a few photos of my air guitar exploits, and hope it will have a viral effect. After all, a million people saw me air guitar on national television, so if just a few of them donate, I'm off to Oulu.

I send out an e-mail to my coworkers, friends, and family announcing my decision to go to Finland.

Within minutes, I receive my first donation.

"You're a wacko and a genius, and that video of you made my day," said Russell of New York City. He offers twenty-five dollars.

"Do I need to call a psychiatrist?" asks Michael, originally from Germany. He offers nothing.

After a couple of days, to my disbelief, I've received nearly three hundred dollars.

Though I still haven't checked with my boss about getting more time off from work, I am pretty much locked in to going once I start receiving donations. I have already missed two weeks in May when Les Sans Culottes played a West Coast tour and recorded a new album in Los Angeles. Then there were the additional days I needed last month to fly to LA to compete in the air guitar finals. Maybe if I had won in LA, my boss would be more supportive of a trek to Finland? I send him an e-mail requesting more time off. He does not reply. But I do get more donations. Someone in Texas whom I've never met emails me and says she's donating five dollars. With that, I know I have truly harnessed the power of the Internet. I need to buy my ticket, as the date is drawing near, but my boss has yet to give me the green light. He and I have the following terse IM exchange:

Björn_Türoque: hey there

MrBossMan: hey

Björn_Türoque: any word on those air guitar dates?

MrBossMan: yeah, you can take the time, unpaid, but I hope we're nearing the end of these requests for leave time . . .

Later, in the hallway, my boss reminds me that I really need to "rein in my focus on the job" and emphasizes that this *really* has to be the end of my requests for time off.

How can I focus on my job? I have an Air Guitar World Championship to think about.

A couple of weeks later, with my airplane ticket for Oulu purchased and song selection process in full swing, I get a call on my cell phone from an unknown number with a 310 area code. That's Los Angeles.

"Hi, is this Björn Türoque?"

"Um, yeah. That's me."

She explains that she is working with a Japanese girl-band called Buffalo Daughter, and that she wants me to come to LA to play air guitar in their music video. "The director saw your work, and he said he just had to have you."

"Wow," I say. "Um, when would this be exactly?"

"This coming Monday," she says. Today is Wednesday. "We can't pay you, but we'll pay for your flight out here and a rental car. A bunch of the other guys from the LA competition will be there, but we've simply got to have you."

I am honored, sort of. Having not won, I wonder if maybe they are confusing me with Krye Tuff. Either way, who wouldn't want to get flown across the country to play air guitar in a music video? It would mean missing another day or two of work, so I ask if it's possible to shoot me on Sunday instead of Monday. She says she'll look into it.

I fly to LA on Saturday, crash at a friend's place, shoot the video on Sunday (they arrange a special day of shooting just for the day I

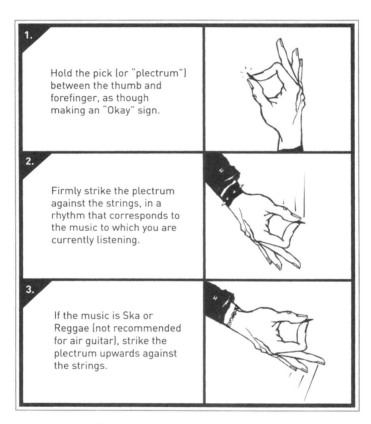

1. Hold the pick (or "plectrum") between the thumb and forefinger, as though making an "Okay" sign.

2. Firmly strike the plectrum against the strings, in a rhythm that corresponds to the music to which you are currently listening.

3. If the music is Ska or Reggae (not recommended for air guitar), strike the plectrum upwards against the strings.

Figure 4. How to use the strumming hand

am in town), and take the red-eye home that night. The best part of the eight-hour shoot is getting to teach a skinny model girl who stars in the video how to play air guitar. There's a crew of about five people with lights, reflectors, a camera, playback—the whole bit— all crammed into a small, sweaty hotel room, and I imagine that the hotel must think we are shooting a porno. The skinny girl and I stand up on the bed and bounce around to the song (which, incidentally, has only one chord in it and is probably the worst choice of air guitar songs I've ever heard—which is maybe the joke?). I instruct the girl on how to feel the weight of the guitar and how to strum with her right hand, like she is holding a pick. Luckily, since the track only has one chord, I don't have to explain much about what to do with her left hand besides position it.

Air Guitar 101.

Several months later a friend of mine e-mails me from Japan to tell me that he thinks he saw me playing air guitar in a music video—or maybe I was playing air keyboard? Apparently it was the most watched video in Japan the month it came out. I was onscreen for a total of about six seconds, indeed playing air keyboard.

Björn Türoque is big in Japan.

Chapter Eight: "And You May Ask Yourself,
'Well, How Did I Get Here?' "

*One must still have chaos in oneself to be able
to give birth to a dancing star.*

—Friedrich Nietzsche

A few years before I met Jane Air, and long before I had discovered
competitive air guitar (which, according to 2001–2002 world
champion Zac "The Magnet" Monro, "can save your life"), I experienced, in true rock-and-roll fashion, my dark period: I slept
around, got drunk a lot, had an on-and-off flirtation with cocaine,
did ecstasy whenever it was available. I even snorted a horse tran-
quilizer, ketamine, which made me feel slanted, crooked—not
good at all. Though I frequently managed to imagine I was having
fun, it was, overall, a pretty grim time.

On the surface, it would have appeared all was well. At the time,
Les Sans Culottes was riding the peak of its popularity—not an
Eiffel-Tower-scraping-the-sky kind of peak by any means, but we
were headlining shows at New York's Bowery Ballroom—one of
the better venues in the city for local and national acts to play—and

we even received interest from some A and R folks on the West Coast. I had a job working at a start-up educational Web site that would share the fate of almost every other Internet start-up and go belly-up within two years. I made good money. I wore expensive sneakers.

On the inside, though, like any rock star (or wannabe rock star), I was tortured.

Despite our successes, I hated playing in what I saw as a gimmick band. I wanted to play real music, but I had quit playing with my more serious venture, Calamine, a year or so prior, after an argument with the singer over the band's direction. And, as much fun as Les Sans Culottes was, it never felt creatively fulfilling. I was also fed up with my career, just as everyone my age seemed to be. I thought that doing work somehow rooted in "education" would make me feel better about it, but I had been producing software for eight years, and I couldn't stand it. If you've ever had something go wrong with your computer and spent hours and hours trying to get the thing to work again, imagine that *every day* is like that—this is your job, making software work. It was endlessly frustrating. Every year I said, *I cannot be doing this one year from now*, and another year would go by and I'd still be making software.

I was also in the middle of a long string of one-night stands, and my average relationship in this period had the lifespan of a Sea-Monkey. I pretty much hated everything about my existence.

My lowest point probably came in the summer of 2000.

Back in 1995, due to New York City's "quality of life" zoning laws, most of the city's strip clubs were forced to move out of the neighborhoods in which they had resided and into commercial districts where, presumably, they would not harm families by tempting fathers with depraved, naked women. Conveniently (or unfortunately) for me, I happened to live near one of these districts, and a strip club called Privilege arrived just one block from my apartment about a year after the ban was enacted. I had, on a couple of other occasions, stopped in for a nightcap and a lap dance at Privilege. It's not a habit of which I am proud, but it was, as I said, a dark period in my life BB (Before Björn).

One summer evening after a Les Sans Culottes gig, I arrived home around two a.m., feeling tipsy, horny, and alone. There's no letdown bigger than coming home after a show, lugging your bass and amp upstairs, and then realizing you are totally on your own for the rest of the night. So I walked over to Privilege. I was carded by the Mafia-esque thug outside and then allowed to enter. I opened the black glass doors that concealed the inside of the club, and paid the twenty-dollar entrance fee to an emaciated woman behind the desk reading *Us Weekly*. She hardly looked up from the magazine to take my money. Everything in a strip club is impersonal.

It was an average strip club—the kind you see in movies, only slightly more downscale (though not nearly as skanky as the Pussycat Lounge). There was a bar in the front, with girls in lingerie talking up guys in suits. Around the tables sat groups of men, mostly Wall Street types, smoking cigarettes and cigars (this was back when one could still smoke in New York City—*that* vice would come under fire a few years later), with topless girls straddling them. White girls, black girls, Latina girls, and Russian girls: all with at least six-inch heels, all smelling of a perfume that might as well be called *Stripper*. On a small stage, a too-skinny girl in bikini bottoms and high heels wrapped herself around a pole. It was beyond formulaic.

I sat by myself in one of the cushiony lounge chairs. I was still feeling the several drinks I had downed earlier; nonetheless, I ordered another from the waitress who came over showing lots of cleavage.

My vodka tonic arrived. I tipped the waitress and sipped on my weak, overpriced drink. The song changed, and the DJ announced another girl coming out. Her "name" was Christine, announced the DJ, his voice doused in reverb. Granted, I was drunk and alone in a strip club, my judgment impaired, but she was just . . . insanely hot. She had long, dark hair and bright blue eyes, and was the kind of girl that made one think, Jesus, why is *she* working here? The sober answer was obvious: she made really good money from assholes like me.

During Christine's stage show, girls kept sidling up to me, rubbing their chests in my face, and asking if I wanted a dance. Going rate: twenty dollars a song. I said no. I knew I had to wait for Christine. It was pathetic, the whole thing.

I waited for her to finish her show, and she walked offstage. When she reemerged, she approached the first guy she saw and offered a dance. He accepted. Nearly forty-five minutes and two more vodka tonics went by, and I kept denying dance offers from all the girls. A goon sitting in the corner smoking a cigar kept looking over at me. He seemed annoyed that I was taking up space in his bar and not paying for any dances. Then an older woman approached the goon and whispered in his ear, and he whispered back. She walked over to me and sized me up. "Those very nice shoes," she said with a thick Russian accent.

"Um, thanks," I replied, looking down at my expensive sneakers.

"I bet you are rock star," she said.

"Well . . ."

"I *know* you are rock star," she said, attempting to be provocative. "What is name of your group?"

"Uh . . ." I paused, weighing my response options. Strippers didn't use their real names. Why should I admit I was in a fake French band? And if I did, wouldn't my credibility be diminished? If I was in a *real* band, would I admit that to a Russian lady in a strip club?

"I can't really say." I had the upper hand now—I could be famous, and it was clear she thought I was.

"Wow. See. I can tell you are rock star. I know by your shoes," she said, pointing. I looked down at them again, and then up at her. She came in close, her hand massaging my shoulder. "Don't forget, have fun tonight," she whispered, and walked away.

Another few minutes went by, and Christine was still occupied. I was growing impatient. Maybe I should just go home. I kept trying to make eye contact with her but was having no luck. More girls approached me, and I turned them all down. Finally, The Goon, who looked like Tony Soprano's long-lost fatter cousin, came up to me and said, "Don't see anything you like, my friend?" He had a shaved head, was at least three hundred pounds, reeked of stale cigar smoke, and could probably crush my skull with his thumb and forefinger.

"I like her," I said, pointing at Christine.

"Awww yeah. Christine. She's da best. Da *best*. You wanna spend some time with her?" he asked.

Spend some time. What did that mean? I knew what "getting a dance" signified, but not "spend some time." I was no pro at this. And I was also completely intoxicated at this point.

"Yeah, sounds good," I murmured, my eyelids struggling to stay open.

The Goon went over and whispered in Christine's ear. She looked over at me, smiled, and then went into the back. The Goon waved me towards him and I stood there, cocktail in hand, awaiting instruction. At least progress was being made.

The Goon sat me down in a small room with a red velvet sofa. There was no door, and he emphasized repeatedly that I couldn't touch Christine and that "they'd be watching me." I would have one hour with her. I sat waiting, confused. Drunk. *One hour?* Christine walked in and plopped down next to me. Even up close, she was still incredibly attractive. She was probably about twenty-two years old. Her skin was sweaty. Her eyes were glowing. We talked for about ten minutes. She had been told that I was a rock star. She kept trying to guess what band I was in. She'd throw out band names, and I'd just keep answering, "Maybe . . . you've probably never heard of us." I wasn't lying.

She told me she was having a *great* night. She was doing "some really good E," she said, and asked if I was having a great night. I said I was having an okay night, but I would also love some ecstasy. She said she'd go see if she could find some. Brilliant.

In the meantime, the cocktail waitress walked in with a bottle of champagne, uncorked it, and poured two glasses. Instantly, I recalled a scene in the recent movie *Go*, where one character tells another *never* to order the champagne in a strip club. Shit. I sat there sipping horrible champagne, wondering where Christine went. It seemed like about ten minutes had gone by before she returned to tell me there wasn't any more E to be had. Oh well. Does that get taken off my time? I wondered.

Christine thanked me for the champagne—"Aww—! That's *so* sweeeeet"—but decided she didn't want to drink any. She was becoming less and less attractive by the minute. I wondered if the waitress had slipped something into the champagne and I was going to wake up the next morning in the alley bruised, broke, and naked. I wondered if anything was going to happen in this back room, or if Christine and I were just going to keep having insipid, phony conversation. I was filling the shoes of the rock star I had convinced everyone (The Goon, the Russian woman, Christine, myself) I was, and Christine massaged my ego while I wished she was massaging anything else. Finally she gave me about ten minutes worth of unenthusiastic lap dancing.

Prince's song "Kiss" played loudly over the club's sound system, muffled here in our private back room hangout. Christine's "ecstasy high" somehow magically wore off. She was all business, all fakery. I was bored, tired, hating myself, and hating her.

Christine put her top back on, kissed me on the cheek, offered a bubbly, "Thanks!" and vanished like a vapor.

As quickly as Christine had exited, in walked the Russian lady with a black folio containing the bill. I blurrily glanced down at the damage.

It was twelve hundred dollars.

Twelve hundred dollars?

TWELVE HUNDRED FUCKING DOLLARS?

I rubbed my forehead furiously and drummed the pen on the table, immediately scheming how I could get out of this. Oh, wait: I was a famous rock star! Surely I could afford a twelve-hundred-dollar, hour-long, useless, mindless, inconclusive tease! No problem!

I pictured The Goon. I pictured my ribs getting broken by The Goon. I was trapped and too drunk to come up with any alternative to just paying the bill. I handed my credit card over to the Russian lady, signed, and ran—literally, ran—the block and a half home to my apartment.

I had blown twelve hundred bucks to feel like a rock star for almost an hour. In air guitar currency, I guess I got a good deal.

NEW YORK CITY August 27, 2005. I kiss Jane Air good-bye, take a cab to Newark, and board the overnight flight to Finland. I had received a total of $430 in donations from people who wanted to see me win the world title. It was only about a third of the money I needed for the ticket, but it helped. Was I out of my mind? No, I was on a mission.

In my notebook on the plane, I write a short, somewhat morbid journal entry:

28 August 03

Approaching Stockholm for plane switch to Oulu. Jesus my handwriting sucks. Will people in twenty years know how to write? This will now mark 40 air hours I have logged in the name of air guitar. Why is not clear. Seems like a thing to do before one is gone . . .

After landing in Stockholm, where I will catch the short flight to Oulu, I slouch slowly towards the immigration window.

"Reason for visit?" asks the gaunt, sullen man at the counter.

"Air guitar?" I say, unsure whether that's a good enough reason.

The customs agent cocks his head slightly and squints his eyes. We have a brief staring contest until, with an abrupt slam, he stamps my passport, allowing me to continue on my way.

I stop to grab some coffee and observe ten Scandinavian-looking guys sitting around a table downing pints of beer. It's seven thirty a.m. I take this as an omen that I will be very drunk on this trip.

I meander around the airport for an hour during my layover. The Stockholm airport is clean, almost beautiful. Everything is well designed, as if by IKEA (not unlikely, with IKEA being Swedish). It's easy to find one's way around. The restrooms are immaculate.

Soon it's time to board the puddle jumper to Oulu. I had foolishly assumed that the other fifteen passengers on this terrifyingly tiny plane would be headed there for the same reason I am, but they are all students, businessmen, and grandparents. Not really an air guitar crowd.

I can see Oulu as we begin our descent. It's gray. Gloomy. Raining. It looks cold and foreboding. Looking down on the city, it's all blocky square buildings—as if everything is made out of LEGOs. I imagine that everyone in Oulu has plastic hair that pops on and off, and that all the men carry square briefcases and drive forklifts to work.

How did this become the global epicenter of air guitar?

I deplane, carrying my backpack containing a few days' worth of clothes, my air guitar costume, and, naturally, my air guitar. After nearly ten hours of traveling, I am completely exhausted.

By American standards, the Oulu airport is about the size of a Pizza Hut. It's quiet. As I exit the terminal, I see a young troll-like dude with a blond goatee and long stringy hair standing alone. He is holding up a small cardboard sign with my name, Björn Türoque, written on it.

I shake his hand. "You are Bjern Turick?" he asks.

"Uh . . . yeah. How's it going?" I say, and shake his hand. He tells me his name in a hushed, fearful whisper.

"I'm sorry," I say. "What's that?" He repeats his name. Again, I can't understand him at all.

"It is an honor to meet you," he says as we walk away from the terminal. Later, I find out his name is Antti Tuominen. He is a Finnish air guitar intern. He studies communications.

My face is wet with Finnish mist. One of the documentary makers is standing nearby, shooting us. From here forward every move I make will be captured on video. Antti and I hop into his small European-looking car (which does look as if it's made of LEGOs) and drive towards the city center.

Oulu appears just slightly *off* from other European cities I've visited. Though the occasional brick or stone structure can be spotted, most of the buildings look as though they have been constructed in the past fifty years and have a more Eastern European feel than Western. Oulu is a university town, so there are lots of student-aged kids riding bicycles. Antti tells me that one of the main national pastimes is to sit in a hot sauna drinking beer.

"So, this is a big event for Oulu, right?" I ask Antti, about tomorrow night's championship.

"Yes, I think so," he responds, as if he's not quite sure what I mean.

"So you're pretty excited?"

"Exciting. Yes," he says, laughing robotically. He obviously lives for air guitar.

We arrive at Oulu's Hotel Cumulus, the official hotel of the Air Guitar World Championships. I look for a sign that reads WELCOME AIR GUITARISTS. There is no sign. I approach the front desk, and a cheery woman wearing a polyester pantsuit greets me. As she hunts for my reservation, I ask her if it's just a coincidence that the official hotel of air guitar is called the Cumulus, what with cumulus being a type of cloud. She's baffled. Then I realize she doesn't really speak English.

She hands me my key, and I take the elevator up to my room. On the door is the number 222: a lucky number, I think, since it adds up to 6, a perfect score.

My tiny room feels like the cabin of a third-rate cruise ship.

The foot of the bed nearly touches the wall. I had been hoping to get a little practice in here, but there's hardly room to change one's shirt, much less run through an air guitar stage routine. Nonetheless, I take out my iPod, put in my headphones, and prepare to practice the two songs I've brought with me, one for the qualifying round and one for the championship—should I make it in.

I select "The Mole" by The Bags and click PLAY.

The Bags were a Boston band who released their first album in 1987. (There was also an LA punk band called The Bags fronted by two runaway Catholic schoolgirls who wore bags on their heads for their first few shows. This is not that band.) In *Playboy*, Charles M. Young described the band as falling "somewhere among the Ramones, Hüsker Dü, and early KISS." Young goes on to say, "Their debut, *Rock Starve* (Restless), consists of thrilling guitar-bash riffs that pound like the sound of a herd of giant woolly mammoths going over a cliff, just enough melody rasping though shredded vocal cords and lyrics wholly unbesmirched by any pantywaist college-poetry influence." Of their 1990 eponymous EP, *Rolling Stone* said, "At their best, The Bags rip it up like the Meat Puppets meet Motörhead, a marriage surely made in bar-band heaven."

The band went on to release another full-length album, 1991's *Night of the Corn People*, which I consider their finest work. I stole the CD from my older brother when I visited him during college. I always loved this album, particularly the track "The Mole." It's a brilliant piece of rock and brimstone that *I think* might be about masturbation.

> *Every night I lie awake*
> *in a clammy lake*
> *of guilt and grief*
> *it's helpless*
> *Till the day I choose to speak*
> *I remain a freak*
> *and it just gets worse*
> *I'm helpless*

> *So now I finally bare my soul*
> *Help me sing it loud—help me out*
> *The Mole, The Mole, The Mole, The Mole*

After releasing *Night of the Corn People*, the band, tragically, broke up. Coincidentally (or not), in 2003, the same year I chose "The Mole" for my Finland air guitar debut, The Bags reunited and began writing songs again. In 2004 they played a sold-out show at Boston's Middle East club, and months later released their first record in thirteen years, titled *Sharpen Your Sticks*. I'd like to think I had something to do with their renaissance, but I suppose that's unlikely.

Returning nostalgically to the air guitar mode of my childhood, I am on my bed in Oulu's Hotel Cumulus, bouncing away, iPod on maximum volume, watching my moves in the reflection of the framed mirror hanging on the wall. I alternate between "The Mole" and my other song choice, "I Get Along," by Brit band the Libertines. I imagine that at this very moment, if one were to cut the building in half down the middle and view it like a dollhouse, one could see scores of air guitarists flopping around their rooms, heads banging simultaneously.

I work myself into a sweaty lather and then fall asleep for a few hours.

One of the documentary crew members knocks on my door and wakes me up—it's time for me to explain on camera why I am here. My hair is standing on end, as if I've been electrocuted, and I look like Nikki Sixx circa 1983. I splash some water on my face and try to look somewhat less disheveled than I feel. My eyes are red and I feel like death. As I walk out into the hall, out of the elevator comes the man I've idolized for months—the man whom I first read about and whose performances I studied online, the best air guitarist in the world two years running: London's Zac "The Magnet" Monro. I knew he wasn't a typical metalhead air guitarist, and in fact he looks even more normal than I had imagined. He's got short hair and vaguely resembles Jude Law.

"Björn Türoque, I presume," he says, and shakes my hand. I'm surprised he knows who I am.

"An honor to meet you, sir," I say.

"I've heard a lot about you," he says. "Good luck tonight. Don't worry, a lot of the guys that turn up for the dark-horse round are kind of crap."

"Okay. Cool, thanks."

Zac is not here to compete.[1] He has returned this year to be one of the judges at this evening's qualifying event and to lecture at the High Altitude Camp—an overnight full-immersion air guitar training course, which I unfortunately had to skip because I couldn't miss any more work than necessary. I get back to the interview and Zac goes on his way, presumably to begin drinking.

Aer Lingus asks me to sit down in front of the camera, and then he begins questioning:

Lingus: How have you been training for tonight's event?

I'm squinting from the two extraordinarily harsh, bright lights shining in my face. I feel jet-lagged, exhausted. I'm not sure I have it in me to conjure up Björn at the moment. But I must.

Björn: I've been getting in shape, better than I was before. I've been running, doing a lot of sit-ups and push-ups, practicing every day. My strumming arm is getting very strong.

I hope it's not too obvious that I've mostly been sitting around my apartment, drinking beer and listening to The Bags.

Lingus: What do you think will be different about Finland's event compared to the US?

I picture myself onstage at the Pussycat Lounge and the Roxy.

Björn: The world air guitar competition is a different arena altogether. In America people took it as a joke and had

---

[1]After Zac's second consecutive win in 2002, he vowed that he would stay off the stage until someone else won two titles, at which point he would come out of retirement.

their funny outfits, but that's not how they approach it here. They're really more into the art and the true spirit of it. You know, Nietzsche once said, "The more abstract the art that you want to teach, the more thoroughly you must seduce the senses to accept it." So that's really what I am about. I am about seduction; I am about taking the art form to a higher place.

Lingus: This is the first time America has sent an official entrant to the competition—how do you think America will be perceived?

I remember Finland's air guitar principle—that if everyone were to hold an air guitar instead of a gun, there would be world peace.

Björn: There's a general consensus in America that the rest of the world hates us. One of the messages I want to bring from America is that I am antiwar; I am the Underdog of Peace from the US. I am hoping I can build that kind of bridge, a bridge really spanning from Newark, New Jersey, where my flight left, all the way to Oulu.

Lingus: What if you don't make the cut tonight? Will the trip to Finland be in vain?

That would suck, entirely.

An hour or so later, documentary crew in tow, I make my way over to another LEGO building, NUKU, where I am told I need to check in for the competition. There I meet two Austrian guys: one has greasy slicked-back hair, and sips from a McDonald's cup; the other just eyes me with disdain and doesn't say much. I learn that the quiet one came in second place in Austria and, like me, has come seeking a rematch.

"So you lost and you're coming back for more?" I ask him.

"I came in second, I didn't lose," he says, defiantly, in his Schwarzeneggerian accent.

"Yeah? So you're the Austrian version of me?" I say, building bridges.

"Yeah, so your name is Niko too?"

"Well, no. Björn."

"Ah, okay." He is not interested in bridge building.

"I was second place in New York," I explain.

"But you see it mostly as a competition—a tough competition?" Greasy Hair chimes in. *What else would it be? He thinks I flew all the way from New York just to hang out?*

"Yeah," I say. "Very difficult. It's probably the toughest competition I'll ever face in my life."

"You think so?" He laughs at me, and then finishes his Coke. I wish them luck and walk away, sensing I overdid it. I worry that I came off as the typically cocky American obsessed with winning above all else. I was mostly kidding, but really, this Niko guy came in second in Austria and trekked his ass to Oulu. There's some part of him that wants to go all the way, right?

How's Niko any different from me?

Are Americans the only ones who actually *want* to win this damn thing?

Is it wrong to want to win?

Downstairs is a small room where we are to go over the rules of the competition and have a brief press conference. I immediately run into my American nemesis, C-Diddy.

C-Diddy: What can I say? I am touched. I am impressed. This man is incredible.

Björn: You're scared, is what you are.

C-Diddy: No. I'm trying to be modest; I'm trying to be supportive. Don't make it hard for me, Björn. There's a lot of respect here, a lot of mutual admiration.

Björn: It's true; we're like a mutual admiration society.

C-Diddy: If you *were* to take the title, I would be very, very happy about it. I think you've earned it.

Björn: I've certainly paid my dues.

C-Diddy: Absolutely. But I'm not going to give it to you, you know.

Björn: I wouldn't want you to take a fall for me. I want to earn it honestly.

C-Diddy: It would be the Cinderella story of the millennium.

Björn: I am the underdog, if there ever was one.

Marika Lamberg, the producer of the competition, interrupts our banter by launching the orientation. "Welcome, everyone. Dere are eighteen brave air guitarists tonight. Six of you will make it to de finals." We all introduce ourselves, and I notice an overwhelming number of German competitors. There are only a few Finns, including "Gore Kitty"—perhaps the evil Finnish counterpart to C-Diddy's Hello Kitty—and a guy called "Terrible One," who announces in a thick accent: "I play Rainbow tonight!"

We all write our stage names on pieces of paper and put them into a bowl to decide the order in which we will compete in tonight's qualifying round. I draw seventh.

Zac Monro shows up and we give him a big round of applause. It's as if General Douglas MacArthur is readying the troops for battle. "Tonight," he announces, "we're looking for a sense of air, really, and we're looking forward to it immensely."

After the press conference, Marika verifies with Zac Monro that he's planning on heading out to the "Service Center" with her this afternoon to judge their air guitar competition. As we are all leaving, Zac asks if I want to join him.

"Fancy coming with me to the home for handicapped people?" asks Zac.

I tell him I don't think I can, as I'm supposed to go shoot some b-roll with the documentary crew.

C-Diddy walks up to join our conversation and Zac asks, "What do you think of this battle of the century?"

"Hey, Ali–Frazier—they went three," says C-Diddy.

He has a point. Even though I didn't get to face him directly in LA's competition, this is technically our third rematch. Our "Showlu in Oulu" to Ali and Frazier's "Thrilla in Manila."

C-Diddy tells Zac that he has much respect for me, and that if I don't make it to the finals tonight, this whole thing is a sham. I feel humbled, in a way, standing in the shadows of these air guitar giants. I thank C-Diddy for his kind words, head back to the hotel, and try unsuccessfully to catch up on some sleep.

A few hours later, with the documentary crew perpetually on my ass, I walk over to the club, 45 Special, where the qualifying round is to be held. The three-level venue has a kind of drinking-establishment-as-theme-park feel to it. Downstairs is a dark grottolike area with brick walls and fly-wing-shaped iron grills between each of the several booths that line the left-hand wall. The main floor has a bar enclosed in a kind of miniprison. Handcuffs, chains, and leg irons hang around the bar, giving you the sense that with every cocktail, you've been served with both a drink and a jail sentence. It's like *Midnight Express* meets the Hard Rock Cafe. On the top floor there's a small stage and an area that probably holds 150 or so people, with a row of steel grating separating the performers from the potentially rowdy audience. That's where the dark horses will be facing off.

I walk around the bar, beer in hand, chatting it up with my competition. I want to find out what makes them tick. Why have they, like me, traveled thousands of miles just to play air guitar for sixty seconds with no guarantee of even making it to the finals? Angus Hung from Glasgow offers, "One of my major reasons for doing this is to prop myself up there for public humiliation. You can only be stronger afterwards. If you've stood up there and made a fool of yourself in front of five thousand Finns—"

Startled by his estimate of crowd attendees, I interject, "Five thousand?!"

"I think there's gonna be five thousand tomorrow night."

"That's insane," I say. "Where do they come from? I mean, that's gotta be most of Finland."

"Yeah. They come from the villages . . . from the mountains. It's going to be huge. I think this is the biggest thing since Finland's fattest-pig competition."

This country really has no shortage of oddball competitions.

Upstairs, the emcee lays down the rules.

"Your air guitars, they must be *invisible*. You can play electric or acoustic air guitar. Air roadies and air groupies are allowed. I also would like to have some air groupies after the show." He introduces the jury, which consists of Zac Monro, a female TV producer from New York, and an actor from a local theater.

The dark-horse round begins. The other competitors—including Gore Kitty, a red-haired dude from London called the Red Plectrum, Angus Hung, and a Brit known as "Lobsterman," who is here for the third time—are not all that impressive. It's hard to believe people have come this far to play sixty seconds of mediocre air guitar. The only interesting competitor is a skinny twig of a Finnish dude with the stage name Rainbow Man, who gets up onstage wearing nothing but his name tag around his neck, a clownish grin, and his air guitar. He quickly loses the name tag, grabs his penis with his right hand, and strums it madly to Nirvana's "Territorial Pissings." Standing only a few feet away, I hope he's not going to take the title of the song too literally. He's pretty good

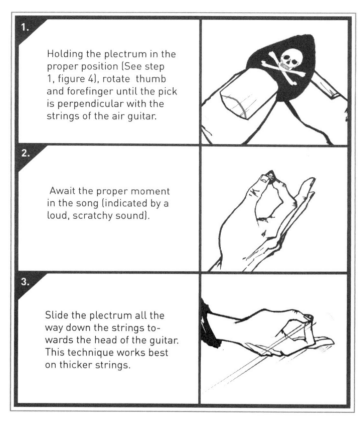

1. Holding the plectrum in the proper position (See step 1, figure 4), rotate thumb and forefinger until the pick is perpendicular with the strings of the air guitar.

2. Await the proper moment in the song (indicated by a loud, scratchy sound).

3. Slide the plectrum all the way down the strings towards the head of the guitar. This technique works best on thicker strings.

Figure 5. How to perform a pick slide

Note: For added effect, one may elect to make a "surprised" facial expression as if to say, "Holy Shit! I had no idea I rocked quite this hard."

for a naked guy, but I do wonder if he's violated the rule of "no props." His scores range from 5.8 to 4.4, which means those five thousand Finns will likely not have the opportunity to witness his performance at the finals tomorrow night.

Apparently, in Finland, "Björn" is pronounced Bjern, and "Türoque" sounds something more like Turick.[2] So my stage name is lost on everyone when the emcee asks "Bjern Turick" up to the stage. Wearing a white oxford shirt with the bottom and the sleeves cut off, my skinny white leather tie, dark corduroys, and black boots, I signal the DJ to launch "The Mole." I am instantly in complete control of my air guitar. I feel confident, powerful. My practicing has paid off. About twenty seconds in, I slide my air pick down my air E-string and transition from the slower-tempo bridge back into the verse, kicking my right boot into the air just as the snare drum hits. The audience goes nuts.

I would bet the cost of a plane ticket to Oulu that not a single person in that room has ever heard of The Bags or listened to their song "The Mole" prior to this evening; yet, when the chorus arrives, they are joining in, as The Bags command:

> *Help me sing it loud—help me out*
> *The Mole, The Mole, The Mole, The Mole*

I almost start laughing at the sight of a roomful of people shouting, "The Mole!" at me, and then the song ends and I raise my hands in the air, victorious. I know I was good, but was it what the

---

[2] The umlauts didn't help. Mötley Crüe faced the same problem at an early concert in Germany, where the audience chanted for "Moetly Cru-eh."

judges are looking for? I glance over to my right, where they are sitting, to see the scores: 6.0, 6.0, and 5.9. I am elated.

The points are tallied, and I've taken first place. It's a strange feeling, winning. I know it's only the qualifying round, and that I must translate tonight's victory into triumph tomorrow night, where I can only assume the competition will be stiffer.

In the crowd afterwards, C-Diddy and I hug as he declares, "USA in the house!" I can't tell if C-Diddy is being genuinely nice to me, or just trying to make me feel overly confident so that I'll blow it tomorrow.

"You could not have been any better. The crowd started off mellow and then you totally turned them around. No jet lag at all. You looked excellent."

"Thanks, man. You know, my room number is 222, and that adds up to 6, so I knew that was a lucky number."

"It could also mean second place, three times. . . ." he says with a raised eyebrow.

"Hadn't thought of that," I say. *Damn you, C-Diddy!*

Zac Monro joins us, congratulates me, and then explains why he thinks I didn't get a totally perfect score. "The reason you didn't get a 6 from one of the judges was that she thought you looked a little cocky. But I think it works. I saw the girls fainting, and I have to say it hurts—you know, I used to be there."

I put my arm around Zac to console him. It must be hard to be surrounded by so much air and yet unable to inhale. "So tomorrow you're gonna be all right," says Zac. "You've got the right moves, the right kind of footwork. . . . Can I ask you how many beers you had to drink before you went on?"

"Um . . . three," I answer after counting them in my head.

"Didn't I say three beers?"[3] he says to C-Diddy, who nods affirmatively. "See, you're a natural. Three beers is perfect." He pauses and looks me in the eye. "You've been chasing this fucker, haven't you?"

"It's like a carrot I keep chasing."

"You won't take no for an answer."

"I'm the underdog. You gotta root for the underdog."

Then Zac suddenly makes a startling pronouncement. "You know, I have to say . . . I look at you, and I see myself. I see the future of air guitar—and that future is Björn Türoque."

With this, C-Diddy appears visibly shaken. Is Zac Monro some kind of divine prophet of air guitar? C-Diddy has traveled across the globe, accompanied by his fiancée and parents; will Björn, the future of air guitar, shame him? It's a glorious moment.

I stroll downstairs to treat myself to beer number four. The naked competitor, Rainbow Man, instead buys me a Salmiakkikossu, the inebriation tool of choice in Finland.[4] He's probably had about ten Salmiakkikossus and is fully loaded. Rainbow Man drunkenly puts his arm around me to tell me how great I was onstage, and then begins getting *exceedingly* buddy-buddy with me. He seems to be trying to kiss me, in fact, and while I am aware of just how

---

[3]At the training camp, I later learn, Zac established The Three Beer Rule, which states that no air guitarist should compete without first being primed with no more and no less than three beers. A one-ounce cocktail may be substituted for a twelve-ounce beer. This rule is similar to Chuck Klosterman's dancing principle, as laid out in *Fargo Rock City:* "If I am sober enough to drive, I am too sober to dance."

[4]Legend has it that this drink is based on an episode of *The Simpsons* where Homer makes a fortune off a cocktail containing, among other things, cough syrup. *Salmiaki*, the main ingredient of Salmiakkikossu, is actually Finnish for ammonium chloride, which is sometimes used as cough medicine, and is also a primary ingredient in a popular salty licorice-flavored candy called Salmiaki. The other main ingredient is vodka. The drink became popular in Finland in the nineties, just after the aforementioned *Simpsons* episode first aired.

"gifted" he is, Rainbow Man is not exactly the air groupie I was hoping to mingle with after the show. I thank him for the drink and quickly make my escape.

As I head towards the bathroom, three young blond Finnish angels approach me. They are giggling with excitement and tell me my performance was excellent.

Could these be Björn's first air groupies?

We grab a table and I ask the girls about Finland. They are all students at the University of Oulu. Having graduated from college a full ten years prior, I feel more than slightly too old to be having a conversation about what Finnish girls are majoring in, but I am drunk on victory and getting drunker on Salmiakkikossu. One of the girls is really cute and very shy and keeps looking at me coyly, nervously, as if she is talking to Lenny Kravitz. Another has a totally alluring gap between her front teeth and tells me that her favorite air guitar song is "Crazy Horses" by the Osmonds. (I find the fact that this lovely girl in Finland is on the same musical wavelength as The Airtight Messiah only slightly disturbing.) The third girl is a bit on the zaftig side, but does have a very nice smile.

I buy them all shots, and we toast to victory for Björn Türoque. Björn is hoping that they'll all go back to his hotel room afterward for a massive rock and roll–style orgy—drugs will be ingested, they'll all roll around naked in Björn's giant suite, the girls will videotape the whole thing and then blackmail Björn for millions of dollars.

Instead, the gap-toothed girl's boyfriend shows up and gets very jealous that we are talking. He insists that she leave immediately. She says no. He storms off in a fit of teenage male angst, and

Figure 6. The Three Beer Rule: How to get appropriately inebriated but not incapacitated

she explains to me that "they are just friends." I start to wonder how I got mixed up in all this high school drama.

The four of us end up downstairs in the basement of 45 Special in an air bacchanalia. Nearly everyone from the competition is down there—the documentary crew, Rainbow Man, Lobsterman, the Red Plectrum, Aer Lingus. The music is cranked, and all are fully adrift in an air guitar free-for-all. My Finnish air groupies and I join in, and for the next hour and a half, we rock together in a frenzied air jam session. The Scorpions' "Rock You Like a Hurricane" (a song that would come to haunt me) is blaring over the crappy sound system and I'm leaning against the dank brick wall of the club basement, playing the solo note for note, when suddenly the gap-toothed girl is on top of my thigh, riding it like a kid on the bobbing horse of a merry-go-round. The song ends; she dismounts and laughs. I laugh. It's vaguely reminiscent of sex—or at least the kind of sex one has before losing one's virginity. Air sex. It's actually, in a way, better than real sex.

It's the greatest night ever.

Eventually the boyfriend of the gap-toothed Finnish hottie returns and drags her off. Her friends follow, and I am left alone with my air guitar, which—considering that Jane Air is waiting for me back home in New York—is probably for the better.

Chapter Nine: Pikku G Means "Lil' G" in Finnish

I wanna tell you this once and then, uh, I ain't gonna say it again. But Rock, you got another shot. This is the second shot. At, uh, I don't know, the biggest title in the world, and you're gonna be swappin' punches with, with the most dangerous fighter in the world. And just in case—you know, your brain ain't workin' so good. . . . So I say for God's sake, why don't you stand up and fight this guy hard?

—Mickey (Burgess Meredith) to
Rocky (Sylvester Stallone), in *Rocky II*

The next day, Marika, the producer of the competition, stands at the front of the small theater in the basement of NUKU, where she reviews the rules and announces the pecking order for the finals this evening. I am suffering from a titanic hangover. "Tonight's order is: going first, from United States, Dan 'Björn Türoque' (pronounced correctly this time) Crane; second, from Austria, Niko

'Air.Alm'; third, from de UK, Ian 'The Red Plectrum' Stafford . . ."

Wait a minute. I won last night. Shouldn't I be the *last* of the dark horses to compete? Doesn't winning the qualifying round guarantee me a better starting position in the finals? That's how it worked in the US. This sets off a deafening "What the fuck?" alarm in my haggard, throbbing, hungover brain. Going first is a death knell. I must wage a protest. When Marika finishes going over the evening's order of events, I ask her why, if I had won the previous evening, I had to go first.

"Dese are de rules, Mr. Crane."

"But they don't make any sense—what's the logic?"

"It is not logic. Dey are simply de rules, and de rules are de . . ."

"But . . . I won the . . ."

"We can make it so you do not go at all, is dat better? I am very busy, and . . ."

"No, that's fine," I relent. "Okay. Okay, I'll go first."

I return to the hotel for a quick sauna in the basement, and then go in search of coffee and greasy food. I have fifteen-gallon sized bags under my eyes and feel like a high-speed European train wreck. At least I've managed to evade the documentary crew, so I can finally get a few moments alone in peace. The Hotel Cumulus has a restaurant on the ground floor, and I am not up for exploring so I grab a table by myself and order some eggs, sausages, and coffee—what they call an "English breakfast." Two tables next to me, a gangly old rocker dude with dyed black hair, a wrinkled black leather jacket, and a gnarled face to match talks loudly on his cell phone.

"Yeah, Hanoi Rocks. It's the manager calling," I overhear. "They're wondering about the sound check. . . ."

Hanoi Rocks, the eighties hair metal band? I assume they are playing in town somewhere tonight. Unfortunately, I'll have to miss the gig.[1]

Do I repeat last night's highly successful performance of "The Mole," or go with my alternate track by The Libertines? From what I can gather about the Finnish air jury (based on my conversations with the locals and what I've read online), they are most concerned with an authentically balls-out rock-and-roll performance, but "The Mole," I fear, might just be too obscure. Conversely, The Libertines were huge in England and were presumably popular throughout Europe, and "I Get Along" couldn't have more adrenaline. After much deliberation, I decide that since I am going first, it doesn't really matter. I might as well try something new and go with The Libertines.

Back in the lobby, I run into a bleary-eyed Zac Monro, who asks if I want to join him for a coffee. I am honored that he wants to hang out with an air rookie such as myself. I feel like Stallone

---

[1]Hanoi Rocks, originally from Helsinki, is the only Finnish band that ever came close to making it big. In 1984, while on their first major tour of the US, drummer Nicholas "Razzle" Dingley was killed while riding shotgun with a drunken Vince Neil, lead singer of Mötley Crüe. Hanoi Rocks never recovered from Razzle's death and called it quits the following year, while Mötley Crüe went on to sell over forty million records worldwide. Hanoi Rocks reunited in 2002 with original members Andy McCoy (né Antti Hulkko) on guitar and Michael Monroe (Matti Fagerholm) on vocals.

about to get coaching from Burgess Meredith. I imagine a montage: Zac and I are running through the streets of Oulu, air guitaring to "Eye of the Tiger"; I stop to do push-ups on the steps of the town hall and the mayor comes out and joins me; we share an air jam and then the mayor joins in; soon the whole town is following us down the street, air guitaring in perfect synchronicity.

We walk though a gray, sleeting day in Oulu. The city seems lethargic, lifeless, as if everyone is busy tending to a bad hangover. Finland does, after all, have among the highest rates of suicide and alcoholism of any industrialized country, which isn't all that shocking considering that the two leading pastimes are sitting in the sauna and drinking.

We enter the mostly empty café, order two coffees, and grab a table.

"You were brilliant last night, man," says Zac. "Totally brilliant."

"Thanks," I say.

"I told you, I see a little bit of me in your style. I think you could take this thing tonight."

"Yeah, I don't know. I can't imagine doing very well going first, but whatever, I'm just glad I made it into the finals."

"You'll be great, just make sure to have three drinks beforehand, right?" I tell him that won't be a problem. Zac then proceeds to tell me about how air guitar changed his life. How he befriended Brian May from Queen and helped him curate *The Best Air Guitar Album in the World . . . Ever* (volumes I and II) at the offices of Virgin Records. How he became a local hero in London after winning two years in a row, and how he met "loads of groupies." But I'm curious about what happened to him yesterday at the so-called Service Center.

"Oh yeah. Now *that's* a weird story," he says, sipping his coffee. "So Marika picks me up in this van that drives us out of Oulu—not the most urban of urban centers, as you can see—and then takes us deep into the Finnish forest. We end up in this really strange place. It's like an IBM-looking building in the middle of the woods. She says, 'We're here,' and I'm like, 'What is this? Where is *here*?' We get out, and there are some very odd people around. Some are kind of costumed (which I am obviously used to in this game) and some not. They all seem to be coming out of the forest."

"Like *Night of the Living Dead* or something?" I ask.

"A bit like that, yeah. They are coming from all sides, some of them walking in a slightly funny way, and they're all going towards this weird archway in this building. They're all going where I'm going, and I don't know where I am going. Some of the people look okay, but some don't, honestly, and I realize Marika's taken me to judge an air guitar competition in a lunatic asylum! Well, that's the old term, at least. And I'm thinking—those at the cutting edge of this whole air guitar thing are quite aware of the close proximity we come to total insanity; you're toying with the edge, and it's kinda nice in a comfortable fashion. But these guys are very much *over the edge*."

"How do you mean?"

"Well, some of them have mental tics that involve their arms flailing all around, and some are screaming to me in Finnish, which clearly I don't get. I initially felt incredibly uncomfortable, not in a patronizing way, but I just wasn't sure they *wanted* to perform. I mean—their ability to communicate is hindered as is. Finally a curtain goes up, and there's this woman who's about fifty years old, oddly proportioned in her ill-fitting skirt, with a lot of makeup added to make her look like a pop star. She's swaying gently to some classic rock, slowly making her way to the edge of the stage to leave, and then she gets prodded to go back and play some more. It's a bit like being at school where some authority figures are pushing some slightly reluctant child performers onstage. Then someone else gets up there, and the whole crowd starts making zoo animal sounds, kind of like screaming hyenas. That's partly okay, because it is an air guitar competition; but it's partly not, because their helpers are yelling at them to calm down."

Zac is a brilliant storyteller. It is, I suspect, what makes him a great air guitarist. Air guitar is really about telling a story, about creating a reality in which the audience can place themselves. It's all about fantasy, and to succeed in it you must be able to translate your personal dreams into something that an audience wants to live inside. In sixty seconds.

"This one guy who had Down syndrome went onstage with some Led Zeppelin rattling through the crappy PA, and when he started going a bit, he got that *click* that we all get, and then everyone clicked, and they all started rocking in their chairs, and he was loving it—this huge baying crowd responding in such a basic way to him, and then him responding to them. The music locked in for him the same way it would for you or me, you know what I mean?"

I do know what he means. He's talking about people with Down syndrome in the middle of some random forest in northern Finland playing air guitar, and they really fucking *feel* it. It's universal.

"So here was this guy who spoke a totally different language from me—and was also *impaired* in that language—communicating to me and everyone else. It was rather amazing, actually. So then they tell me I've got to deliberate on who should win this, and I'm like, 'What do you mean, *deliberate*?' They take me into this back room and lock me in with four patients who are also judging the thing, and one of their caretakers. And I'm thinking . . . anything could happen in here. Maybe this is all just a ploy to lock me up? So they say, 'What do you think of so-and-so?' and I have no idea who 'so-and-so' is, and they're like, 'He's the guy who kinda leaned a bit at the beginning and then jumped excitedly, and then relieved himself onstage.' So I say, 'I thought he was all right, I guess.' Finally, I don't know how, but we arrived on a winner and made the announcement. So then some guy starts shouting in the crowd— but I don't even know if that was the guy we chose or not. It was very weird. Very strange . . ." He trails off, still seeming troubled by the whole experience.

"I just wished it had been a rebellious thing," he adds. "Not the ironfisted hand of the institution being held over them, stopping 'em from going nuts. They should've been allowed to just freak out. That's what they wanted, it seemed to me."

"That's what we all want, I guess," I respond.

"Yeah, you know, man," says Zac, pausing to reflect, "one of the most beautiful things about air guitar is that it's all about the moment; it's all about the unknown. For me, I mean, how could I know

I'd end up there judging that thing, right? You can't predict where it's all going. It's like blind faith. Air guitar is like jumping off a cliff. The minute you start thinking about it, you're lost. I'm pretty sure those people at the Service Center knew that. I mean—air guitar is so much about angst, and frustration, and the desire to be saved, right?"

Is he right? Is it my own angst and frustration that attract me to air guitar—a hope that I might somehow be saved?

Zac is staring out the window of the café. He is squinting, his forehead slightly wrinkled. "And you know," he says, nodding his head slowly, "we all need to be saved in some way."

A few hours later after a good shower, a little hotel room MTV-watching, and a surprisingly decent fried whitefish in the hotel's Hemingway's restaurant (part of a chain of Hemingway-themed dining establishments throughout Finland), a group of us walk en masse over to Kuusisaari, the giant outdoor arena where tonight's event will be held.

It's like Woodstock, only smaller and colder, and with a lot fewer hippies. Hundreds of people are walking towards the venue, which sits on an island just over a bridge from the historic Oulu town center. There's a light rain falling, and the anticipation is palpable. Along the way, I see throngs of young blond Finnish girls. Naturally, I ask some of them to cheer for me.

"Hi. I'm Björn Türoque. I am competing tonight. Will you cheer for me?"

They look at me like I'm a sex offender who's just moved into their neighborhood, and start walking faster.

We arrive around five p.m. and congregate in a tent backstage, where we are told the order of events for the evening. Pikku G, a teenage Finnish rapper, will perform a set; then there will be a demonstration from last year's winners of the differently abled air guitar competition. After that the competition will begin. Once it's finished, Hanoi Rocks will play.

"Wow. Hanoi Rocks?" I say to C-Diddy, who stands nearby.

"I thought they were dead," he replies.

"Tonight's judges," announces Marika, in her Finnish accent, from the back of the tent, "are Juha Torvinen, one of de founders of de air guitar competition; Henrik Andersson, guitarist from Swedish band Hank; and Angela McCoy, wife of Andy McCoy, guitarist of de Hanoi Rocks. For now, have a good time, and please be here when Pikku G is done making his set."

I ask one of the other Finnish girls who help run the competition what Pikku G means. She tells me, "It means Lil' G."

"You mean like Lil' Kim or Lil' Bow Wow?" I ask.

"I think so, yes," she says. "He is sixteen and is biggest rap star in all Finland."

Now I realize why there are so many people here.

Zac walks over to tell me that the warm-up is about to begin, and asks if I could please join in.

"Put your beers down," shouts Zac to the international group of wannabe rock stars. We gather in a circle, awaiting further orders from the Master. "This is very simple, a bit of a warm-up so you feel ready. Just do what I do, and when I say change, change." Zac prepares to lead us in precompetition yoga and tai chi.

As instructed, I begin to loosen my quadriceps by pulling my foot up behind my ass. I watch as guys dressed in everything from leather to hockey jerseys to hot pink boxer shorts bend over to try and touch their toes, stretch their arms high in the air, windmill their arms, and get more exercise in ten minutes than they have probably gotten in the past ten years.

The men grunt. Someone cries, "Fucking hell!"

"This will *really* help!" reassures Zac.

We complete our warm-up, and everyone lets loose a loud group "Woo!" We return to our beers, try to relax a bit, and wish one another good luck. I check out a few minutes of sixteen-year-old Finnish rapper Pikku G's set. To me he sounds like a slower and clumsier Eminem, but I'm about as qualified to judge Finnish hip-hop as Pikku G is to judge air guitar.[2] Finally Pikku G walks off the stage with several young female cheerleaders. The real games are about to begin.

To open the ceremonies, a man and a woman take the stage. It is announced that the couple are the winners of the past year's air guitar competition at Tahkokangas, the nearby institution for the differently abled.[3]

"Why last year's winners?" I quietly ask Zac.

---

[2]Later I consulted my friend Charlie (a hip-hop aficionado), who told me that Pikku G sounds more like Latino rapper Big Pun (aka Big Punisher) than like Eminem.

[3]According to Marika, the Air Guitar Competition for Disabled People has been happening since 2001 in Tahkokangas Central Institution (where more than two hundred disabled people live), and they plan to expand it around Finland in the coming years. To me, it's a true testament to the healing powers of air guitar. Unfortunately I can't really imagine this happening outside of Finland.

"Dunno," he says, and shrugs his shoulders.

We both watch the couple onstage. The guy is wearing an AC/DC shirt and the woman has a Metallica shirt underneath her suede jacket. Both are wearing tight jeans, and both of them have Down's syndrome. A fog machine emits a cloud of smoke as they play air guitar together for the entire five minutes and thirteen seconds of the Metallica song "Attitude." They strum around the stage, and the audience cheers them on with gusto. They look happy and free.

I watch and wonder how I'm going to follow two Finns with Down's syndrome playing air guitar to Metallica for more than five minutes. It feels awkward. And then it's my turn.

"Our first competitor tonight, from the United States, Mr. Björn Türoque." At least he pronounces it correctly.

I tell the audience I want them to count down the song with me. They seem to understand. I turn my back, raise my hand into the air, and together we count, "Four-three-two-one . . ." and then "I Get Along" by The Libertines engulfs the outdoor arena. I begin to jump around madly, playing my invisible guitar in time to the song. But my left hand feels frozen—it's hardly moving at all. It's not until nearly halfway through the song clip that I finally hit my stride.

After the short chorus, I slide my air pick down the strings of the air guitar, and then kick (literally, with a high front kick) in to the bridge, which ends with a four-count pause during which I grab an air microphone and mouth along with the lyric, "Fuck 'em!"

I close with the guitar solo.

I am dripping both with real sweat and artificial sweat (beer), in which I doused my head just moments prior to taking the stage. The judges each hold up their scores on white cards: 5.9, 5.3, 5.3.

These are not the scores I had traveled thousands of miles to receive, though I take some solace in the fact that Angela McCoy, the Hanoi Rocks guitarist's wife, gave me the 5.9.

I approach C-Diddy backstage and look him in the eyes. He has the focus and concentration of a brain surgeon about to extract a tumor. Beneath his long red kimono, a Hello Kitty breastplate waits to be unleashed. "It's up to you now, man," I tell him. "Good luck."

"Thanks, man. You were great," he says. "No one likes going first."

"Yeah," I say. "Whatever. I'm just glad that's over." I continue drinking, more heavily now. The scores are a letdown, but I start to think about my interaction yesterday with the greasy-haired Austrian dude (who will be performing shortly as Mike "The Judge"). I now know what he meant—that this whole thing is not actually about winning. The mere fact that I came here and met all these people and got to be a part of it is probably what it's really about, but I can't help but feel an honest sting from those 5.3s. It feels like a long way to fall from last night's victory.

I walk around to the front of the stage to watch local Petri Kalmari, a gargantuan bald mountain of a man with a goatee and a sadistic smile. He plays to a Finnish death metal song I've never heard and hope never to hear again. His arms—like oak trees—are so huge that every strum requires a Herculean effort just to raise them in the air, hurl them across the air strings, and then haul them back up again. It's as if he is playing in slow motion. His scores, like mine, are not spectacular either: two 4.9s and one 5.7 (perhaps there was a touch of regional favoritism).

Following him in the lineup are luminaries the Airminator from Austria, the Red Plectrum, and Australia's Roxy McStagger.

McStagger is at least six and a half feet tall, with another four or so inches for his curly red hair. He looks like a cross between *The Simpsons'* Sideshow Bob, Ronald McDonald, and comedian Carrot Top (without the weird makeup and extensive plastic surgery). He turns his back to the audience and shakes his bony ass in his taut leather pants and begins to windmill, knee-slide, headbang, and front-flip across the stage to an obscure Australian song I'm unfamiliar with. He ends by doing the splits, spinning on the floor, and then having air sex. His moves are less like watching a Foo Fighters or Faster Pussycat show than they are like watching *Flashdance*, but it's pretty damn entertaining. McStagger's scores are nearly as inconsistent and confusing as mine: 5.9, 5.1, and 5.6. What do these judges want from us?

In between performances, cheers can be heard from the crowd for the band that will be playing a set *after* the competition with nonair instruments: "Hanoi Rocks! Hanoi Rocks! Hanoi Rocks!"

Then, the man I've followed around the world from New York to Los Angeles all the way here to Finland, the man who claims to have been trained in the Suzuki Method and to be powered by a force known as Asian Fury, the man who thus far has defeated anyone who dared compete against him, the air guitarist known as C-Diddy, takes the stage. C-Diddy opens his kimono and someone screams, "Hanoi Rocks!" More cheers erupt, but they are quickly silenced when C-Diddy begins his assault. His performance is flawless, just as it was on both coasts of the United States. With three 5.9s, he wins the round hands down.

Unlike the US competition, where only the top five make it to the compulsory, all sixteen of us will compete in the next round. The surprise song is "Get Your Hands Off My Woman," by recent British chart-toppers The Darkness, a band that hasn't yet made it to the States. But on my first hearing of the song, I know it's ludicrously great. During the between-round intermission, I ask C-Diddy to write the words "Make Air Not War" on my chest so that I can rip open my shirt to reveal my antiwar statement. I hope to let Finland know that not all Americans support the war in Iraq.

I see Zac Monro backstage between rounds, and he looks at me with pity. "It's rough being the first up, yeah?" he says. "Like I said, no way of knowing how it'll go."

"Nah, it's fucked up. I knew I had no chance once I found out the order. The scores always escalate as the round goes on."

"I thought you were pretty good. Seemed a little stiff, maybe. What happened to 'The Mole'?"

"I don't know. . . . I should've stuck with that."

"Doesn't matter, man. You'll be back next year. I can tell."

"Maybe, who knows . . . ?"

"Looks like your man might go all the way, yeah?" he says, referring to C-Diddy.

"Yeah, he is pretty amazing, right?"

"I dunno. It's a different approach, really. There's just something about his face, right? But look, between you and me," he says quietly, "I don't fancy it. You'll be back."

He winks and pats me on the shoulder, then goes to make an announcement to the crowd.

"We have banished evil tonight!" he shouts into the microphone. "And I think very soon we will make history." The audience is uninterested—they want Hanoi Rocks. But I admire Zac's persistence. "It's very hard to know *why* we are doing this. But remember: there is *nothing as important* or *as powerful* as air guitar!" And with that he raises his hands, waves to the crowd, and walks off.

The crowd of five thousand Finns probably thinks Zac is being facetious (actually, most of them probably don't understand a word he is saying), but I am reminded of Zac's story this morning about the Service Center—about the real universality of it all. For some reason, when Zac talks about salvation by way of air guitar, it seems tangible. It makes sense. It feels like truth. He's probably the best spokesman air guitar will ever have. I envy him.

In the compulsory round the stage is soaked, as a heavy mist has started to fall. The beers that people have been throwing at us aren't helping either. By the time I get up onstage, it's incredibly slippery, and I slide all around in my Converse high-tops, falling on the ground in accidental somersaults. I get up, rip my shirt off to reveal my political message, and earn a substantial cheer, but my moves are all over the place. I am like a slapstick routine on ice. I stumble and try to maintain my balance, fumbling my way through the song until it ends with singer Justin Hawkins' beautifully grating last line, "Get your hands off my woman motherfuuuuuuuu. . . . . . . KAH!" My scores are okay—two 5.6s and a 5.8—but they are nothing to write home about. I hope the people who donated money to send me here will not be demanding refunds.

London's "The Red Plectrum" (whom the other air guitarists have taken to calling "The Red Rectum") swan-dives from the drum riser to the stage. It looks incredibly painful.[4] He remains supine and simulates jacking off for the rest of the song.[5] Petri Kalmari, the giant, is so bulky that he simply cannot keep up with the breakneck tempo of the song, and walks offstage clutching his chest as if he is about to have a heart attack. Donaldo, a guy with long braided pigtails, comes out in a skirt, apologizes to his mother, and dances like Britney Spears. He repeatedly lets the audience know he is not wearing any underwear by spinning around and kicking his leg high into the air. Austria's Niko "Air.Alm" pretends to be asleep until an air roadie awakens him with a beer shower, and then he falls off the stage.

C-Diddy doesn't wander around much during his sixty seconds. Instead, his movement is focused in his hyperspeed hands—his "weapons of mass destruction," as he calls them—and his contorted facial expressions. I just can't understand how a man's tongue can flap so quickly, but I imagine that his fiancée must be a very happy woman.

C-Diddy is declared victorious, and announces to the crowd: "Greetings, Finland! I am very honored to be here, and I marvel at the beauty of the country and its people." He closes with what might, for all I know, be the Finnish national motto: "World Peace, Air Guitar, *Forever!*" and the crowd cheers, mostly because this signals

[4]Normally the stage dive entails leaping from the stage onto the raised hands of the audience. Some credit the origin of this ritual to Peter Gabriel, who would repeatedly stage dive during live performances of his song "Lay Your Hands on Me" from the 1982 album *Security*.

[5]Later that night, the Red Plectrum claims that he *actually* ejaculated.

the end of the air guitar competition and the beginning of Hanoi Rocks' set. But it's not over yet; we have a tradition to follow.

We all join together onstage to play "Rockin' in the Free World," as fireworks explode at the front of the stage dangerously close to where we are standing. At one point, while I am kneeling on the ground in a deep air jam, Stan Kreich,[6] a Belgian competitor who came out during the compulsory round dressed as Jesus (complete with thorny crown, stigmata, and a diaper), wraps his legs around my neck. I stand up, and he is playing air guitar on my shoulders.

Aussie Roxy McStagger, who tied with Stan Kreich for second place, leaps off the stage into the audience and starts hugging the girls of the front row. The Red Rectum, who came in dead last, tosses out to the crowd a Red Plectrum T-shirt that immediately gets thrown back at him. C-Diddy holds up his trophy: a handmade Flying Finn guitar that he has no idea how to play. The song comes to an end, and as I join arms for a final group bow with these men whom I have battled, my envy of C-Diddy fades. We are all equals tonight. We will all keep on rockin' in the free world.

As we walk offstage, Petri Kalmari, the Finnish Humvee of a human, envelops me in his hulklike arms and gives me a rib-crushing embrace. He is welled up with joy. As he puts me down, like Lenny dropping a limp dead rabbit, I see a tear fall from his eye. The spirit of it has overwhelmed him. I nearly cry, myself. I am suddenly filled with international pride. As I think about all of us up there onstage making complete asses of ourselves together, it seems, somehow, honestly beautiful.

[6] I learn later than Stan Kreich has extensively toured Europe, Japan, and the US in an Iron Maiden *air tribute band* called Air on Maiden.

Then Austria's Mike "The Judge" comes up to me to tell me he liked my "Make Air Not War" message. "That's really good to hear from an American," he says.

I thank him. We hug.

Hanoi Rocks starts rocking and "washed-up" doesn't begin to describe them. It's painful. If we were the imitation rock stars, they are the caricatures—sounding as haggard as they look. So Zac and I decide to split after a few songs and head to the after-party. As we are leaving, C-Diddy, the new world champion, is getting mauled by international press and eventually has to escape in a taxi like the Stones fleeing fans and paparazzi (except C-Diddy is with his parents and fiancée).

On the way over to the house where the after-party is going to take place, Zac and I finish off a bottle of whiskey as he tells me more stories of his past as an air guitar champion. He so clearly misses the spotlight. The fans. The thrill of victory. Maybe it's better that I didn't win, I think to myself. It might be too hard to come down from that.

The after-party is a sloppy, drunken mess. Zac walks around with his leather jacket on, and no shirt. He and Björn are having air guitar duels on the tops of tables, talking incessantly about the philosophy of air guitar and mugging it up for the documentary crew, which refuses to stop filming even this late in the evening. Eventually, as you may remember, Björn is found lying on a table, incoherently muttering the chorus of The Darkness' "Get Your

Hands Off My Woman," when someone tells him, "Mr. Monro is about to throw up. We need to go."

After his brush with greatness at the Grilleriina (getting drooled on by Hanoi Rocks' Andy McCoy) and a nauseating trough of gravy-covered fries, Björn and a few of the remaining air guitarists stagger back to second-floor lobby of the hotel for one final nightcap with the hangers-on. Fueled by the ephemera of fame that only an air guitar competition can provide, everyone has taken on a rock star patina. Zac and Björn are break dancing and Aer Lingus is playing air guitar on top of the coffee table in the center of the room. Empty whiskey and beer bottles are all over the floor. A pizza box flies through the air, seemingly from nowhere; then the elevator doors open and one of the hotel managers steps out to say, in the most polite voice ever, "Hallo. Could you please be a little more quiet? You can stay, but please more quiet. Thank you." And then he disappears. Everyone looks at one another, bewildered. The hotel is getting trashed. There are burgers and fries and gravy ground into the floor, and drunken lunatics standing on the furniture. But he doesn't tell anyone to stop throwing shit or to clean up or to get out of the hallway—just to "be a little more quiet."

This isn't the official hotel of the Air Guitar World Championships for nothing.

Shortly thereafter, it dawns on me that my return flight to Stockholm is in two hours—poor planning, to say the least. I spend a few drunken, hazy minutes gathering my shit together. I am sure I've lost something (my leather zip-up tie, I'll realize when I get home[7]), but I walk out of my room with my bags to say good-bye to everyone before catching a cab to the airport.

There in the hallway, lying next to each other on the floor, in their underwear, are Zac "The Magnet" Monro and Andy "Hanoi Rocks" McCoy playing air guitar on each other's thighs. They are blathering and moaning incoherently, laughing and . . . playing air guitar on each other's thighs.

On the floor.

In their underwear.

---

[7]Three years later, Zac "The Magnet" Monro will remind me that before leaving Oulu, I gave him my leather tie as a symbol of our eternal air guitar bond. I have since replaced it (there seems to be an endless supply of these on eBay).

*If you gaze long enough into an abyss,
the abyss will gaze back into you.*

—Friedrich Nietzsche

In my sophomore year of high school I went to a party at a friend's
house one weekend. I was into my fourth can of Milwaukee's Best
when I noticed an attractive blond girl with green eyes, from the
senior class, sitting on the arm of a sofa. I tried to talk to her but
mostly ended up following her around the party like a lost puppy.
At one point, I trailed her upstairs and into a bedroom, where she
sat down on my friend's parents' bed. Thinking that my strategy
was paying off, I sat down next to her and shyly stared at my knees.
I was two years younger than she was. I was drunk. I was basically
an idiot.

"So . . . what do you think I should do?" I finally asked after
what seemed like minutes of silence.

"I think you should be *much* more aggressive," she said seductively, and then paused and looked into my eyes. "*But* . . . not with

me." And with that she got up and walked out of the room and back downstairs.

I always approached everything I did with a touch of fanaticism. But was I chasing after the *wrong things*? Maybe I just wasn't cut out to be the best air guitarist in the world. Maybe, as others often suggested, it was a stupid pursuit. If my air guitar could talk, would it tell me to give up the dream? Would it tell me to wise up and "be *much* more aggressive" in my pursuit of *something else*—like my own music or my relationship with Jane Air? I was the seventh-best air guitarist in the world, sure, but in reality nothing had changed. And even if I had won, my real, *nonair* existence would have remained by and large the same. Something hit me in Finland. Maybe it was all the Salmiakkikossus or all the time spent sweating out toxins in the sauna in the basement of the Hotel Cumulus; I didn't know what it was, but I returned to New York with a renewed urgency for change. I needed to figure out what the fuck I was doing with my life.

One desire that burned within me was to find a way to bring air guitar to the masses. In Finland I discovered that air guitar was really the second international language. It brought people together to shed their inhibitions, their preconceived notions of themselves, and occasionally their clothing—all in the name of the only religion I ever believed in: rock and roll. Mike "The Judge" from Austria was right—air guitar was not about the triumph of the individual; it was about the collective spirit of music. Everyone, whether they knew it or not, had an inner air guitar just waiting to be released. Could I be a catalyst for this self-discovery? I wanted a way to relive that night in the basement of 45 Special on a regular basis. I wanted others to feel what I felt when teary-eyed Petri Kalmari nearly hugged me to death after the group rendition of "Rockin' in the Free World." I wanted people to play air guitar together in an open and collegial environment.

I also wanted never to be trounced again by Asian Fury.

So I followed the "if you can't beat 'em, join 'em" rule, and I invented Aireoke: where karaoke meets air guitar.

Aer Lingus, Teddy Ruckspin, and I joined forces and had our first Aireoke night in December of 2003. It was, in a word, fucking awesome. People got up onstage and played the shit out of their favorite songs. They performed solo, as duets, and even as full-on air groups—with air drummers and air bassists. They rocked fast songs, slow jams; they even rocked songs without any guitar in them at all. The Aireoke All-Stars, where all air guitarists are invited up on stage to play together, was also born that night when we played AC/DC's "You Shook Me All Night Long" and everyone in the room went berserk in unison.

As I looked towards the future, I hoped Aireoke would become a nationally recognized pastime, popular around the world in cities large and small. I imagined it would become not only a venue for people to share their air, but a farm system for the majors—a place for aspiring air guitarists to hone their chops for competition. Indeed, it eventually became just that.

As the year drew to a close, I decided it was time to let go of everything that wasn't working in my life. My first order of business was to officially retire from competitive air guitar, which I did

	KARAOKE	AIREOKE
Inventor	Japanese singer Daisuke Inoue.	American air guitarist Björn Türoque.
Talent(s) Required	*Singing*. Most people who perform karaoke severely lack this requisite ability.	None.
Equipment	Expensive machines, video monitors, and a microphone.	Music, air.
Cheesy Videos	Yes.	No.
Duration	Songs are played from start to finish and frequently feel interminable. (Ever suffered a drunk guy stumbling his way through an entire "Bohemian Rhapsody"? Enough said.)	As in a standard air guitar competition, songs only last about sixty seconds—unless the person is rocking so hard that he or she simply can't be stopped. The most frequent exception is for the fourteen-minute-and-eight-second live version of "Free Bird," which as a rule will never be interrupted.
Songs	Instrumental cover versions lacking the punch of the original.	Songs are by the original artist and remain unpolluted by off-key, untalented interpreters.
Alcohol	The more drinks, the worse the singing. It's the karaoke law of diminishing returns.	Performances tend to improve on an equally proportional curve to the number of drinks consumed until vomiting, death, or both occur.

with little fanfare or notice from the media. Though I had failed to secure a top spot in the air guitar hall of fame, and was only the seventh-best in the world, I hung up my Pro-Line air guitar for good. I also quit my life as a computer geek, took a hiatus for a while from the French band, and moved to Los Angeles to work on a friend's documentary. Not surprisingly, Jane Air wasn't happy about it. The move took a major toll on our already fragile relationship, and two months after my relocation, we broke up.

Part 2:

Once Bitten, Twice Shy

Ever tried. Ever failed. No matter.
Try again. Fail again. Fail better.

—Samuel Beckett, *Worstward Ho*

In ninth grade, my friends and I used to play an unnamed game that began with me standing alone on the moderately well-trafficked corner of Denver's Seventh Avenue and Emerson Street, and them hiding behind the trees and bushes nearby. When my friends saw a car coming, a pack of seven or eight of them would run out from behind the shrubbery and attack me. They'd throw me to the ground and pretend to violently kick the shit out of me as I screamed at the top of my lungs, "Help! Somebody *help*!" If we got a car to stop, as we did one day when a guy jumped out of his truck and chased the gang away, the game was considered successful.

"Are you okay?" the man asked. "Get in!" he shouted, and I hopped into his truck.

"Those guys just like to beat me up sometimes," I explained. Mock tears welled up in my eyes as we drove away. "Just far enough away so I can walk home would be cool," I told the guy, pointing up ahead, and knowing I'd walk back and meet up with my friends at the house on Emerson. As I sat riding in his truck, watery-eyed, trying to maintain the pretense of being injured, I started to enjoy believing I had been rescued. I was faking it at this guy's expense, but he felt like a hero and I felt saved. Everybody won. The guy dropped me off, and I thanked him and walked back home smiling. When I returned, victorious, my friends high-fived me, and we all laughed and made fun of the idiot in the truck who had fallen for our stupid game. I was the comedy and the tragedy. I got my ass air-kicked, and I had shed air tears. It was an act of comic, physical self-deprecation—a performance that generated both sympathy and laughter. I was the joke *and* the punch line. And I liked it.

In early May of 2004, air guitar season started up again. I was living in LA, working on my friend's documentary, and was officially no longer together with Jane Air. Aireoke was running strong, and people were beginning to talk about the upcoming competitions. I tried to ignore the chatter, but it wasn't easy. The US Air Guitar Web site announced that five cities would be participating this year: New York, Los Angeles, Chicago, Minneapolis, and Denver—my hometown.

I thought I could keep him stowed away, buried in the closet collecting dust along with my air guitar, but Björn could not be held back. He just showed up one day, unannounced, and I have to admit I sort of missed him. Our reunion was celebrated on my porch with an ice-cold beer and a couple of hits off a homegrown

California joint while we debated our existence in psychological terms and listened to Led Zeppelin's *Presence*.

While we were stoned, Björn convinced me to come out of retirement, return to Denver, and bring air guitar to my people. Did they want it as much as I did?

BURBANK, CALIFORNIA June 10, 2004. In the Burbank airport, I call my friend Matt to let him know what time I'll be arriving in Denver. He owns the Hi-Dive, the club where the first Denver Regional Air Guitar Competition will be held. I've known Matt since we were in ninth grade (he was one of the members of the gang that pretended to beat me up) at Denver's East High School.

Long-standing friend that he is, Matt defies official air guitar competition rules and informs me that another competitor is planning on performing to the song I've been rehearsing for the past week: "Dueling Banjos." Though I have recorded my own version—lifting the banjo part from the original and editing it with my own recording of a wailing and distorted electric guitar—I suspect that my act (involving a George W. Bush Halloween mask on the back of my head and frequent 180-degree rotations as I switch between the electric guitar and the banjo) will fall flat if another competitor has already performed the same track.

Panic sets in as I board the plane bound for Denver. I don't know if I should stick with "Dueling Banjos" or resort to the alternate track I've practiced in case the impossible happens and I lose in Denver and need to compete again in the New York competition that takes place a few days later. Would it really be so bad if someone else does that song? Maybe my other song is better. Maybe "Dueling Banjos" is too gimmicky? Maybe I should've eaten something before I got on the plane—I'm starving.

DENVER, COLORADO June 10, 2004. Upon arriving in Denver, I finally decide to commit to my backup song, Air Supply's "Making Love Out of Nothing at All."[1] It's a terrible song, really, but the title (not to mention the name of the band) just feels so right. Back home in LA, I had spent half a day editing the song down and adding my own guitar solo for sonic enhancement. Now that time will not have been wasted. I then realize that the only stage outfit I have with me (Western shirt with cutoff sleeves, Budweiser hat with George W. Bush mask hand-sewn into it) was intended for "Dueling Banjos." I don't have a costume that says "Air Supply."

I am met curbside by a local documentary crew that has been hired to follow me around Denver and video the competition. I get wired with a microphone under my shirt and hop into their van. The cameras get turned on and now Björn Türoque is back, and he's feeling cocky.

"The air is thinner in Denver," says Björn, "and this will be to my advantage—as I have been training in the thicker, sea-level air of Los Angeles."

They ask why Björn has come out of retirement, what his chances of winning are, and why has he traveled all the way from

---

[1] "Making Love Out of Nothing at All" was written by Jim Steinman, who is most notable for writing and producing the bulk of Meat Loaf's loaf, and for penning the most annoying song of 1983, Bonnie Tyler's "Total Eclipse of the Heart."

Los Angeles to compete when there's a regional semifinal there in a few weeks? Björn artfully avoids giving genuine answers to all of their questions and then explains that he needs to go by the club to check in, but then must be immediately chauffeured to the nearest thrift store to obtain appropriate Air Supply—worthy eighties garb.

The car pulls up to the club, and my eyes immediately gravitate to a remarkably hot young redheaded girl standing outside. (That's after my eyes finish digesting the unsavory meal of what must be my competition—a guy dressed head to toe in a robot-pirate suit made entirely of cardboard boxes with the words "Captain Metal" painted on the front. He looks impressive, but I'm unsure how Captain Metal will be able to move his limbs at all in that getup.) The hot girl is being interviewed, and it's obvious she's either a competitor or one of the judges. I pray for the latter. We catch each other's eyes briefly. I sense that she, like me, is intrigued. Or maybe the thin air is getting to me. I drop my bags off inside, and the cameraman and I climb in the van and head over to the Buffalo Exchange thrift store a few blocks away.

Denver doesn't have much in the way of culture, but it does have excellent thrift stores. We pull up to Buffalo Exchange, videotape me running into the store, and then shoot it again to make sure we got a clean shot. Reality this documentary ain't. I hastily peruse the racks but don't find much. I ask the girl hanging up belts—who is sort of sexy in her "I work at a thrift store but I'm actually really smart *and* into kinky weird sex involving ropes, blindfolds, and candle wax" kind of way—if she can help me find something to wear for tonight's air guitar competition. "Oh my god. I totally heard about that!" she says.

"Yeah? You should *totally* come. It will be the greatest night of your life," I tell her.

It's as if Thrifty Girl has been scouting this outfit her entire Buffalo Exchange career. Within moments, clothes are flying off the racks and into my hands: black leather pants with lace-up sides and crotch, a brown leather vest with fringe, a sleeveless purple shirt that reads (in eighties block letters) "Eat Your Heart Out—I'm Married," white-framed aviator sunglasses, a blue pleather jacket with leopard-print trim, a bandanna, and a sort of leather-and-silver-chained G-string. I go to the dressing room to try on the entire ensemble. I look like the guy who got kicked out of Village People for looking *too* gay. They convince me I just look "very eighties" and the clothes are perfect for any song by Air Supply. I am a sucker.

I ask if I can give the outfit a test drive. One of the other employees puts on "Master of Puppets," by Metallica, and I leap up onto the counter to see how my moves fly in this garb. The store's other patrons seem nonplussed but fundamentally unfazed as I shout, "Hello, Denver!" and begin air guitaring. Thrifty Girl gives me the thumbs up, and I convince her to let me "borrow" the clothes on my credit card, to be sweated in and returned tomorrow. She lets me take everything except the sunglasses and the bandanna, which I have to purchase.

"Denver doesn't suck as much as I remembered," I say to the camera as I walk out of the store.

We head back to the club. I'm insanely hungry, as I always am before a performance. Within Les Sans Culottes I was known as "The Stomach of Paris," due to my need for a constant intake of food while on the road. Now the Stomach of Denver needs something to eat tout de suite. Outside the club, the red-hot red-head I spotted earlier is still hanging out. She advises me that I can get a decent slice across the street. I thank her, smile, and go to fuel up. I am plugged into my iPod, playing the song over and over as I wait for my pizza to get heated. I make a few practice air guitar gestures as I pace around the place. Nobody seems to notice me.

Once you choose to fully accept air guitar into your life, you'll begin to notice air guitarists all around you. And not just air guitarists, but entire air bands: air drummers, air bassists, even the occasional air saxophonist (who should be avoided, shunned, and/or beaten up). I won't even say what should be done with air flautists. One late night when I was driving home in Los Angeles, a guy standing under a streetlamp on a desolate road waiting for the bus mesmerized me. He had headphones on, and as I drove past, he laid down some badass air guitar moves, right there on the sidewalk in the middle of the night. I like to think of that guy as the Aircrow.

I down my slice and return to the club. A few of my high school friends have arrived to cheer me on, including Stacy, a girl I used to drive around on the back of my moped in high school and haven't seen since we graduated. We try to catch up on the past fifteen years of each other's lives, but it's pretty clear I am the more accomplished one. After all, I was crowned the second-best air guitarist on the East Coast last year and ranked seventh in the world. Forget marriage, kids, money, real estate—I've really *done something* with my life. In fact, I feel very conscious of the fact that my friends are all married, one is pregnant, and one has already spawned two kids—and they're cute fucking kids too. I'm newly single and have quit my lucrative educational software career to move to Los Angeles and work on a low-paying documentary about Hollywood. It seems pretty obvious as we all sit in a booth having drinks that I am in some kind of midlife crisis. Though I am only thirty-three, and life expectancies are rising every year, so maybe it's a third-life crisis? I have dedicated a good portion of the past year to the pursuit of air guitar glory, and tonight I'll be wearing leather pants with lace-up sides and crotch. My friends think it's funny, and then I realize that in fifteen years, nothing's changed: I'm still eager to step in as the butt-end of any joke.

"I gotta go downstairs and get my Björn Türoque on," I tell my friends. "Wish me luck."

One of them offers the predictable but always funny "Break a string" (I much prefer "Break wind"), and I head to the dressing room, aka, the piss-sticky-floored men's room of my friend's club.

On the way into the bathroom, carrying my plastic bag full of borrowed ridiculousness, I spot Jesse "Demon Strait" Pulley. He's wearing a white puffy shirt unlaced to the lower part of his clavicle. He has long, stringy blond hair and looks as if he might hold a

summer job working the mutton booth at his local Renaissance
Faire. I picture him jousting, not playing air guitar. I have in fact
been warned about Demon Strait. Apparently, months prior to this
year's regional air guitar competitions, The Demon had contacted
Aer Lingus, asking for a "guarantee" that he would win, as he was
an "authentic" air guitarist and was "much better than any of those
wussies." Lingus, who described the Demon as "an enormous
freak," told him he could offer no guarantees. So the Demon
threatened to "just take acid and come anyway."

Only days ago the Demon drove from Mobile, Alabama, to Chicago in order to compete. He lost by a mere one-tenth of a point
and registered complaints of partisan judging—bitching that the
guy who had won was a friend of the club owner. Now he's driven all
the way from Alabama to Denver to take another shot at the title.
Here in *my* friend's club, the circumstances sound eerily similar,
and I worry that the Demon might throw a metal shitstorm if and
when I win. I sensed he was a sore loser out for revenge. He
sounded, well, like me.

Björn is feeling way too sober for this event. Now fully outfitted,
I head out to the bar to grab a beer and a shot of vodka. The place is
completely packed. I'm standing at the bar, wearing my sunglasses
and full leather/pleather combo, when the hot girl I spotted out
front turns around and sees me standing next to her. She smiles,
then visually ingests my sizzling couture and nods her head in an
impressed "wow, it takes balls to wear that outfit" kind of way. With
a shot glass full of whiskey in one hand, she takes her other hand

and pokes her finger between the laces on the side of my pants, rubbing my upper thigh.

I am actually going *sans culottes* and it's finally paying off.

"Nice pants," she says. I feel as if I am in some kind of porn version of a Dockers commercial. Then she follows up with, "Shouldn't you be offering blow jobs to the judges right now?"

"Why, are you a judge?" I ask.

"Yup," she affirms.

"Interesting . . ." I say. "So . . . can I offer you a blow job?" I ask her.

"Maybe later." And she walks away.

Okay, it's possible that a little bit of our dialog is misremembered, but that's the essence of what "went down," so to speak. She most *definitely* suggested that I should be offering the judges blow jobs, which—considering that blow jobs refer specifically to the oral stimulation of *male* genitalia—is confusing, as she was indeed a female. But based on my knowledge thus far (our glance exchange, her fingering my upper thigh through my leather pants), I sense her flirtatious advances were not simply full of hot air.

The inside of my leather pants has begun to steam up. I swig my beer and go back downstairs riding a cocainelike boost of confidence. Slightly aroused (luckily the leather pants are thick and heavy enough to keep my fondness for the female judge under wraps), I feel pretty fucking good about my chances of winning, or at the very least getting some action after the competition.

Round one, which I watch from the back until my name is called, features a guy called "Death," made up to look like Skeletor, doing one of my all-time favorite songs about death (it's the ringtone on my cell phone), Blue Öyster Cult's classic ballad "(Don't Fear) The Reaper." I had seen Death lurking downstairs, wrapped in a black cloak, speaking to no one, and looking not dissimilar to how I imagine Death *actually* looks.

Death does not stop for me. He walks right past me and up onto the stage. I fear he could be an air guitar genius. He removes his cloak, revealing an impressively well-toned body for an air guitarist, and then begins to do some kind of modern interpretive dance to the song. It is graceful, inspiring, and nearly brings a tear to my eye, but it is no air guitar. The crowd shouts homophobic epithets and boos the near-naked reaper, and then Death dances off the stage and bites the dust.

Captain Metal, the pirate-in-a-box, can barely get his arms in the air to simulate the existence of a guitar, but it's fun to watch him climb on and off the stage in his cardboard suit. Jesus, or at least a skinny Hispanic guy with the stage name (or possibly real name?) Jesus is up next, performing to "Closer," by Nine Inch Nails. He's not bad. He looks possessed, which is how I would expect Jesus to look when playing this most unholy instrument of all.

Now it's my turn. I get up onstage, strap on my axe, and cue the emcee to start my song.

My performance is transcendent. I feel that everything I learned in the past year on the professional air guitar circuit has paid off. Things start off slowly, but build perfectly just as I had planned. I work the crowd, and they are hanging on every note.

When the song gets to the moment where the guitar sits out for a few bars, I look down at my air guitar in shock: I've broken a string. From my ass pocket, I remove a paper wrapper that once held a guitar string, open it up, and quickly restring my air guitar. I end with the brilliant solo that I've overdubbed, and the crowd goes wild. Really, they *go fucking wild.* It's by far my best performance yet.

I watch from the back of the club as Demon Strait closes out round one. He is technically adept at mimicking Yngwie Malmsteen's epically dull[2] "Queen in Love," but the dude hardly moves at all. He fails to represent the rock star persona in the slightest. He does, however, invoke the image of a complete loser sitting in his room all day long, stoned, playing along to Yngwie Malmsteen to the severe annoyance of his mother. I can picture the incense wafting underneath his door as his mother shakes her head in disappointment, muttering, "I've raised a moron," as she goes off to prepare him some mac and cheese.

The top performers of round one are announced in reverse order. Jesus is in. Death is still kicking. The Demon is on board. I start to think I might be passed over, but I am announced as the winner of the first round, which means I'll be the final contestant to perform round two's compulsory song, "Eruption."

Van Halen's "Eruption" is cliché to the true air guitarist. For those few ignorant of the track, this one-minute-and-forty-two-

[2]While a few guitar geeks out there consider Malmsteen a genius because he can play an inhuman amount of notes very quickly, his music is actually incredibly boring and, in my opinion, the worst choice for competitive air guitar. As Chuck Klosterman notes in *Fargo Rock City*, Malmsteen's music "seemed to create a whole new way for music to suck."

second baroque guitar solo was composed and performed by the infamous Eddie Van Halen. It includes finger taps, extreme whammy dives, midsong detunings, and incendiary picking, and it liberally quotes from Bach and Paganini. "Eruption" is a song any air guitarist knows by heart, and I'm a little disappointed in the choice. It's almost too easy.

We each have our way with the song. Jesus runs around the stage, flailing his arms and rolling on the floor. It's as if he is air guitaring in tongues. The crowd is amused, but I'm convinced his scores will be low. Death is hardly memorable. Demon Strait gets to the stage, stands like a cancerous lump in all his nonchalant puffy-shirted glory, and plays "Eruption" with both the precision and enthusiasm of a Swiss watch. He's dead-on, note for note—the finger taps, everything. I worry this could be trouble, and I'm right—the crowd is lapping it up. I stand at the back of the club, bewildered: this is not what air guitar is about. There's no rock and roll. It's more mime than air guitar. I've never seen an air guitar performance like this, so focused on accuracy and so ignorant of persona. And yet . . . his performance ends, and cheers spew forth from the boozy audience like vomit.

I must crank up my persona to eleven, at least. From the back of the room, I head towards the stage, spitting beer on the audience. That pisses a few people off, but fuck 'em. Rock is coursing through my veins, and these Mile High neophytes are about to get schooled. And I am great. Fucking brilliant, to be perfectly honest. I start with the classic boot-on-the-monitor stance and full-on nail the song. There's my signature midsong ripping open of the shirt, the classic

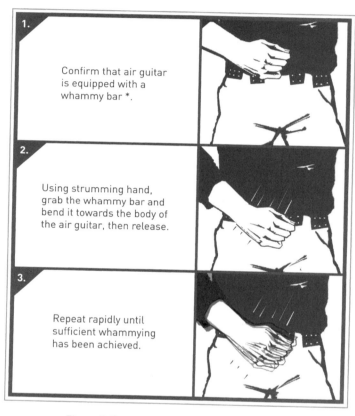

1. Confirm that air guitar is equipped with a whammy bar *.

2. Using strumming hand, grab the whammy bar and bend it towards the body of the air guitar, then release.

3. Repeat rapidly until sufficient whammying has been achieved.

Figure 7. How to use the whammy bar effectively

*If no whammy bar is installed, do not proceed to step 2 as serious damage to reproductive organs (male) may occur.

heavenward air guitar toss, catching it on the downbeat (borrowed from Krye Tuff), and the well-honed Björn Türoque facial gestures and Jagger-esque kicks. The audience goes insane. It is as good as air gets. I high-five my way back to the rear of the club and wait.[3]

It takes nearly ten minutes to tabulate the scores. It's like waiting for the microphone while a drunken couple does karaoke to Meat Loaf's "Paradise by the Dashboard Light." I mean, how long could this go on? Finally the emcee takes the stage to announce the results.

"In third place . . . you know him, you love him: Jesus!"

Cheers and rock concert *woos*.

"And in second place . . ."

Now, if you're paying any attention at all, you probably know what comes next. So let's just make it easier on everyone and cut to an hour later, when the hot female judge and I are in the bathroom of the club making up for my loss by making out. She is my first *real* air groupie (those girls in Finland were all talk), *and* she's one of the judges. As she unlaces my leather pants in the dark, beer-stenched bathroom, I feel no shame in my third second-place finish, but I do feel a bit of an identity crisis: Here I am, a rock star, with my leather pants down around my ankles, making out with a groupie in the bathroom of a club—but is she kissing me or Björn?

---

[3]Denver's compulsory round is scored slightly differently from those of standard air guitar competitions. Rather than having the judges display their scores immediately following the round two performance, à la figure skating, or, say, *The Gong Show*, the scores are tabulated in secret. This leads to greater suspense and, I suspect, cheating.

I'm pretty sure I am not the only one to score that night. It seems that Death and Captain Metal might also have gotten busy after the show. The Demon doesn't get any action that I know of, but he does get a one-way ticket to Los Angeles to compete in the nationals.

Being number one is everything. There is no second place. Second sucks.

—Bob "Bull" Hurley (Rick Zumwalt), in *Over the Top*

It was just as C-Diddy predicted in Finland when I told him I was staying in room 222: Second place, three times.

Second place has followed me like a shadow for most of my life. As a kid, my family's refrigerator was adorned with red ribbons—the color awarded for second place in my school's biannual field day competitions; I took second place in several of East High School's photography and oratory contests; my first choice of colleges deferred my early admission application, so I became impatient and decided to apply to my second choice, where I enrolled after being accepted. There, I competed in the American Studies department's annual pie-making contest and was awarded Second Best Pie for my "Italian-American" (an Oreo cookie crust with tiramisu filling—my invention) while another guy inconceivably won first place with his totally average blueberry pie—its surface decorated with an American flag made of fruit and food coloring. "You were robbed," several students told me.[1]

Maybe, subconsciously, I seek out second place. I avoid "serious" or "important" ventures in which I might succeed, like tackling a more meaningful career or playing in a band I really care about.

Early on, I thought a novelty/cover group like Les Sans Culottes would go nowhere. Though we eventually started writing our own songs, headlined at some of New York City's best venues, released four albums, had a huge photo in *The New Yorker*, and were interviewed on NPR, I still always felt like we could never be taken seriously. Others confirmed this feeling—like the manager of a successful band from Iceland called Sigur Rós, whom I met in a bar one time. I told him about our faux French concept band.

"Do you really think there's a market for an American band singing in, and pretending to be, French?" he asked, his question both condescending and rhetorical.

"Is there really a market for a symphonic rock band singing in Icelandic?" I replied—much later, in my mind.

Joining a fake French rock and roll band in which I could wear wigs, tight shiny pants, psychedelic shirts, and silk scarves, and bounce around onstage meant that I could play the role of a faux rock star without really doing much of the real work. Not to say that we didn't work hard—we worked our asses off onstage—but it was

---

[1] Adding insult to injury, the winning blueberry pie belonged to Daniel Handler, who, several years later, went on to become one of the most successful children's book writers ever. You might know him as Lemony Snicket.

much easier to write songs in the style of an existing genre rather than defining our own. It was easier for us to have fake identities than to be ourselves. The result was that we remained, for the most part, a novelty band—a second-place joke before the "real" headliner.

DENVER, COLORADO June 10, 2004. The next morning, following the brutal upset handed to me by the Demon from Alabama, I suffer the insufferable Denver International Airport (where the line for security is guaranteed to be at least an hour long) and prepare to leave my hometown, bound for NYC. I had planned to go to New York from Denver anyway to see some friends and watch the New York competition, which, coincidentally, was the following evening. Also, if for some strange reason I hadn't won, I could compete again in New York. It was a backup plan of sorts.

I settle into an uncomfortable chair near my departure gate and realize how sore my neck is from last night's show (too much headbanging, as usual). I decide to call my father to give him the bad news.[2] My dad lives in Phoenix—a city I've only visited once since he moved there ten or so years ago, where I experienced the hottest July day on record: one hundred and twenty-six degrees Fahrenheit. Since then I can only refer to Phoenix as Hell on Earth.

"Yeah, so . . . how was Denver?" he asks.

---

[2]When my father was in high school, he was a drama geek and "competitive orator" who came in second place in East High's annual Woodbury Oratory Competition in 1953. Like father like son—I actually took second place in the very same competition thirty-six years later, during my senior year. Later in life, he was nearly cast as the Marlboro Man (if only he could have ridden a horse).

"Good, I guess. I didn't win, again."

"Oh, that's right, you were there doing your air guitar thingie?" he asks, with a tone that approaches condescension but is probably more a reflection of his confusion.

"Yup. The air guitar thingie. I came in second place again."

"Yeah? So, now, explain to me what would have happened if you'd actually won this time? You'd go to Finland again?"

"No—I'd be flown to LA to compete in the finals. There are five regionals this year," I explain to my dad, who will, promptly after hanging up the phone, forget we had this conversation. "Then if I win the finals, I go to Finland."

"But, so, you're going to New York now?"

"Yeah, I'll compete again there. Hopefully I'll win this time. . . ."

"So . . . you mind if I ask, uh, who's payin' fer all of this travel?"

Though I've never borrowed a cent from him since graduating college, my dad is typically paternal in his never-ending concern about my money. This probably stems from the fact that he once had some and now has none. I have been doing a fair amount of traveling, though—I was just in New York four weeks ago to play at a Les Sans Culottes CD release party. Luckily my new job in LA has a flexible schedule, so I can take off when I need to. I won't be making any money if I'm not working, but fuck it. It's air guitar season.

"The Dan Crane International Air Guitar for World Peace Fund is paying for it," I offer.

"Uh, say that again?" he asks.

"Um . . . that'd be me. I used frequent flier miles for this trip, so it's not so bad."

"Well, can I ask a strange question?" If he had allowed me time to answer, I would have said no. Alas, he continues, "Why are you doing this?"

It was a fair question.

"I honestly . . . I have no idea," I say. "It's fun . . . I guess."

I really wasn't altogether sure what kept me going. Eventually, I thought, all bridesmaids had to become brides. Eventually, I was told by my overweight gym teacher in high school, persistence paid off. But would it? And did it matter if it did? And why should I trust an overweight guy who taught gym?

"Okay, well," he says, "as long as you're having fun."

I know parents make it their jobs to not understand what their kids do with their lives, and granted, *most* people have a hard time even grappling with the notion of competitive air guitar. But it reminded me of a time when my brother and I went to the Guggenheim with my dad several years ago. My brother is a painter (art, not house), and my dad—staring dumbfounded at some piece of abstract art—said to him, "Now, explain to me why this is art. I mean, I could do that!"

"Yeah, but you didn't," said my brother.

NEW YORK CITY June 12, 2004. The day of the New York competition, I give a friend of mine a call to wish him happy birthday, and he invites me to his celebratory afternoon picnic in Central Park. My friend writes for a major music magazine, and his friend, the editor in chief of the magazine, is coincidentally one of tonight's three judges and will also be attending the picnic. I think maybe I can butter him up at this preshow get-together or perhaps, if necessary, bribe him.

I head to the picnic, which is being held near a little pond at the north end of the park. It's perfect picnic weather. There, I say a polite hello to the man who holds one-third of my air guitar future in his hands, but mostly we avoid each other. I don't want to be accused of winning because I know one of the judges, so I must operate stealthily. It doesn't really matter, though, as he has—along with most of the other picnic attendees—gotten thoroughly trashed. In addition to the vast quantities of alcohol being consumed, I am told that one or more picnic attendees might have also ingested a variety of hallucinogens.

One picnic attendee repeatedly tries to get me to join the trip. I explain that no, I can't start tripping now, that I have an important air guitar competition in a few hours.

"So you're *actually* telling me that you can't eat magic mushrooms because you have to play an *invisible* guitar tonight?" He grabs me by the shoulders and shouts again, "An *invisible* guitar?!" Other picnic attendees look on and laugh. "Jimi Hendrix would be *sorely* disappointed, my friend!"

Maybe I should just eat the mushrooms. Maybe it will help me to better visualize my air guitar if I am genuinely hallucinating. It's certainly worth trying—one day. Not today.

The picnic debauchery continues. I say good-bye to the man who will be judging me in just a few hours, and he wishes me luck. I don't bother bribing him, as he is utterly soused and will no doubt quickly forget the transaction. How he is going to accurately score such a serious event in a few hours is beyond me. *It's the competitors that are supposed to be drunk*, I think to myself, *not the judges!*

Later that evening, one recovering picnicker tells me how the day ended: A huge crowd of people arrived and inexplicably sat down around them. Then someone wearing a giant bear costume came running over the hill towards them, waving arms, making funny bear grunts. My friends momentarily panicked, thinking that they were in fact under attack by a person in a giant bear costume. Then the play started—it turned out they were all tripping smack dab in the middle of a roving Shakespeare in the Park.

The last time I had been at the Knitting Factory, a medium-sized rock (and occasionally bad jazz) club in TriBeCa, was for a Halloween 2003 show with Les Sans Culottes. But tonight I am entering the Knitting Factory as an air guitarist. The place is starting to fill up with press and fans, and it's only six-thirty. Just after I walk in, I spot the reigning world champion: Mr. C-Diddy.

I haven't seen the Diddy since the Aireoke he attended in LA a few months back, where I had definitely established my retirement from competitive air guitar forever. That night C-Diddy gave a spectacular air demonstration, putting the Aireoke attendees under his spell. Later we reminisced about Finland, New York, and everything in between, but I always sensed that C-Diddy was laughing at me for letting air guitar take over my life. Perhaps his ability to distance himself from it all is one of the sources of his power.

I say hello to C-Diddy, who (despite my earlier claims of retirement) is not surprised to see me. I get down on my hands and knees on the dank floor to bow before the Master. He is, after all, another of tonight's judges. I stand up and express my admiration for his greatness, he wishes me luck, and I head backstage.

The Knitting Factory is a multifloored musical complex with a tiny stage in the basement, a slightly bigger room one floor down, and a decent-sized main stage with a ground-floor area and a balcony. It's definitely a step up from the Pussycat Lounge and strip club. On the balcony level, behind the main stage area, is a dressing room as shitty as any other dressing room at a New York City music venue—maybe shittier. At least it's well stocked with beer. It's here that I encounter tonight's competitors.

The first guy I recognize is The Shred, air guitar elder from Maryland. I am happy he has made it back for another year. Despite his age, The Shred's body is rock solid from daily air guitar workouts. Wearing black pleated shorts, a sparkly patterned vest, a black tie, and no shirt, the Shred looks like he might be mistaken for a male stripper from Eastern Europe or maybe Canada. But I admire The Shred, as I admire anyone over the age of forty who still willingly partakes in public displays of idiocy. I wish him luck and dive into my first can of courage.

Burping up lamb (word to the wise: never eat lamb shwarma before a competition), I grab my bag and go to the bathroom to get changed. (I'm freeballing in the leather pants and don't want to frighten the ladies in the dressing room.) I lace up my cow-skin trousers and look at myself in the mirror. I realize that these pants, held over from my Denver performance (I had to call the thrift store and tell them I was keeping the clothes I had "borrowed," and they ended up charging my credit card eighty-seven dollars), are way too big for me. In the crotch area, they lack a certain . . . *shapeliness*. While the pants' bulge deficit didn't prevent them from being stripped off me by the judge in the bathroom of the Denver club, I feel I can do better. I finish off a bottle of complimentary water, find some duct tape, and strap the empty plastic container to my inner left thigh. That tape is not going to feel good coming off, but my crotch does look massive.

I swagger down the hall like John Holmes. A muffled "Fell in Love with a Girl" by The White Stripes pounds through the walls from downstairs, and it gets my juices flowing. Back in the dressing room, I meet a guy wrapping himself in tinfoil like a walking Andy Warhol factory. He goes by the name Space Man Rock, and he's "blasted down" from Chicago, where he took third place about two weeks ago, behind Demon Strait. I wonder what it is about the Chicago winner that inspired both the Demon and Space Man to seek revenge. For me, these dudes make the idea of traveling around the country for an air guitar do-over just slightly less preposterous. At least I am not alone.

My friend Yoktan arrives, wearing a long stringy wig and a tight pink Hello Kitty T-shirt, obviously trying to reference C-Diddy's Hello Kitty breastplate. Actually, his shirt says "Hello Titty" and has two ample breasts forming the face of the kitty. He is going by what might be the most brilliant stage name of all, Airsatz, and though he looks like he could be Asian, he is really Tunisian—which I don't think counts. At least, I've never heard of Tunisian Fury. I tell him I noticed three Asian-looking names on the contestant order sheet that's going around, and because of C-Diddy, I still fear the Asian Fury.

"Yeah, and one's a girl," he says.

"What? An Asian female contender? Fuck! I am just going to call it quits. This is not happening."

I feel edgy and anxious tonight for some reason. Maybe it's lack of sleep from the traveling, maybe I'm still bitter from my Denver defeat, or maybe it's the lamb shwarma that keeps talking back to me; but I decide to ignore Zac Monro's Three Beer Rule and begin to down nearly every alcoholic beverage in sight. I am fully buzzed and taken by surprise when I see the female emcee up onstage. We've started already?

Though there are no chairs for the audience to sit on, the emcee asks them to remain standing for the Hendrix version of the national anthem. Irish-born Air-Do-Well (who in 2003, you'll recall, blew his chances by staying out all night the night before) crawls up onstage to perform the anthem of his adopted country. He seems in the same condition as last year—totally incapacitated. Air-Do-Well wraps up his touching but sloppy paean to the Land of the Free and the Home of the Brave, and now it's time to get ready to rumble.

A few dudes into it, Chicago's Space Man Rock is announced as coming "all the way from Venus to teleport you to Rocktopia," and does a medley that goes from the psychedelic countdown in Bowie's "Space Oddity" to Motörhead's "Ace of Spades." Is there a connection between the two songs? I can't think of one. Most of his foil sheds like heat tiles falling off the shuttle *Discovery*, and then Space Man Rock falls to the floor and waves his arms like he's dog paddling. It's baffling, really. Baffling not only that he managed to get third place in Chicago, but also that he bothered to fly here to try again.

The Shred goes old-school with his sampling from side one of the prog-rock classic 2112.[3] How he was able to whittle Rush's twenty-minute-and-thirty-three-second opus down to sixty seconds remains a mystery. What is clear, however, is that The Shred has still got what it takes. He moves with the agility of an eighteen-year-old on an athletic scholarship. He plays the air guitar with his teeth and it *actually* looks like he's hitting the right notes. As I stand on the side of the stage, watching, I can't help but think, Long live The Shred!

I am waiting for my turn, and the anticipation has started to build, mostly in my bladder. I've had way too many beers, and there's no time to for me to take a leak before getting onstage. Luckily I'm on next.

"This man needs no introduction," begins the emcee. "He's the second-best air guitarist in the US.[4] Playing Air Supply's 'Making Love Out of Nothing at All,' Björn Türoque!"

I feel a lot looser tonight than I did in Denver. As I dig in to the track, I can't tell if the crowd is with me or not. Everything feels like it is moving very slowly, like I am watching myself perform from above. Am I dead or just drunk? This time, when Air Supply's

---

[3]In this era of early-seventies prog-rock from which *2112* hails, bands like Rush and Yes put out epic orchestral albums with some of the most ridiculous-sounding song titles ever, like "The Temples of Syrinx" and "The Revealing Science Of God," many of which lasted entire album sides and were frequently based on loose interpretations of Eastern religious scriptures or books by Ayn Rand.

[4]Technically, this is probably not true. Even though I have come in second place in three competitions, Krye Tuff, who won the LA competition last year, is probably the true sovereign runner-up.

anthem hits the bars where the guitar sits out, I pull an air vial out of my jacket, pour some air cocaine onto my hand, take a big snort, and then launch back into the closing solo with newly acquired zeal. It works. But I come down quickly when, at the end of the song, I dive out into the audience, which parts like the Red Sea for Charlton Heston in *The Ten Commandments*, only much faster. The foolish thought that anyone might catch me quickly perishes as I land just barely upright on the floor. I climb back up onstage, and it appears my disastrous stage dive has not cost me: I take the lead with three 5.9s.

The final contestant of the night is the Asian female I was worried about: MiRi "Sonyk-Rok" Park. She walks out onstage dressed as every man's fantasy: the Catholic schoolgirl. Sonyk-Rok has the short plaid skirt, the unbuttoned white shirt tied above her belly button, the knee socks, and the high-heeled shoes. Looking like Britney in the "Baby One More Time" video, she coyly walks towards the back of the stage and gingerly sets down her eyeglasses. Tight floor toms beat out the opening of Van Halen's "Hot for Teacher," and she straps on her guitar. As the opening power chords unfurl, she pulls a chopstick from her tightly pinned hair and unleashes it, heralding the arrival of her Asian Fury. She's not that technically adept and I don't really *see* the air guitar, but when she gets down on her knees and does a full back bend in mid–Eddie Van Halen solo, it doesn't matter. I, like everyone else there, am smitten. When she flashes her Hello Kitty underwear at the end of the song, the last nail is in the coffin: three perfect scores.

At that point, I already know how it ends. But before it's over, I have to suffer through the intermission, where backstage a mysterious roving freelance judge assaults us all with his personal critiques. He's a short, weaselly looking guy, and he carries a notepad on which he has scrawled his distillations of our performances—for what reason it is not immediately clear, as he's not competing here tonight.

"You should be sweatin', man," he says to me. "I am training harder than Dolph Lundgren in *Rocky IV*, buddy. I am fucking Russia right here. In my mind I am going to Finland. It ain't finished till I'm Finnished." The dude is more wired than David Bowie recording *Station to Station*.

"Who is this guy?" I ask. Nobody knows.

Space Man Rock walks by, and the weasel quotes to him from his notes, "I like robots. I gave you a 5.0. Who's next? Who else wants some?"

"Is this guy accredited?" asks Aer Lingus, laughing at him. But soon everyone wants to know the guy's evaluation. People start peering over his shoulder to see what he thought of their performances.

"What'd you give me?" asks The Shred.

"Keep the dream alive: 5.0."

"Dude," I say, trying to get his attention. "What's your deal?"

"I am the Reaper," he explains. "I was nervous, but now I am fine. Eight million people in New York, and *this* is what they could find? If Vernon Reid[5] were here, he'd have a heart attack."

I reach the conclusion that The Reaper has not been taking his meds.

---

[5]Lead guitarist of the band Living Colour.

"So, what are you doing here?" I ask.

"I'm scouting. You can't pitch a four-game series and not know who the talent is! LA will envelop my *macheeezmo*! I am on a steady diet of rice cakes—it's all air! I have to travel three thousand miles to find some competition!"

"So how'd I do?" I have to ask.

"Which one are you?" he asks.

I am vaguely insulted. "Björn Türoque. Air Supply. Number thirteen."

He looks down at his notepad and is flipping through pages until he finds it. "Will have air betties by the end of the night. He's going to LA."

I am starting to like The Reaper.

"What about Sonyk-Rok?" I ask, thinking that maybe The Reaper is some kind of crazed oracle.

"The Margaret Cho look-alike." He finds the entry and reads, "She uses sex for a 6.0. I'm gonna dominate her dojo in LA."

The Reaper wanders downstairs to watch round two, which culminates in Sonyk-Rok doing a full split onstage at the end of "Crazy Train," the evening's compulsory song. And I am—it comes as no shock at this point—the runner-up, again.

She does have it all, though: sex appeal, flexibility, adequate technique, Asian Fury, *and* Hello Kitty panties. It didn't matter what The Reaper said; I knew she was on her way to Finland.

Upstairs after the show, I am fully saturated in alcohol and getting belligerent. C-Diddy announces to the few of us hanging out in the dressing room that it's about time Asian Americans made a statement, and if it needs to be in air guitar, then so be it.

"Koreans," he declares, "we know pain. We are the new Jews of America."

"What?" I shout. "I am the Jews of America!"

He points to Sonyk-Rok and jokes, "This is my fiancée." And then he puts his arm around me. "And this is my bridesmaid." Everyone in the room laughs.

"I feel like I've been a bridesmaid for a long time," I say.

"You were good," he says, consoling me. "But I feel like you dropped it on the second round."

"What do you mean I dropped . . . There was *no way* I was beating that . . . fucking slut over there. . . . *Fuck her!*" The alcohol is doing the talking at this point, and I immediately regret what I've said. Sonyk-Rok gives me the finger. "I am kidding! I am kidding! She is awesome."

"You are your own myth, man," says C-Diddy, and I wonder if he is being genuine or patronizing.

"I am, yeah. As are you."

"But were you actually *aiming* for second? 'Cause that's hard to do."

Make that patronizing.

"Honestly, there was nothing I could've done in that second round to win against her, right? Not a goddamn thing."

"Yeah, it would've been tough. I mean, on top of her performance, you couldn't do the splits. Which neither can I."

"Oh, I can do the splits," I say, "just . . . not in these pants." At least I get a laugh from the room. It would've been a good line to leave on. Instead, upon exiting, I shout, "Who wants to have sex with me? Come on! I'm the second best!"

Silence.

Afterwards, a bunch of friends and I (including Airsatz, who was recovering from being booed off the stage, and the perennially bitter Air-Do-Well, who still claimed to have invented air guitar) stay up until sunrise, boozing, playing music way too loudly, dancing on a friend's dining room table, and exchanging air guitar war stories. Nothing beats seeing the sun come up in the morning in Manhattan, and realizing you are still raging against the machine. It's man versus city here, and staying up all night means another small victory for the rock and roll team.

And then . . . somehow, Monday morning arrives. Still aching from air guitar battle wounds (battered knees, sore neck and shoulders, bruises of mysterious origin all over my body—maybe I didn't really land on my feet after that stage dive?) and riding a two-day hangover over from Saturday night's sorrow-drowning, I feel like I've been hit by a garbage truck followed by a taxi followed by a Chinese-food delivery guy on a bicycle. To be a true air guitarist, one needs dedication and devotion to everything the rock fantasy has to offer: one must *live* the life of a rock star, following in the winding, staggering, and lumbering footsteps of Mötley Crüe or Guns N' Roses as they hobble their way from city to city, bottle to bottle, upper to downer, and groupie to groupie. I'm trying my best.

The flight back to LA from New York is brutal. I have to leave on the seven a.m. flight out of JFK in order to get back in time to get even a partial day's work in. *Oh yeah*, I realize. *I am not Slash. I have a job*. . . . It dawns on me that I have been missing so much work because of air guitar competitions and band commitments that I am quickly running out of money. What the hell am I doing?

Days later I find out that Sonyk-Rok performs in a comedy troupe with C-Diddy and trained with him one-on-one for weeks before the competition. I consider mounting a protest, but what would that really accomplish? Was there a larger Asian air guitar conspiracy looming? Probably.

What does not destroy me,
makes me stronger.

—Friedrich Nietzsche

LOS ANGELES June 14, 2004. My third installment of LA Aireoke is scheduled to start at ten p.m. Emceeing Aireoke requires a level of wit and intoxication that no amount of coffee or ibuprofen could prepare me for under such hungover conditions; nonetheless, the show must go on.

We've started to get some repeat attendees at the LA Aireoke since its inauguration three weeks ago. The very first night, a guy showed up and sat at the empty bar looking around, confused. Our fliers had said, "Doors at nine, Aireoke at ten." It was 8:45 p.m.

I walked over and introduced myself. "Hey, you here for Aireoke?" I asked the guy. He looked like he was in his midtwenties. He had a black jacket, black jeans, black facial hair, and a solemn look in his eyes.

"Yeah, what time does it start?" he asked.

"We'll probably start rolling around ten, I would think," I told him. "But feel free to hang out and get drunk. I'm Björn, by the way." I shook his hand.

"Psycho Dave," he said, and shook back. Strong handshake too.

Aireoke LA began at the Tempest bar on Santa Monica Boulevard in West Hollywood. The manager of Les Sans Culottes had recently started booking the venue, which was trying to change its image from an upscale lounge to more of a rock and roll club, and he suggested we set up shop there. A recent arrival to LA's shores, I had no way of knowing that it was a completely lame venue. The place had no walk-ins, and it was clearly struggling for business. Yet the best they could offer me was Monday nights.

I had to start somewhere.

Aireoke, unlike a standard air guitar competition, is really air guitar *by the people* and *for the people*. It was my way of democratizing airness, of giving something back. Air guitar, as I had learned in Finland, was really about freedom. It was about letting go. It was about embracing nothingness. And Aireoke simply provided a forum for anyone to do just that—the freedom to get up onstage, hear the roar of the audience, and feel like a rock star for a minute or two without having to be judged.

Psycho Dave was our first regular in LA, and tonight, my first night back to LA after two crushing second place finishes, he is his usual punctual self—right on time at nine o'clock. He is wearing

Dockers khakis and a long-sleeved black T-shirt. Deeming my Aireoke selection of over six thousand songs inadequate, he hands me his own CD containing a sixty-second edit of "Freight Train" by a metal band I am ashamed to admit I've never heard of, called Nitro. I initially feared Psycho Dave, who early on informed me that he worked for John Tesh.[1]

Also in attendance that night are two red-haired twin brothers going by the stage names "Power" and "Control." At one point in the evening, Power does the most incredibly accurate, awe-inspiring four minutes and thirty-four seconds of air drumming I have ever seen, to Rush's "Tom Sawyer." As a joke, since air drums as far as I know are not permitted in formal competition, I attempt to convince Power that he must compete. He takes it under advisement.

Then, in an act I can only suspect stems from deep-rooted fraternal competition, Power's brother Control headbangs continuously for the entire length of Metallica's "Master of Puppets." I find out the next day that he has severe whiplash and cannot get out of bed. It's the first Aireoke injury that I know of, though I suspect many go unreported.

I'm on my second or third hair of the dog, struggling to keep it together in my role as emcee. Onstage, in between air guitar performances, I announce that the best air guitarist that night (as decided by my highly accurate measure of audience cheering) will

---

[1] John Tesh, or "The Tesh" (as I like to call him), was the host of *Entertainment Tonight* from 1986 to 1996. An accomplished pianist and saxophone player, The Tesh also composed "Roundball Rock," the theme song of *The NBA on NBC*. Nowadays The Tesh is focused on his radio network (where Psycho Dave is employed), which touches millions of fans every day with its focus on light rock, smooth jazz, and talk with a "family-friendly" bent.

get a free entry[2] into the LA regional competition three nights from tonight, sponsored by US Air Guitar. Several Aireokeists later, a short young Asian dude blows everyone away. He's got long, curly hair parted down the middle, and wears jeans and a T-shirt with an iron-on portrait of his cousin on it.

"Ladies and gentlemen," I announce from the stage to the thirty or so Aireokers, "I'd like to introduce a little Diddy. Yes, it's C-Diddy, Junior! Let's show some love for another Aireoke regular: the Rockness Monster!"

Rockness starts Pantera's "Suicide Note Pt. II" slowly, strutting back and forth, but when the song (which has the edgy, aggressive, and incredibly dark vibe of your average Pantera track) finally reaches the solo, Rockness explodes into a fireball of air guitar ferocity, windmilling his arm until it becomes a blur. He eventually falls to the floor and air dies. Moments later he is resuscitated by the head-splitting distortion of Pantera's wall of guitar. He is unquestionably the evening's champ, and I suspect he will be a contender on Thursday night. He is, after all, Asian.

At the end of the evening, I am outside with Rockness talking about Thursday's competition. I've had about four hours of sleep in two days and at least that many vodka-and-sodas since the evening began. My eyelids feel like they are filled with a dense mud, and I am making drunken declarations.

"There is no way in hell that I will compete on Thursday," I tell him. "It's just not happening."

"Well, that's pretty sad," says Rockness.

---

[2]The standard USAG entrance fee: twenty-five dollars. For the world championships in Oulu, Finland, it's twenty-five euros.

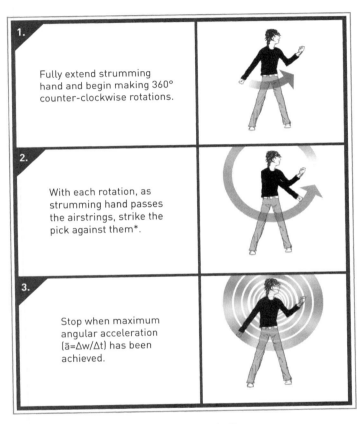

1. Fully extend strumming hand and begin making 360° counter-clockwise rotations.

2. With each rotation, as strumming hand passes the airstrings, strike the pick against them*.

3. Stop when maximum angular acceleration ($\bar{a}=\Delta w/\Delta t$) has been achieved.

Figure 8. The Windmill

*Caution: Not to be combined with whammy bar techniques—Pete Townshend, the move's progenitor, impaled his hand on the whammy bar during a windmill in 1989.

"I've learned my lesson, my friend: you can only come in second place four times. That's when you gotta stop."

"Understandable," he says.

I then make a loud announcement to several random strangers walking down Santa Monica Boulevard at two a.m.: "In my stead, Rockness is gonna fucking carry the torch, but he's gotta *win*. It's a burden, but he's *got* to win it for me."

"For you, man," agrees Rockness. *Is he sober? Humoring me?*

"For Björn Türoque! I am just passing the torch," I blather. "Björn Türoque! Björn Türoqueness Monster! It just fuckin' flows like that." A car drives by, and the people shout, "Woo!" out the window at us. I wish both Rockness and Psycho Dave good luck on Thursday, drink a couple of glasses of water, and eventually get in my car to head home.

LOS ANGELES June 17, 2004. Tonight's event—the 2004 US Air Guitar Championships, my seventh official competition—takes place at Key Club on the Sunset Strip. (Okay, I was lying to Rockness Monster and the random passersby on Santa Monica Boulevard the other night at Aireoke. Maybe I got carried away. But the only reason I would miss competing in the LA regional heat is if Demon Strait mysteriously died in a bizarre hedge-trimming accident and I had to step in as Denver's runner-up in the finals. Unfortunately, despite my best efforts, this never managed to happen.) Key Club is two blocks west of the infamous Viper Room, where, on the sidewalk in front of the club, River Phoenix died of acute multiple drug ingestion in 1993. Key Club was once a rock club known as Gazzarri's, where The Doors and Van Halen used to tear shit up. Now the club looks like something inhaled by a tornado from Las Vegas and vomited down on LA. Blue neon panels cover the exterior. Inside it's all colored gel mood lighting, wrought-iron railings, and cheesy brushed aluminum. All of the staff wear headsets. It feels like a disco. And though lots of cool bands have played here since it became Key Club (Def Leppard, Ratt, the Scorpions, and even Rick James), it's no Roxy.

Worst of all, there's no free beer.

We are supposed to get ready downstairs in the leather-padded and lavender lit "Plush" room. How are we supposed to give good air guitar performances sober? We hang out, get oriented, and begin doing interviews with the press. I spot Psycho Dave sitting alone on a banquette. He is deep in concentration. I approach to greet him, and we shake hands. He's wearing black jeans, a black leather jacket with Wile E. Coyote painted on the back, a Jack Daniel's T-shirt, and a bullet belt.

"Nervous?" I ask.

"A little bit," he says. "I think I spent too much money on my costume."

Nobody outspends Björn Türoque when it comes to air guitar costumes.

"Oh yeah? How much did you spend?" I ask.

"Well, all told it was about a hundred fifty dollars."

I start to feel bad for the guy. I've seen his work at Aireoke, and I can just tell he doesn't have a real shot at the title. Psycho Dave, like me, has the desire. It burns deep within him. But his air guitar performances are all inwardly directed, delivered with a contorted face of suppressed rage. He seems the quintessential angst-ridden teenager, taking out his frustration on his invisible guitar, and that's why I like Psycho Dave. He feels something profound when he gets up onstage, and I think he wants to win—needs to win—way more than I do.

"You been training?" I ask.

"Every day," he says.

I wish Psycho Dave luck, and then a Japanese video crew comes over to interview me. I feel like Bill Murray in *Lost in Translation* trying to understand their questions.

"Where are my form?" I ask, shrugging my shoulders.

"Form, from! Where you are from?" they repeat.

"Ah!" I say. Duh. "I am from Sweden," I tell them. "I am the only Jewish air guitarist from Sweden. I take my style from Bjorn Borg, but also Jimmy Page, Frank Zappa, and Larry David." They politely thank me, and I bow and walk away, wondering if they know who Larry David is, much less Frank Zappa.

Also chilling in the Plush room is Mother Rucker, a friend of a friend who has been the DJ for Aireoke since I started hosting it in LA. He won the regional championship in his hometown of Minneapolis, so he has to compete in the finals only. I say hello and toast him with a beer. He tells me about how during a tiebreaker in Minneapolis, playing to Queen's "Stone Cold Crazy," he jumped from a seven-foot-high stage onto concrete, and suffered stress fractures in both heels, a strained tendon in his right ankle, and a hyperextended elbow. This was all while stripped down to his socks and Calvins. He is also complaining tonight of "air guitar elbow." That makes the second air guitar injury I've heard about in recent days.

As I walk around the Plush room, I look over the other competitors. There's a guy wearing a fake fur animal costume and a furry mask, being led around on a metal leash by a hot girl in a white jumpsuit. I am told he is the Yeti. I see another familiar face: it's The Reaper, the idiot who was in New York a few nights ago offering postperformance evaluations. The Reaper is wearing black stockings over a diaper, and a tight T-shirt on which he's written his catchphrase, "Not Finished Till I'm Finnished." (I prefer "Oulu or Bust," myself). Who is he channeling? What rock star wears a diaper? His manager, a guy wearing a dark suit and tie, helps him get warmed up by forcing him to do push-ups.

Control and his twin brother, Power, are there, wearing matching blue tennis outfits and headbands. Control, Power's manager, chews on a cigar and scrutinizes the several pages of rules to determine if there's any mention of air drums being prohibited. After going over the rules several times, Control informs Power that he's in the clear.

The Airtight Messiah, my childhood friend and adult nemesis, has returned for more punishment. He is sitting at a table with a pen, looking carefully over some papers.

"What are you doin', man?" I ask The Messiah.

"Catching up on work, man . . ." he says, seeming embarrassed to be working instead of drinking in these last minutes before the evening gets rolling.

"Wait, are you still at *Hustler*?" I ask, remembering that the last

I had heard, The Messiah was an editor at the porn magazine run by the infamous Larry Flynt.

"Yup," he says.

"Cool . . . I guess editing an article for *Hustler* is as good of a warm-up for an air guitar competition as any." He nods affirmatively, and I leave him to edit his porn in peace. If you've ever wondered who writes the articles in porno magazines, now you know: The Airtight Messiah.

Aer Lingus enters the Plush room to go over tonight's proceedings with the performers. "Any questions?" he says to the crowd of nervous costumed freaks.

"Who are the judges?" I inquire. I have participated in enough of these damn things to know how critical it is who's judging. What are their credentials? Would they know Airness if it bit them in the ass?[3]

"Tonight's judges," answers Lingus, "are two guys from The Firm named Andy Gould and Simon Renshaw, and the guitarist from the Vandals, Warren Fitzgerald."

"Yo, Lingus. What's The Firm?" I ask.

"It's a music management company. They manage bands like the Dixie Chicks, Rob Zombie, and Limp Bizkit."

Everyone laughs. Not surprisingly, nobody here likes those bands (though I suspect a few are into Rob Zombie, and I think one of the Dixie Chicks is pretty hot).

The first five competitors are called up to stand in line next to the stage, and the rest of us sit downstairs watching a video feed on

---

[3] Some have likened Airness to pornography: you know it when you see it.

a large monitor at the back of the room. It's not long after the competition begins that we realize the judges are not taking their jobs seriously. The Reaper, who puts on a comically ridiculous and by any standard terrible performance in his diaper, gets fairly high marks, as does Rick London, a guy who has plastered fliers of himself all over the venue and performs wearing nothing but overstuffed tighty-whities and knee pads. The judges evidently like watching men strumming in their underwear.

But Psycho Dave is the first unfortunate victim of their shoddy adjudication. During his performance I hear others around me saying things like, "Wow—he rocks," and, "Awesome." And Psycho Dave is, in fact, really good. His moves are solid, and the audience is receptive. He could actually get laid tonight. He's no C-Diddy—and he's no Björn Türoque either, for that matter—but the hours of practicing have paid off. That is, until the performance is over and his scores are announced: 5.2, 4.9, and 5.7. The first two scores are from The Firm dudes, and the last is from Warren Fitzgerald.

"What the *fuck*?" shouts a fellow air guitarist. I too am confused—he really deserved better. A demoralized Psycho D walks downstairs and looks . . . well, psycho, to be honest. His eyes are open wide, and he looks like he might hurt someone.

"Those judges fucking *suck*!" he says as he throws himself into a banquette to nurse his beer and lick his wounds. I tell him he was robbed, but he just sits and sulks. "It's bullshit," he mumbles.

It's going to be a long night.

"Ladies and gentlemen, the hardest-working man in air guitar, Mr. Björn Türoque!" is how I am announced onstage. I am wearing a Mexican-style poncho and a giant sombrero as I saunter out onto the stage. I point to the soundman to start my song and gingerly pluck the opening triads of the Gipsy Kings' cover of "Hotel California" on an acoustic *aire guitarra*. About fifteen seconds into it, I strum the nylon air strings and sustain a chord with a flourish, remove my poncho and sombrero, and reveal my torn-up white shirt with cutoff sleeves and a tie, as the opening drumbeat of the Dead Kennedys' "California Über Alles" fades in and takes over. "Hotel California Über Alles" is what I am calling my medley.

I slow it down during the bridge where singer Jello Biafra sings about the "suede denim secret police," and then fly into a rage the moment he screams, "Die!" I end the song with a Nazi-style military march back and forth on the stage and a short air drum fill, and then I toss my air guitar into the crowd on the final chord. It's one of the best audience reactions I have yet to receive. I am surely improving with age. I thank my fans, grab my poncho and sombrero, and walk offstage feeling elated. And then I hear my scores: 5.3, 5.1, and 5.9? It's a death sentence. It's obvious that the Vandals dude gets it, and he's got cred: he's played with punk legends the Vandals since 1987 and he's played guitar in Tenacious D's massively kick-ass band with Dave Grohl of the Foo Fighters. But the Firm guys, responsible for the two low scores, are just out of their element. They are air pollution.

"Whatever," I say as I walk downstairs. "The gods are against me . . . against me . . ." I echo in despair. "It's all backwards—it's like we're in the Bizarro world of air guitar." Then I see Sonyk-Rok in the corner putting on some eyeliner, and I'm reminded that none of this matters. Soon she'll be flashing those Hello Kitty panties.

The Rockness Monster is up next. He stands on stage as Slayer's

"Raining Blood" begins to bleed slowly through the club's PA. I am standing by, watching with anticipation. Will the Firm judges get their heads out of their asses and give the Rockness his due? His performance starts off leisurely and I think he's not that great, until the song really kicks in and he begins convulsing in a paroxysm of pent-up aggression. A moment later he reins it in, pauses, and gives the crowd a wide-eyed stare. And then he explodes again! It's an intense performance with brilliant dynamics, like the structure of a Nirvana song: quiet, loud, quiet, *loud!* And the audience can't get enough. His two 6.0s make sense, as Rockness is clearly superior to all who have preceded him. But the middle score, a 5.2, is from Simon Renshaw, the Firm guy who undoubtedly thinks he's Simon Cowell and is relishing the chance to just be a dick.

Power's air drum version of "Tom Sawyer" is also stupendous—even better than what he did at Aireoke. Every single drum hit is dead-on. It's the most accurate air performance I've ever seen, and it makes me think that maybe competitive air drumming will be the next big thing (though I imagine a disproportionate number would choose songs by Rush). Power scores high marks from the judges and lots of *woo*s from the crowd, but, despite what the official rules do or do not say, I think he will ultimately be disqualified for not playing air guitar.

Round one comes to an end, and a few moments later they ask the top five air guitarists to the stage in ascending score order: I have tied for fifth place with the diaper-wrapped Reaper, who is in fact passed out in the basement; in fourth place is Rick London, who has thankfully put on a gold lamé robe so we don't have to look at his overstuffed undies; Clayton Sweeny, an unremarkable rocker from round one, is third; Power, the air drummer, is second; and Rockness, the undisputed winner of the round, gets a tsunami of screams from the crowd when he returns to the stage in the pole position.

The five of us are standing onstage when the chanting starts. From somewhere deep in the crowd it begins as a murmur and grows increasingly louder until the entire audience is shouting in unison: *"PSY-CHO DAVE! PSY-CHO DAVE!! PSY-CHO DAVE!!!"* After about fifteen seconds of this, Psycho Dave runs upstairs from the Plush room. The audience is cheering madly as Psycho Dave marches angrily over to stage left and snaps both hands in the air to flip off the Firm judges. They laugh heartily at him. Psycho Dave then raises his hands and looks out into the audience to elicit more cheers, which he gets. Then he storms off.

With that drama over, our compulsory song is played. It's "Monkey Wrench" by the Foo Fighters. In the middle of it, The Reaper staggers woozily out onstage. And even though he and I tied for fifth place, and he was passed out up until two minutes ago, I have to go first in round two.

And I suck. Completely.

Suddenly I am tired of air guitar. Tired of losing. Tired of these feeble judges. I just want it to be over so I can go complete a more imperative mission: finish getting drunk and find a nice air groupie to make out with. This is all fairly transparent in my performance. I have one decent foot-on-the-monitor moment towards the end of the song, but then I lose my balance and nearly fall into the crowd just as the song finishes. My scores are pathetic. My third attempt in 2004 to become a champion is an utter disaster, but at least it's over.

Rockness wins the LA regional portion of the evening hands down. He is adored by all. Personally, I think he is similar to Sonyk-Rok in that what he lacks in technique, he makes up for with a highly distinctive and captivating style. Rockness will now battle it out with the winners of all the regional competitions for the national title.

The Chicago champion, Steven St. Lyxx, is up first in the national heat, and he's profoundly mediocre. The judges have now gone full *American Idol*–style and begin making idiotic commentaries into their microphones after each performance. "I don't know about you guys," says Simon Renshaw, "but I think it might be time to bring back Psycho Dave!"

Someone in the audience shouts, "The judges suck!" and Psycho Dave leaps to the stage to seize whatever accolades he can get. Like an aging actor being welcomed back to the theater after a long hiatus, Psycho Dave laps it up. As he makes his exit, Simon the judge eggs him on by telling the crowd, "You know, he'd be so much more compelling if he had any talent."

With this, Psycho Dave flips his wig. He grabs the microphone from the emcee and begins ranting.

"This is just like the last presidential election, you motherfucker—you don't know *shit*, and you don't know shit about rock and roll!" The emcee wrestles the mic away as Psycho Dave alternately points back and forth between the two Firm judges, shouting, "You suck, you suck, you suck, and *you* suck!"

"So . . . back to the concert," says the emcee, trying to keep things moving.

"I have *no idea* why they call him Psycho Dave," remarks Warren Fitzgerald.

Next, a bit of just desert when Demon Strait, the long-haired somnolent metalhead from Alabama who edged me out of the Denver crown, takes the stage in his flowing white pirate shirt, and people throw empty beer cups and various crowd detritus at him as he strokes and finger-taps his motionless air guitar.

"I think he was in Whitesnake—or was it Nelson?" says one of the judges.

"That represents everything that air guitar is all about, a stoned hippie just playin' away," remarks another—providing further evidence, at least to me, that these judges have no idea what air guitar is all about.

Sonyk-Rok then performs her schoolgirl-gone-bad performance exactly as she did in New York, complete with Hello Kitty panty flash, and the fans predictably freak out. She gets three 5.9s but no 6s. The judges are just universally unforgiving, though, regarding the panties, they do offer: "That's what air guitar is *really* about!"

Rockness Monster does Guns N' Roses' "Welcome to the Jungle" and receives a *perfect score*. He is an explosive young air virtuoso, and everyone loves his work. "No panties, but this guy's outrageous," offers one judge.

The evening ultimately boils down to two Asians battling it out in a final compulsory round for the national title: the Rockness Monster (Vietnamese) versus Sonyk-Rok (Korean). I'm left to wait in the wings, watching enviously as they each have their way with the compulsory song, Halen's "Ain't Talkin' 'bout Love." They're both masterful, but in my opinion and based on the audience's reaction, Rockness has it nailed. At the end of their performances, they are interviewed, beauty pageant–style, as a way for the judges to make microadjustments in their scores.

Sonyk-Rok is asked, "What is the *not*-air guitar you imagine playing?" and she answers, "It's a white strat with a red strap—I didn't get a chance to use the whammy bar."

To this one of the judges asks, "Are you busy later?"

Another judge, seduced by Sonyk-Rok's thighs, comments, "All I heard was wood."

Then Rockness amuses the audience and the judges with his brilliant answers:

Judge: Who is the greatest guitar player of all time?

Rockness: Glennn Lagrimas.[4]

Judge: Who?

Rockness: He's my friend.

Judge: That's a good answer!

Judge: Do you play *not*-air guitar?

Rockness: I pretend to.

Judge: He's funny! Okay, if you were the air guitar champion of the world, what would you do with that belt or whatever it is?

Rockness: I would promote world peace and happiness.

---

[4]Yes, according to Rockness Monster, there are indeed three *n*'s in his first name.

He has good answers and a superior performance, and the audience unmistakably prefers him, but he loses out to the flash of Hello Kitty panties, and Sonyk-Rok is declared the winner. She will go on to flash her panties on the Conan O'Brien show a few nights later, and then once more in Finland, where she will become the disputed world champion of 2004.[5]

As for the Rockness, there's no question he'll be back for more.

Downstairs after the show, I am several sheets to the wind. Cameras are everywhere, ignoring Björn Türoque. The judges head downstairs to congratulate Sonyk-Rok and are ambushed by a drunk and belligerent Psycho Dave. He still won't let it go. He grabs the Vandals' Warren Fitzgerald and puts his arm around his neck, shouting, "This is the *one* judge who knows anything about rock and roll." Then he points to the Firm guys. "*These* two guys are corporate assholes. They are probably the same guys that passed on Nirvana! They'd pass on Metallica! They'd pass on any-

[5]Shortly after the championships in Oulu, the following press release was issued by the US Air Guitar committee:

"*September 2, 2004*—After the celebrations, the cheers and the awards ceremony, MiRi 'Sonyk-Rok' Park—the 2004 US Air Guitar Champion—was awarded the ninth Air Guitar World Championship. Playing an inspired rendition of Van Halen's 'Hot for Teacher,' Brooklyn's Park beat last year's US and world champ David "C-Diddy" Jung in a much-hyped battle between master and pupil.

"But in the days that followed the event, a judging controversy eerily reminiscent of this summer's Olympic men's gymnastics threatened to tear apart the very fabric of international air guitar competition. Upon reviewing in detail the scoring in the final rounds, the independent jury discovered that the New Zealand champion, Tarquin 'The Tarkness' Keys, should have edged out Park for top honors.

"In an unprecedented move, the jury has decided to share this year's first prize between the USA and New Zealand. Both contestants are expected to return to Finland next year as defending world champions. This controversy may never die down until these two consummate professionals duke it out on the world stage once again."

Apparently, air guitar producer Marika Lamberg was so horrified by the scandal that she threatened to quit.

one except fuckin' Yanni!" A crowd of cameras and spectators has gathered around to witness Psycho Dave's rant.

Fitzgerald gives Psycho Dave a consolatory hug as Psycho Dave remarks, "If I was gay, I would have sex with this man." Fitzgerald then tries to escape Psycho Dave's vicelike grip, to no avail. "Unlike *these* two guys," he says, pointing again to the suits from The Firm, "who probably haven't gotten laid since 1971 and are taking out their sexual frustrations on me. These are the same guys that have to pay transsexuals to blow them!"

The crowd starts hollering. It's like we're watching a live version of *The Jerry Springer Show.*

"Who's blowing me?" asks Simon Renshaw.

"A transsexual!"

"Perfect!" says Simon, and he toasts the crowd and walks away, instantly extinguishing what might have turned into an exciting chair-smashing brawl.

Thus 2004's battle for the crown of best air guitarist in the United States comes to a close. From Denver to New York to Los Angeles, I fought long and hard, but in the end I just didn't have it. Is there a magic formula? What if I spend the next year training with an Asian guru? Maybe all I needed was a Hello Kitty jockstrap? Am I too committed? Not committed enough? Maybe I just don't have Airness after all, and I never will. Maybe I should, as so many had already suggested, just set my air guitar free. *Just let it go. . . .*

My air failure is all too perfectly analogous to my real life as well: I am broke, my job in LA is over with, I'm not really playing in the French band anymore, and Jane Air and I have been broken up for almost three months. I'm not the best air guitarist in the country. I'm not even the *second*-best air guitarist in the country. Sure, I'm the second-best air guitarist in Denver (*wow!*) and New York (*okay*), but things just seem bleak all around. I don't make out with any groupies after the show, and there's definitely no way I'm making it to Finland this year.

The day after the competition, in a lonely, hungover moment of doubt and despair, I close my eyes. Suddenly I am transported back to Finland. There's a cold beer in my hand, the spirit of world peace is in the air, and I'm talking with Zac "The Magnet" Monro as his immortal wisdom echoes in my head as if fed through a delay pedal:

"I look at you and I see myself," says Zac. *"I see the future of air guitar . . . tar . . . tar . . . tar . . ."*

Well, there's always next year.

To air is human,

to air guitar divine

—*BT*

Part 3:

Carry On

My

Wayward

Son

The only performance that makes it, that really makes it, that makes it all the way, is the one that achieves madness, right? Am I right? Are you with me?

—Mick Jagger, in *Performance*

TOPANGA CANYON, CALIFORNIA September 3, 2004. A friend of mine in LA has invited me to join twenty or so musicians for a Neil Young tribute concert, part of a series of fund-raisers for Theatricum Botanicum, a cool outdoor theater tucked in the hills of Topanga on the outskirts of Los Angeles. Well-established local musicians and a few bigger names like folksinger Michelle Shocked and seventies folk icon Jackson Browne will be participating. I feel *vaguely* intimidated by the prospect of performing on the same stage as Mr. *Running on Empty*, in a tribute to someone as formidable as Neil Young. But, then again, I have shared the stage with the greatest air guitarists in the world.

The night of the concert, I show up at sound check with my iPod and my air guitar. Most everyone else has brought an acoustic guitar, mandolin, or banjo, and a large dose of sincerity. There is an old Wurlitzer electric piano waiting to be played. Backstage, amidst some of LA's finest musicians, I load up on complimentary wine and stumble upon the set order tacked to the wall. *This must be some kind of mistake*, I think. Apparently, I am to close the show.

One by one the performers are called onstage to do a sound check. They tune up, adjust the balances between their various instruments, swap out bad cables, and ask the soundman for more vocals in the monitor. (As usual, vocalists can *never* have enough of themselves in the monitor.) I am blown away by a few of the players, particularly Jackson Browne, and this is only the sound check. Since I am last in the set, I am last to test out my gear. I walk onstage, plug in my iPod, and let a few seconds of my song erupt over the speakers. It's loud. Embarrassing. There are drums and distorted guitars—a stark contrast to the mellow *unplugged* vibe I was getting from the other players. I quickly stop the iPod and lower my forehead in to my hand. This will be a complete fucking disaster.

Night descends, and the audience slowly begins to arrive. I am shocked that the theater—which seems on the edge of nowhere, surrounded by dense, lush trees—is actually filling up. Cicadas provide an acoustic backdrop to the evening as almost three hundred of Southern California's aging hippies, hipsters, and helplessly unhip sit on uncomfortable built-in wooden benches. Two older ladies who take care of running the outdoor theater open the show, playing a sloppy but endearing version of Neil Young's "Old Man."

Several songs in, a skinny blond-haired guy named Evan (who fronts an LA-based band called Marjorie Fair) gets up and sings a song called "Soldier." The song's spare lyrics ask a soldier why his eyes "shine like the sun," and Evan's voice is one of the most amazing I've ever heard. The lyrics and his voice, juxtaposed with the knowledge that the war in Iraq is getting worse every day, make his rendition of "Soldier" beyond haunting. The mood suddenly turns somber.

Then a surprisingly well-aged Jackson Browne, wearing the classic blazer, T-shirt, jeans, and blindingly white sneakers of every man over fifty who still wants to be cool but who will no longer endure the torture of shoes that lack at least an inch of foam cushioning, plays his version of "Only Love Can Break Your Heart." It's mesmerizing, and I stand there biting my nails, thinking, *Wow— that guy really sounds like Jackson Browne.*

Michelle Shocked has the entire audience join her in a version of "Helpless," and that's about how I am starting to feel backstage as I pace around, nervous as hell. My friend Mike, a genius musician (he wrote the music for the film *Donnie Darko*), who played earlier in the evening, laughs, gives me a high five, and jokingly asks if I am ready to go out there and kick ass. Yeah. Sure. I've only played air guitar for people who were *expecting* air guitar. I feel way out of my league. Can I go home instead?

Nope. It's time for the finale—time to coax Björn out of hiding. I run out onstage, approach the mike cautiously, and announce, "Okay, people, it's time to get stupid." My hands are shaking as I grab the microphone to steady myself. I practiced by singing along in the car on the way here, but I somehow feel ill prepared for this.

I can hear murmuring among the crowd.

"This song requires a little setup. . . ." I continue. "In the past two years, I've somehow gotten mixed up in the crazy world of competitive air guitar." The audience, thankfully, seems to find this funny.

"As those of you who have attended an air guitar competition know, it's a tradition for every competition to end with this song, which you will hear shortly. All air guitarists are asked to get up onstage and play this song together."

Laughter is erupting throughout the outdoor venue. I intentionally return a look of confusion, as if I am not in on the joke, and the more they laugh, the more relaxed I become. They actually seem to be in the mood for a little comic relief after all the solemnity.

"In Finland, where the Air Guitar World Championships are held, it is said that if everyone in the world were to hold an air guitar instead of a gun, there would be no war."

Cheers and laughter.

"This is my own cover of the song, which I recorded, so it is in fact me playing the instruments, and I will be singing; but in the spirit of world peace, I'll be playing air guitar for tonight's performance."

I pick up my iPod off the floor of the stage and hit play.

Then I strap on my air guitar, walk up to the microphone, and rock the shit out of "Rockin' in the Free World." The audience is laughing and clapping to the beat. The second I start singing, they are mine completely. By the time I get to the scorching guitar solo (which I recorded using a guitar filter called, appropriately,

"Scorching Guitar Solo"), people are completely freaking out. I run back to the mic to finish the last chorus, and everyone is singing along. I wish I could get them all onstage with me so that we could play air guitar together.

With my last chord, they offer an extended round of wild applause. I take a bow, grab my iPod, and walk off, not knowing exactly what just happened.

"Holy shit! That was fucking awesome!" says Mike, who gives me a double high five when I arrive backstage. The other performers offer congratulations, smiles, nods of approval, and pats on the back. It feels like what a great performance *should* feel like. I'm actually shaking a little, overwhelmed by it all. "Dude, Jackson really dug it!" Mike whispers to me, laughing slightly and pointing to Jackson Browne, who looks over and smiles as if to say, "You're insane—but nice work, kid."

Later, as I am leaving the theater, I hear someone shout, "There goes the air guitar guy!" The stranger comes over to shake my hand. "Oh my god—you rocked, dude! That was amazing!" he says. We shake hands. I say thanks and then walk away.

No, it wasn't an official air guitar competition. I'm not walking away knowing I was the best, or the second best. It wasn't an earnest display of Neil Young adulation, but it wasn't entirely a joke. It may not have been as powerful an antiwar declaration as "Soldier," but in my own way I did make a statement. It was one of the most gratifying performances ever, and I didn't mind at all that air guitar had leaked out of the competitive world into my everyday life.

"The Air Guitar Guy" had a nice ring to it.

Chapter Fifteen: A Star Is Björn

The easiest kind of relationship for me is with
ten thousand people. . . . The hardest is with one.
—Joan Baez, as quoted by Joan Didion
in *Slouching Towards Bethlehem*

Air guitar, I had learned, was about commitment. It was about forging a promise between oneself and the music, the result of which was the manifestation of *nothing*, rendered visible. For most, air guitar exists solely in a private world behind the locked door of a teenager's pot smoke–filled bedroom, or in the sanctity of a car-as-rock-arena stuck at a traffic light. In its most natural form, air guitar happens subconsciously, spontaneously, unexpectedly. But it doesn't matter if you are playing for an audience of one or of one thousand; what matters is that you are dedicated to the act and that you give yourself over to it fully. Anything shy of that is wasted air.

It's not unlike love, really.

After a lot of talking and fighting and more talking, Jane Air and I finally got back together in the autumn of 2004. We had put a lot of work into the relationship, and it seemed stupid just to let it fall apart without giving it one more try. In March of 2005 I made plans to move back to New York so that we could be together.

As I prepared to return home, I also began communicating with members of Les Sans Culottes about rejoining the faux French fold. Several of them were into the idea, but there was the sticky problem of Clermont Ferrand, the lead singer, who was still angry about a joke I had made in an online diary linking him, a fish taco, and a "hideous smell from stage left." Ferrand had reportedly said on numerous occasions that if I was ever to try to share a stage with him again, he'd kick the shit out of me.

LOS ANGELES February 10, 2005. Before I leave LA, I host one of the weirdest Aireoke nights ever. It makes departing all the more bittersweet. I started doing Aireoke at a run-down divey venue called the Parlour Club in West Hollywood as part of a night called The Thing, hosted by Don Bolles, the drummer for the seventies LA punk band the Germs.[1] Aireoke at the Parlour Club feels like the punk rock Los Angeles of a bygone era, one I imagined myself a part of when, as a seventh grader in Denver circa 1984, I saw bands like Black Flag, Nig-Heist, the Meat Puppets, and the Dead Kennedys play at the Rainbow Music Hall. Bolles wears shiny gold

[1]The Germs (originally known as "Sophistifuck and the Revlon Spam Queens"—a name I like better, though it's not quite as *catchy* as the Germs) were a veritable petri dish for musicians in LA in the late seventies. Belinda Carlisle (under the stage name Dottie Danger) briefly played drums, guitarist Pat Smear went on to play with Nirvana and the Foo Fighters, and Joan Jett produced the Germs' first full-length album, (GI). The Germs are recognized by many rockologists as being the first West Coast punk band. Singer Darby Crash, like a true rock star, overdosed on heroin at age twenty-two, under a sign on the wall stating HERE LIES DARBY CRASH. Bolles went on to drum for bands like Nervous Gender, 45 Grave, and Celebrity Skin, and is still rocking out today.

leather skintight pants with a lace-up crotch ("Man, these were designed for *David Lee Roth*!" Don boasted one night) and looks like one would expect a guy who played in a seventies-era hardcore punk band to look—which is to say, very similar to Andy McCoy, the dilapidated guitarist from Hanoi Rocks. But Don is the nicest, funniest, coolest punk veteran I'll ever meet. And he loves air guitar.

Tonight, the Parlour Club is packed, and people are signing up one after another to pay air guitar tribute to their favorite songs. Things are in full swing when I call up a guy whose sign-up sheet looks like this:

STAGE NAME:	DICK FIDDLER
BAND:	BLACK FLAG
SONG:	I DON'T CARE

Wearing a scarf tied around his face and head, and holding a pizza box in his right hand, Dick Fiddler climbs up onto the small stage. "I Don't Care" starts playing, and seconds into it, he drops the pizza box onto the floor and opens it up. Then he turns around and, with his back to the audience, he quickly pulls down his pants and releases a vile stream of liquid feces from his ass into the open box. He closes the box with his foot and kicks it away, then begins to play some violent punk rock air guitar, repeatedly throwing himself onto the floor inches away from the dirty bomb. When the song—sixty perfect seconds of uncut aggression—is finished, Dick Fiddler picks up the pizza box, walks offstage, and vanishes.

I return to the microphone, stunned.

The smell is foul and takes nearly ten minutes to dissipate. Despite the stench and the queasy feeling in my gut, I respect Dick Fiddler immensely. Not only did he not *eat* his feces or *throw it* at any of us—as punk lunatic GG Allin would have done—he packed it up in a box and took it with him.[2]

As if that weren't enough, Har Mar Superstar, a chubby, pasty white guy who sings R & B songs in his underwear for a living—*and actually sells records*—shows up and does a shirtless, erotic, Oulu-worthy "The Boys Are Back in Town," much of which is delivered while strutting on top of the club's bar.

The evening closes out when Howie Pyro, who played bass for D Generation and on two Danzig albums (*Live on the Black Hand Side* and *I Luciferi*), agrees to act as judge for a spontaneous air band playing Danzig's most famous track, "Mother." I am on the air drums. Pyro looks a little bored and doesn't give us a score. In the end he begrudgingly tells us, "You were okay, I guess."

Aside from the occasional shit-in-a-box or sporadic slow night, I love Aireoke. As for competing again, I decide that rather than continuing to face continued second place shame, I should focus my energy on becoming an Ambassador of Air, preaching the Gospel of Airness throughout the world. I submit a proposal to lecture about air guitar at a conference at the Experience Music

---

[2] GG Allin will probably rise from the grave and shove a broken beer bottle up my ass when he finds out that he is a footnote in any book, much less one about air guitar, so I'll just mention that the notorious GG would regularly ingest laxatives before shows in order to dump his load onstage. That may have been how the Fiddler got cued up as well.

Project museum in Seattle and am, to my disbelief, accepted. Other speakers will include Greil Marcus (author of influential books about music and pop culture such as *Lipstick Traces* and *Like a Rolling Stone: Bob Dylan at the Crossroads*); Robert Christgau, the *Village Voice*'s elder statesman of rock journalism; and numerous other authors and academics. On my own dime, I will fly to Seattle to give a twenty-minute lecture about the subject that has come to dominate my life for the past two years.

SEATTLE April 14, 2005. I arrive a day early to check out the lecture hall and eat some fried haddock at Seattle's famed Pike Place Market. The fish is fresh, crispy, delicious. I head over to the Experience Music Project museum, a building designed by Frank Gehry that looks a lot like his other signature steel buildings (the Guggenheim Museum in Bilbao, the Walt-Disney Concert Hall in LA); only this one deviates from the monochromatic silver by using molded sheets of colored steel. I am told that the inspiration for the building came after Gehry bought a bunch of electric guitars and smashed them to bits as if he were Pete Townshend.

The day of my presentation, I am pacing back and forth in the hallway outside the JBL Theater, the largest of the three lecture venues. The room holds about two hundred people and at the moment, with the current panel entitled "Lessons in Mayhem," in full swing, it's packed. A guy named Drew Daniel just gave a lecture called "How to Act Like Darby Crash," which I find a strange coincidence as I've been cohosting Aireoke with one of Crash's former bandmates. (I later tell this to Daniel, who seems about as interested as a twelve-year-old kid being told that dinner is ready.) I poke my head in to hear Greil Marcus reading his paper—about contemporary musicians playing old blues tunes. I watch a few minutes of his arid lecture, but I am too nervous to stick it out. I return to the hallway to pace and go over my notes. It's raining. Considering that I am in Seattle, the fact that it's raining is not very surprising. It's dismal here. No wonder Cobain killed himself.

The "Lessons in Mayhem" panel finishes, and people pour out of the hall like drunken sports fans exiting a basketball game and racing to their cars to beat the traffic. Only these people didn't drive. And they're sober. Many of them wear glasses. They are all music geeks. What's their fucking hurry?

It's time for my lecture, which I've titled "Air Guitar: There's No 'There' There—Or Is There?" I get set up and keep waiting for the hordes of egghead musicologists to return, but they don't. By the time I have to start, there are only about thirty people in the room, including, surprisingly, Greil Marcus himself, who sits in the second row. I begin my lecture with a PowerPoint presentation about the history of competitive air guitar. Then I introduce Björn Türoque, who, I explain, "will be giving us a demonstration of air guitar technique." I put on a bandana and sunglasses, transform into Björn, and play the Scorpions' "Taxman Woman" in honor of today's being tax day: April 15, 2005. It's a terrible song (not among the Scorpions' finest by any means—it's from their disappointing 1993 release, *Face The Heat*), and my performance is mediocre at best. Bear in mind, also, that I am *completely sober*, playing an invisible guitar for music scholars at the front of a large, fluorescently lit auditorium filled to about one-seventh capacity in the middle of a rainy afternoon in Seattle. These are *not* ideal Airness-inspiring conditions. Following the performance, I interview Björn Türoque, asking him a series of FAQAGs, taking the head-band/sunglasses combo on and off to signify the transformation from self to Björn. Sympathetic laughter occasionally sputters from the audience like the reluctant final kernels of a bag of microwave popcorn. This is obviously going over their heads. I wrap up by playing air guitar and singing my cover of "Rockin' in the Free World," just as I did so successfully at the Neil Young tribute concert in California several months ago. Despite my best efforts, the magic is gone. Nobody is clapping along or cheering. They are just looking at me, glazed over and baffled. I give it one last push during the scorching guitar solo, when I leap from the stage up onto the arms of one of the chairs in the front row, and then promptly lose my balance. Swinging my arms wildly behind me in an attempt to regain my stance, I awkwardly jump backwards off the chair on to a short cement ledge at the front of the seating section. I regain my stability and hop down off the ledge, thankful to avert what could have been a severe spinal cord injury suffered under the stupidest circumstances I can imagine.

Mild applause ensues. I thank the audience and sit down to catch my breath. The moderator, Dave Dederer, who fronted the mid-nineties pop band the Presidents of the United States of America, gets up to the podium and says, "Thank you, Dan; thank you, Björn . . . If nothing else, the two of you share colossal ball size." And now the audience finally laughs at something.

Dederer continues, "The first person I ever remember playing air guitar was Duff McKagan[3] at a junior high party in Seattle in 1976. He stood next to a record player all night, listening to Aerosmith, Led Zeppelin, and Ted Nugent, playing air guitar, with a silk shirt opened down to here." Dederer gestures to his navel. "Things worked out okay for him. . . ."

Yes, they sure did.

There's a great scene in the Wilco documentary *I Am Trying to Break Your Heart* where the band plays an outdoor daytime gig in front of about twelve people—several of them small but moderately receptive children. It's profoundly depressing, but then the next night their show is magically packed with adoring fans.

Part of life as a musician requires dealing with playing to an empty house or in front of people who did not come to see you. Until you've made it to the very top, it's virtually guaranteed that life on the road will include awkward, sucky gigs such as Wilco's. It's called, I believe, paying one's dues. My presentation felt like just another watermark in my extended series of dues-paying. It was a long way to travel to give a lecture about nothing. About *no thing*. About air guitar. But I was stronger for it—and so was Björn.

From Seattle I returned to New York, where I had moved in with Jane Air a few weeks prior. I had left New York over a year before to get a new identity in Los Angeles: to escape from my

---

[3]The bassist from Guns N' Roses. Duh.

black hole of a career producing educational software, to exile myself from the French band and let Jean-Luc Retard take a breather, and—though I refused to admit it to her or to myself at the time—I had needed to be away from Jane Air for a while to figure things out.

Now I was back in New York as a new man. Jane Air and I were, after a few initial bumps in the road, getting along well. I had successfully shed my software career. That was easy. It just meant that I made a lot less money and had no health care since I had become a full-time freelance writer and professional air guitarist. It was a pleasant hiatus from the French band, but I missed playing music with a nonair guitar. There had been so much Björn and so little Jean-Luc in the past year that I started to think maybe it was time to bring the Retard back.

I seriously entertained the idea of playing with Les Sans Culottes again, as long it was *sans* singer Clermont Ferrand. I had always pushed for the band to be less shticky and more musically complex, and I thought that maybe if I was truly committed to the band, it would be more satisfying. Maybe we could just overthrow Ferrand in a bloodless coup d'état? It seemed fitting, so that was what we did.

Stupidly, we forgot about his day job. Ferrand was a lawyer, so he decided to make a federal case out of getting the boot. We got served papers to show up in the court of the Southern District of New York, i.e. federal court, for an alleged trademark violation. Ultimately, after hiring a lawyer, going to court twice, and repeatedly trying to explain the concept of a faux French band to a curmudgeonly, blind judge (imagine if I'd had to explain air guitar), we decided to settle. We gave Ferrand the band name and Web site, and we started a new group called Nous Non Plus, meaning "us no more."

May rolled around and it was as if spring training had begun—you could actually *smell* the air in the air. America's interest in competitive air guitar was growing exponentially every year. Seven cities were announced as regional hosts for 2005's US Air Guitar Championships: New York, Los Angeles, Boston, Denver, Chicago, Asheville (North Carolina), and Austin. Should I bother? I had come so close so many times. Could I handle having my nose rubbed in another steaming pile of defeat?

What was once for me a joke had become an addiction. It was enough already. So I decided this year would be different. I would kick the habit. Get the air monkey off my back. Watch from the sidelines. Let someone else take over as the bridesmaid of air guitar.

Then I got drunk.

One night, I was at a bar in the East Village with some friends, including Aer Lingus and his new girlfriend, Minji. Lingus et al were taunting me about entering that year's competition. They knew I was in a self-prescribed recovery program, but they also knew how badly I craved a fix. They told me Björn *had* to enter this year, and I just shrugged them off. No mere peer pressure was going to affect this guy. Then Minji went in for the kill.

"I should totally design a costume for you," she said.

Minji is a fashion designer.

"Hmm . . . really?" I grumbled into my vodka. "I think I'm gonna just sit this year out."

"What? No! Björn has to compete!" she said. "It's like a tradition, right?"

Minji had only been dating Lingus for a few months—she didn't really know the full extent of my mental illness.

"I just can't face second place again. It's becoming stupid."

"I think your problem is that you haven't had the right costume designer," she said.

"I've never had a costume designer."

"Exactly."

"Well . . . C-Diddy did have the whole Hello Kitty breastplate thingie," I said. "Maybe I need something like that. Not exactly that, of course, but something that makes more of a statement."

"You should come by my store, and we can figure something out."

"I dunno. You think I should really subject myself to another year of torment?"

"Of course!" she says. "You have to compete. You're Björn Türoque! You're a legend. This is totally your year, I can feel it."

"I think that's the mojitos you're feeling."

I was just drunk enough to be swayed by her pep talk, and I was reminded: Minji *is* Asian. . . . This might just be the Asian Fury edge I'd been looking for.

NEW YORK CITY May 13, 2005. At four p.m., just a little over one week before the competition, I show up at Minji's store, called Min-K, in SoHo. It's one of those small, narrow boutiques with about fourteen shirts and a skirt or two on a couple of racks. How these places stay in business I'll never understand. Pretending I have a reason to be looking at high-fashion women's shirts, I scroll the racks, waiting for Minji to show up. There's a cute girl behind the desk who has told me Minji is on her way. I am paranoid that the girl thinks I'm shopping for an outfit for an upcoming drag queen competition.

Nothing makes a guy feel more like an asshole than being in a fancy clothing store for the ladies. There's always that chair in the corner—set out for the bored boyfriends and husbands of tireless clothes-whores. A friend of mine dubbed this chair the "Asshole Chair." I take a seat in the Asshole Chair and wait.

Minji arrives moments later. "Sorry I'm so late—really insane day," she says.

"Yeah, me too," I lie. I've spent part of the morning helping my friend take her fifth-grade class fishing, and the rest sampling potential air guitar songs.

I explain to Minji that I'm not totally set on a song but that I've been leaning towards "Set Me Free" by the British glam rock band Sweet, off their 1974 album *Desolation Boulevard*. Sweet were contemporaries of other glam rockers like Slade, T. Rex, Gary Glitter, and Queen, and were most famous for their hits "Fox on the Run" and "Ballroom Blitz." They were among the first hard rock bands to start wearing heavy makeup, platform boots, and chain mail shirts—something KISS would take to its furthest possible extreme a few years later. I am drawn to "Set Me Free" for its frequent tempo shifts, its kick-ass ascending power chord riff, the chorus' falsetto shrieks of "Set me free!" and its inspired use of the wah-wah pedal. It's fast, furious, and heavy as fuck. It's a perfect air guitar anthem.

"So . . . check this out," she says as she hands me a coffee table book full of photos of glam rock bands from the seventies. I open it up to find David Bowie in one of his "transvestites from Mars" outfits, quickly thumb to Freddie Mercury in a white bodysuit with giant ruffles, and then turn the page to find Iggy Pop half naked and writhing on the floor wearing skintight shiny pants. I realize I might be in trouble.

"I'm totally excited—this is going to be really cool," she begins. "Okay . . . So . . . how body-conscious are you?" she asks. I flash back to Jamie Kennedy pinching my beer gut on national television.

"Um . . . I'll wear whatever, I guess."

"I'm thinking of making you a tight spandex bodysuit," she says with a little too much enthusiasm.

"Okay, but it's not going to look *too* gay, right?" I say, worried that I will wind up looking like Liberace in a leotard. "I mean, there's a fine line between glam-rock cool and just kind of . . . gay."[4]

"It won't look gay," she replies.

I raise an eyebrow in suspicion.

"I promise. You will *not* look gay."

"Okay," I say. "I just . . . it shouldn't look *too professional*, either. Like, it should look sort of crappy in a way—I don't want to look like I am trying too hard."

"But you want to win, right?"

"Well, yeah, but—it shouldn't *look* like I want to win."

"Right. I think I understand. Don't worry."

[4] I have nothing against gay, by the way, as long as it doesn't affect my chances of winning an air guitar competition.

We continue discussing outfit ideas, and I tell Minji about my vision. A few nights prior to our meeting, while trying to get to sleep, I had a revelation: dry ice. I never did get my wall of fog on that Carson Daly show, and *nothing* is more arena rock than a wall of fog. I ask if there's a way to build little pockets into the costume, in which I could insert chunks of dry ice, which onstage will produce (I hope) miraculous clouds from my windmilling arms. I think it might be my most brilliant (or stupid, or dangerous) concept to date.

Minji is not immediately tuned in to my dry ice vibe. "Doesn't dry ice burn you?" she asks. I eventually convince her to forget about my burning my arms off and to just figure out a way to make it happen.

"We could make little pockets with zippers on them, attached to your arms like little wings," she suggests as she sketches in her notebook.

We work out the details of the outfit, and I agree to come back in a few days for my first "fitting."

Just another day in the life of the professional air guitarist . . .

Four days later I return to get fitted, and Minji's seamstress, a lovely woman from Guyana, takes my measurements. I wonder how much this is all going to cost me. We go over the details of the armbands, which will have zippered pouches for the dry ice. I ask the seamstress if she understands that the outfit she is making is for an air guitar competition, and she replies in a thick Guyanese accent, "Oh, sure, my son watch the MTV, so I know what this about!" After my body measurements have been drawn on a piece of muslin, the three of us hop into a cab and head over to a fabric store in the East Village to pick out the threads.

After much deliberation, we decide that we should use two different fabrics, one for each vertical hemisphere of my body. We settle on a stretchy, shiny silver fabric for one half and a midnight bluish fabric with silver lines on it for the other. For the armbands, we get a few yards of navy fabric with glittery silver stars. The fabrics total thirty-two dollars, which isn't so bad, considering what I ended up spending at that thrift store in Denver.

NEW YORK CITY May 21, 2005. The day of the competition, I go to pick up my air attire. If it's too small, too big, too long, too short, *too gay*, I'm basically fucked: the New York regional battle begins in about eight hours. Minji pulls the costume out of a bag and holds it up. It looks pretty good, I think. I stretch the armbands with the special zippered pockets over my forearms, and tie a piece of star-spangled fabric around my skull as a headband. Fully dressed, staring at myself in the dressing room mirror, I'm reminded not of Bowie or of Iggy Pop or of any of the members of the seventies glam rock band Sweet, but rather of the buxom, lassoing female superhero known as Wonder Woman. I don't look gay, exactly, but I *do* conjure a lesbian icon. Wonder Woman flew an invisible plane, which is sort of like playing an invisible guitar, but . . . it's not exactly what I was going for. Whatever. It's too late now.

I step out of the dressing room to cheers all around. Everyone says it looks great. I try to believe them. The documentary crew (still shooting after all these years) is there to capture it all, and as I'm mugging for the camera, waving the star-spangled cape that gives the outfit its *pièce de résistance*, my friend Yoktan (aka Airsatz, who lives on the same block) walks by the store, looks in the window, and catches me mid—cape twirl. He pokes his head in the door and shouts, "Haven't you given up *yet*? Let it go! You'll never win!"

Airsatz closes the door and starts to walk away, and then returns to add with a snicker, "Nice outfit!" Everyone else laughs.

At this point in my air guitar career, I've taken verbal beatings from just about everyone. I'm used to it. But at the moment, standing in a women's clothing store wearing a tight spandex custom-designed bodysuit and getting made fun of by Airsatz, I feel a shade vulnerable. I give Airsatz the finger, and he walks away—undoubtedly pleased with himself.

A few days prior, I called around the city to find out where I could obtain some dry ice. Luckily, there's a place on Forty-fifth Street and Tenth Avenue, not far from my apartment. I bike up there with an ice chest, which I've purchased solely for this purpose, dangling from my left handlebar. A snaggletoothed guy sells me twenty-five dollars' worth, and, having remembered rumors of dry ice's ability to burn people, I ask just how dangerous it is.

"Just don't touch it, and don't lock yourself in a room with it—you can't breathe that stuff," he says. He slips on giant thick rubber gloves and brusquely throws some chunks of the vaporizing crystals into the cooler, and I suddenly feel a piece of shrapnel fly off and singe my arm. It stings a little, but I don't think it will affect tonight's performance.

Back at my apartment, it's time for a test run. Using kitchen tongs, I place several pieces of dry ice in my armbands, zipper them up, and then . . . voila! I am thoroughly disappointed at the result. The fog does not seep through the fabric as I had hoped. Instead, tiny tufts of vapor periodically puff out of the small space where the zipper meets the top of the armband, and that's about it. I've done a bit of research, studying dry ice and how it sublimates,[5] so I decide to add some warm water to the ice-filled pockets. This is a substantial improvement, but still way shy of the hazy white billows I had envisioned.

I try on the entire outfit, loading up and saturating the armbands to give the whole thing a dress rehearsal. I am dripping water all over the floor of my apartment. I hit PLAY. My cat runs and hides under the bed. "Set Me Free" blares from my stereo, and barely visible contrails poof out of my armbands as I strum. I see my reflection in the dark TV screen, and I really do look like Wonder Woman. I pause for a moment to think, *I've completely lost my mind.*

A couple of hours later, I pack a brown paper grocery bag with the following:

---

[5] Dry ice is frozen carbon dioxide (what we exhale, what plants absorb during photosynthesis), which goes directly from solid to gas, without passing through a liquid stage, in a process called sublimation. According to dryiceinfo.com, along with spooking up jack-o'-lanterns come Halloween time, dry ice can loosen floor tile, kill gophers, shrink dents on your car, brand cattle, and attract mosquitoes—presumably away from people. Maybe one day they'll add to their list: enhance air guitar performances.

- costume (jumpsuit, armbands, headband)
- kitchen tongs
- turkey baster
- Tiger Balm
- Clif Bar (2)
- iPod
- gum
- Badtz-Maru guitar keychain—refashioned into necklace

Unfortunately, I forget my own personal bottle of whiskey.

This year's event is being held at the B.B. King Blues Club & Grill on Forty-second street between Seventh and Eighth avenues in the heart of the Disney-fied Times Square. It's a neighborhood I try to avoid at all costs, as it tends to amp up my already pinning misanthropy meter. I get into a cab with my grocery bag full of crap and my cooler filled with dry ice and head towards the club. I would take the subway, but the ice chest is kind of heavy, and I can't afford to strain my arm muscles this close to showtime.

The cab pulls up on the south side of the street across from B.B. King's. I am taken aback by the enormous marquee reading:

US AIR GUITAR CHAMPIONSHIPS

The club apparently holds one thousand people. It's certainly a far cry from the dank bar above a strip club downtown where I first competed in 2003, and it's at least three times as large as last year's venue, the Knitting Factory. As absurd as it all was, I feel some genuine satisfaction knowing I am going to be on that stage to-night.

I sign in and walk around the place. It's fucking huge. There are schoolchildren eating in the banquettes lining the perimeter of the club, apparently as part of some city education program where kids get to see a rock band sound check, then have a free meal afterwards. (And my childhood field trips were to places like the Museum of Natural History!) I head backstage to check out the dressing room, which I find—considering the enormity of the club—is shockingly small. In the brightly lit hallway, there are pans filled with crusty pasta, a frightening whole roasted fish of some sort (salmon?), and greasy chicken wings, to which we are told to help ourselves.

I grab a chair in the dressing room, eat, and wonder when the free beer will arrive. "Let's trash the room!" shouts a bald guy in a thick outer-borough accent. He's known as Marty "The Dancer" Oster, he tells us, and he plays air guitar as part of tailgate parties before New York Jets games. He looks like a tattooed Homer Simpson wearing a W.A.S.P. T-shirt.

"Can we smoke in here, or they gonna fuckin' bust me or somethin'?" asks Marty. I see he's holding up a giant cigar.

"A cigar? I don't know, dude. That's gonna be harsh," I say, wondering if he might sit on me to death. But honestly I would prefer the smell of Dick Fiddler's Aireoke pizza box to the smell of cigar smoke. Plus, I've always thought that smoking something that A) others around you actually *inhale* more than you do, B) smells putrid, and C) *doesn't get you stoned* is just stupid.

"I'm smokin' a cigar. Where's a fan in this fuckin' room?"

"Are you sure you wanna smoke that stogie? 'Cause we're gonna be in this room for like two hours," I say. "Like, twenty people . . ."

"We gotta be in here two hours? What're we on *Survivor* or some shit?" says Marty, and everyone in the room laughs. "What the fuck!"

Despite the cigar, there's something I immediately like about Marty "The Dancer." He is different from the usual air guitar contestant. He's obviously a big Jets fan, as we know because he keeps inviting us to come to the tailgate parties with him: "Anybody's fuckin' welcome! Twenty-five dollars, all you can eat and drink! It's awesome! Awesome! Awesome . . . *Awesome!* The tailgate is the bomb!" But more than that, Marty is not a hipster, or an actor, or into the Philosophy of Airness—I am pretty sure he doesn't even care about winning. For Marty, I suspect, the air guitar competition is just an excuse to get a little rowdiness out of his system before the preseason games start.

I think I've met most of the contestants at this point, and thus far I am beyond pleased to find no Asians competing. *Thank you, O Lord of Airness.* I do get nervous when one hot girl with a very low-cut sleeveless black shirt enters the room, but it turns out she's the emcee.

Instead of with hot girls and/or Asians, I'll be sharing the air tonight with guys like "Joey Hot Dog," who sells hot dogs at Shea Stadium for a living, and looks (to me) like a skinny version of Vincent D'Onofrio as the utterly bonkers private Gomer Pyle in *Full Metal Jacket.* I ask Joey Hot Dog if anyone has ever told him this. He says no, and then doesn't talk to me for the rest of the night. Two dudes from last year's competition are also in the house—"Jammin' J-Bone" and "Assquatch"—and they give me mad props for coming out once again. I have become somewhat of a legend in air guitar circles. Many of the other competitors have read online about my lecture in Seattle and of my defeats in Los Angeles, Denver, and Finland, and they know I'm hopelessly devoted.

I am disappointed that veteran air guitarist The Shred, who was at both the 2003 and 2004 events, is nowhere to be seen. Perhaps age has finally caught up to the ol' guy. But there is a metalhead here tonight by the name of Andrew "Shredosaurus Rox," so there will be no shortfall of shredding.

The last repeat offender is a guy from Boston wearing a newsboy cap. I recognize him from LA in 2004. He doesn't have a stage name—he just goes by "Jamie" (his real name, tragically)—and I can only recall that he got completely shitfaced at last year's gig, which he had flown all the way from Boston to compete in. His performance was unmemorable, which explains why I can't remember it. Nonetheless, he's back to give it another go. Jamie tells me that he does weekly air guitar shows in Boston where he'll open up for a band by playing a ten-minute air guitar medley. He tells me air guitar is his life. He tells me tonight's contest is just a "warm-up" for Boston's, where he'll be competing again in a few days. And I think, *This guy is a complete idiot. He sounds just like me.*

I run upstairs to check on the crowd. I poke my head out the door to see a large mob forming on Forty-second Street. There is a line halfway down the block, and people seem to be on the verge of stampeding. Then it starts pouring rain. *That should calm them down,* I think sarcastically to myself. *It's funny that you can be sarcastic to yourself,* I think as I head back downstairs.

Outside the dressing room, Aer Lingus is handing out the contestant order for the evening, explaining the rules, and answering stupid questions. Lingus introduces last year's world champ, Sonyk-Rok, who will be one of tonight's judges. She is with her air mentor, C-Diddy, whom she overpowered in Oulu last August.[6] Due to the severe lack of free alcohol, everyone is startlingly sober. There's a timidity in the air that Lingus—keenly aware of such things—immediately hones in on.

"I'm looking at you guys, and I feel like personally I am not seeing any world champions. I'm just not feeling it," he chides. "So you guys need to prove it to me a little bit—get drunk, trash talk, show me your licks or something, 'cause *I'm not feelin' it!* And if you let New York down, you're a *bunch of fucking pussies*."

At this, we all shout like a band of angry pirates, trying to prove him wrong. "Arrrghhh!"

But he's right. We are way too sedate. I chalk it up to the combination of the sterile, fluorescently lit environs backstage, the bad food, and the complimentary-alcohol drought. Whatever it is, something feels off. I try to ignore it.

Minji shows up backstage to assist me with any last-minute problems and to tighten up a few "loose ends" in the outfit. As she

---

[6]Sonyk-Rok will be heading once again to Oulu this summer to defend her title. C-Diddy has officially retired from competitive air guitar in order to help his father with his blossoming pooper-scooper business. (I *wish* I could make that up.)

helps me climb into my tight, shiny threads, other competitors eye me with a mix of disdain and envy. *This guy has his own personal wardrobe chick?* Lingus walks by and points us out to Sonyk-Rok. "See the way Björn Türoque is getting back at Koreans by hiring them as cheap labor?"

"He needed kimchi power," she says. I flash her the rock-and-roll devil horns and say, "Hell yeah!" in agreement. Thanks to Minji, I am feeling an Asian Advantage tonight. Also, I have my Badtz-Maru guitar keychain/necklace around my neck. I hunted it down a few days ago at the Sanrio store, which is, coincidentally, right next door to the B.B. King Blues Club. Badtz-Maru, for those unfamiliar with the world of Sanrio iconography, is the rogue penguin who serves as an occasional foil for Hello Kitty. I have chosen Badtz to serve as my talisman—he is my entrée into the Hello Kitty world so integral to both C-Diddy and Sonyk-Rok.

Then I run into a bunch of kids in the hallway. Like, actual children. I ask a girl with long reddish hair who looks like she's about eleven if they are there supporting their brother or dad or something. It turns out she's Axl Rose.

Li'l Axl: We're Li'l Gn'R.
Björn: Are you serious? Where's Slash?
Li'l Axl: He's missing. We don't know.
Björn: That's the thing about Slash—he's always late.

I had read on the schedule that Li'l Gn'R was going to play at some point during the show. I assumed it was a Guns N' Roses

cover band composed entirely of little people—kind of like Mini-KISS, the all–little people KISS tribute band.

> **Björn:** Do you think maybe one day I can jam with you guys? Where do you play? Are you on tour?
>
> **Axl:** We play all over New York—we played CB's. . . .
>
> **Björn:** I've played CB's. . . .
>
> **Axl:** And we've played . . .
>
> **Björn:** Okay, you've played cooler places than I have.
>
> **Axl:** Yeah—would you open for us?
>
> **Björn:** I would *so* open for you guys—that would be a dream come true. [A group of adults stands behind them, laughing at me.]
>
> **Björn:** These are your parents, I assume?
>
> **Axl:** They're our groupies.
>
> **Björn:** Dude [I whisper quietly to Li'l Izzy, the guitarist] no offense, but *get younger groupies.* I guess there's a logic to it, though: I'm old, so I get young groupies, and you're young, so you get older groupies. . . .

I am tempted to ask Li'l Axl if she knows that Axl Rose is an anagram for "oral sex," but I'm not sure she knows what an anagram—much less oral sex—is. Plus, I think that might scare her parents and/or get me arrested.

"Slash" finally arrives. And, in fact, he really looks like Slash. He's six years old and biracial, and dons Slash's signature top hat. And he is nearly forty-five minutes late. It's perfect. I have to admit that I am looking forward to their set. We wish each other a good show, I high-five them all, and then I head back to the dressing room to see whether things are about to get kicking.

In addition to Li'l Slash, everything is running late, and it's reported that the crowd is drunk and antsy. Finally the hot girl emcee takes the stage to welcome everyone, explain the rules, and introduce Corn Mo—one of the evening's judges, who will be opening the ceremonies by playing air guitar to Hendrix's version of the national anthem. Corn Mo is a plump dude with long stringy hair, who apparently plays piano and accordion, and sings in a band called . . . Corn Mo. He does not play guitar. His lyrics are sort of funny if you are in sixth grade, and his songs sound like a cross between Ben Folds and They Might Be Giants. (In fact, he's opened for both.) Where and why did they find this guy?

Corn Mo massacres the national anthem, and the audience quickly boos him offstage. Actually, most of the first ten contestants get booed, have cups of beer thrown at them, and receive very low scores. Maybe "Go-Veg.com of Steel" started things off on a bad note when he tried to use the event to push his vegan anti-meat agenda. Also, he kind of sucked. Maybe it was Jamie from Boston's lackadaisical performance of his air medley that sent the crowd over the edge. Regardless, this is the meanest, rowdiest, drunkest audience I've ever seen at an air guitar competition. Thank god for intermission.

I'm getting my air on (drinking) backstage and rubbing my arms and shoulders down with Tiger Balm when a refrigerator-sized guy walks in from the front area and commences a bitter tirade. "Thirty years," he says in a heavy Brooklyn accent. "Thirty fuckin' years in this fuckin' business, and this is what I get? Fuckin' air guitah?"

I am standing there looking confused in my sparkly Freddie-Mercury-meets-Evel Knievel jumpsuit. I swallow my beer as he begins speaking to me directly. I fear that any minute he may just grab my neck and start wringing.

"I did sound for Aerosmith, the Stones, Jethro Tull," he shouts, "and this is what I fuckin' get? A bunch uh pussies playin' air guitah?"

"Take it easy, man," I say, trying to calm him down. "It's all rock and roll—we're all just trying to have a good time."

"Stupidest thing I've evuh seen. Thirty *fuckin' years*, and this is the *worst* fuckin' night of my career." And with that, he walks away.

The worst night of his career? Personally, I would've thought doing sound for a band led by a fop standing on one leg playing the flute would have been worse, but what do I know?

The intermission entertainment is about to begin, as some strange bald guy in a suit walks out onstage. I am told he's going to do a "Beatles air guitar act," but he is having technical difficulties. Evidently the guy refused to bring a CD to the venue and insisted instead on playing his music on cassette via a tiny boom box which doesn't work. He and the sound guy spend at least ten minutes onstage fiddling with the thing, during which time the stage manager finds me and says I'm on next. It's time to prep for the dry ice thaumaturgy. I wrap my arms with Ace bandage tape and then slip the armbands over that. I look around, and the only person I can find backstage to help me is Slash's mom, a hippie-looking woman

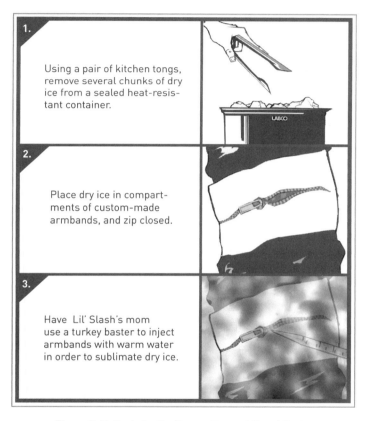

Figure 9. Methods for the Preparation and Use of Dry Ice

with long hair and John Lennon glasses. I ask if she'll give me a hand, and she agrees to load dry ice into my armband's zippered pouches, using the kitchen tongs I've brought from home expressly for that purpose.

"I'm psyched to see Li'l Gn'R," I say. "Your son totally looks like Slash—a *young* Slash."

"Oh, thanks," she says, focused on not burning either of us with the dry ice.

I grab a cup of water and give it to her, along with the turkey baster. Little cascades of mist make their way from the armbands as I stand next to the stage, wrapped in my cape. Having never gotten his music to play, the Beatles air guitar intermission act finally gives up, and they decide to start the second half of round one, with the emcee offering what has become my staple introduction, "Ladies and gentlemen, the hardest-working man in air guitar: Björn Türoque!"

As the emcee makes her announcement, Slash's mom loads the turkey baster with water and injects it into both my armbands. The dry ice quickly begins to sizzle and evaporate. I run out onstage and raise my arms high until I'm nearly pointing at the ceiling. I open up my cape to reveal my outfit and the armbands filled with sublimating dry ice. As I look out into the audience, I imagine that dense clouds of smoke are emerging. In reality, upwards of three people with extraordinarily good vision can probably see something resembling fog next to my arms. The first power chord of "Set Me Free" cranks over the sound system.

It's as if at that precise moment, someone presses the HYPER-SPACE button on the Asteroids arcade game and I pop out at the end of the song having no idea how I got from point A to point B. I look down and see that my right armband has slipped all the way down to my wrist. I can remember water and shards of ice flying in slow motion all over the audience and me, but that's about it. I was lost in the song. The next thing I know, I see the scores: 5.8, 6.0, 5.8, and 5.7. *This*, I think to myself, *this may finally be Björn's year.*

There are really only three other dudes who are at all entertaining in the second half of round one: Andrew "Shredosaurus Rox," who performs Judas Priest's "Painkiller," wearing a skintight Anthrax T-shirt and sheaths of leather with numerous half-inch spikes on each forearm; Ambrose "Magic Fingers" Martos, a dead ringer for Art Garfunkel, if Art Garfunkel was wearing shiny gold vinyl pants and a purple feather boa; and a preppy looking guy on drugs who was not a registered contestant but sneaks onstage from the audience and insists on competing anyway.

Now, how do I know the guy was on drugs? I don't use that phrase lightly. He had been standing next to me on the side of the stage as I watched the other competitors. He was sweating, grinding and twisting his jaw, and twitching his head and arms every few moments as if getting repeated electric shocks from somewhere inside his skull. So, no, I didn't give the guy a urine test, but he looked pretty fucked-up to me.

In between Marty "The Dancer"—who starts with a shirt that says "I Fuck Like a Beast" on the back, then strips down to shorts with "Meet Mr. Bone" emblazoned on the crotch, and smokes a cigar continuously throughout his performance—and Jammin' J-Bone, who does an admirable but unremarkable job with Fugazi's "Margin Walker," On-Drugs Guy (the stage name with which I decide to christen him) walks out and just stands behind the microphone, sloppily gesturing towards the sound guy to play a song. There's a fair amount of confusion as the sound guy tries to figure out who exactly On Drugs Guy is. The emcee knows he's not one of the official entrants, so she fetches security to get him offstage. The audience throws beer at him as he stands there babbling into the microphone, stretching his jaw from side to side. A heavily intoxicated Air-Do-Well, acting as the between-round DJ, is convinced that On-Drugs Guy is being harshly treated (and perhaps identifies with the guy's addled state), so he grabs the microphone and begs the audience to give On-Drugs Guy a chance. Finally security arrives and ushers him off the stage.

Magic Fingers plays "Eruption," which, as I mentioned earlier, sits at the top of my cliché list, but he has cleverly edited an extra ten seconds or so of silence into the already existing pause between Eddie Van's detuning of the low E string and the subsequent velocious arpeggios. During the extended dead air, Magic Fingers rips open his shirt, picks up his beer and guzzles it down, and then finishes off the song in spastic convulsions as the solo ends. This gets him good scores—two 5.7s, a 5.8, and a 5.9—and that will take him to the compulsory round.

Joey Hot Dog comes out dressed like Angus Young, with devil horns glued to his head, one of which immediately falls off. He's one of the few lefty air guitarists I've seen, and while his strumming hand looks good, his fingering hand looks paralyzed, sort of like Bob Dole's.

Between the two rounds, Li'l Gn'R is sent out to keep the audience pumped. Here's how Li'l Gn'R works: A prerecorded instrumental version of a Guns N' Roses song (they open with "Paradise City," naturally) is cued up on the PA system. Li'l Axl sings along while Li'l Steven Adler beats a real drum kit, somewhat in time, over the prerecorded track. Li'l Izzy, Li'l Slash, and Li'l Duff strum toy guitars. It is possibly the lamest, most irritating thing I've ever seen, and it goes on for *nearly a half hour*. It's embarrassing—for them, for me, for the audience, for air guitar, for nonair guitar, even for Guns N' Roses. Li'l Slash is pretty cute, and his mom did help me out, but it's really Li'l Axl who drags the show to the depths of nauseating horror. I don't begrudge Li'l Axl personally. It's not her fault. She's clearly worked for many years trying to make it as a Broadway musical child star. It's just that, well, This isn't *Annie*, for fuck's sake. It's supposed to be rock and roll—or at least a decent imitation of rock and roll. It's perfectly logical that they got a girl to hit Axl's high notes—after all, Axl really does wail—but Li'l Axl's phrasing is square and edgeless: it's worse than Pat Boone singing "Paradise City" on his *In a Metal Mood* album (which is actually rather enjoyable). About a third of the audience has left by this point, but what's left of them boos the Li'l Shits off the stage until it's time for round two.

Backstage, the refrigerator-sized sound guy returns. I fear he wants to sever my limbs, drink my blood, auction my kidneys, and burn my costume for making a mockery of his precious career in rock and roll.

"I gotta say . . ." he begins.

I am praying to the Gods of Rock for mercy.

"You're the only one of these assholes that I liked."

"Thanks," I say, surprised. Humbled.

"And that song—that was pretty damn cool. I fuckin' love Sweet. I haven't heard that song in years. Good luck, man. You deserve it."

He shakes my hand, and we exchange a brief manly hug. I feel I've been blessed.

The top five from round one are called up onstage: Jammin' J-Bone; a guy called "Facemelter," whose earlier performance I must have missed; "Magic Fingers" Martos; the Shredosaurus; and me, Björn Türoque, in first place. I think it's in the bag, but this is the crucial round. I remember the Mile High Battle of Denver and how the metal moron from Alabama stole the title from me with his noneruptive "Eruption." I know I can't *expect* to win. I know (as Zac Monro once explained to me) I can't *want* to win. I must simply—win.

The compulsory song is a 2004 Velvet Revolver[7] track called "Slither," which I've heard once or twice but I am by no means solid on. Then again, I am sure nobody knows this track that well. We stand onstage together listening to it. It's got a cool lick and some heavy-ass guitars, and I feel confident that I can conquer it.

I head backstage as Jammin' J-Bone takes his shot. I decide impulsively that I should go fully balls-out for the compulsory round, so I strip down to my underwear, jockstrap, and cup (which I had been wearing to provide a little extra bulge) and my armbands,

[7]Coincidentally, the first song Velvet Revolver ever recorded (for the soundtrack to 2003's *The Hulk*) was called "Set Me Free," though it sounds nothing like Sweet's version. For those unfamiliar, Velvet Revolver is a band composed of former drug- and alcohol-addict rock stars (including ex–G-N'-Rs Duff and Slash), led by singer Scott Weiland—the heroin enthusiast who once fronted Stone Temple Pilots. To me, VR's sound is overly polished and lacks soul. To put it another way, it ain't Sweet.

which still have some residual dry ice in them. I am about to walk back out when Aer Lingus sees me.

"Is that what you're wearing?" he asks.

"Yeah. I figured I should just, you know, let it all hang out."

Lingus sizes me up and down, pauses, and then simply says, "Nope."

"You don't think I should do it?"

"Definitely not."

I heed Lingus' advice, put the glam rock costume back on, and head out to wait by the side of the stage. Looking back, I have to thank Aer Lingus for saving me a world of pain.

Magic Fingers begins his performance by pouring an entire longneck bottle of Budweiser onto his head and then pouring another into the mouth of a guy in the audience, which makes the crowd burst with *woo*s right out of the gate. "Slither" starts, and there's something about Magic Fingers' eyes that really does it. He looks haunted. He fully engages the crowd, and they love him. But in the end his scores—two 5.7s, a 5.8, and a 5.666—are not that spectacular. I feel a little sad for the clown, but not that sad.

Shredosaurus is hardcore. He looks like the kind of guy who walks around forever looking for someone's ass to kick. I talked to him a little bit before the show, and despite his ominous presence he was a perfectly nice guy. I asked him if he works out, because he is one of the most buff-looking motherfuckers I have ever met. He told me that he alternates between Atkins during the week and carbo-loading on the weekends, and he lifts weights every other day. "It totally works," he said. I told him he should write a diet book and get rich, but he said someone had already beaten him to it. Standing onstage, he looks as serious as a skinhead in a street fight (and considering that his head is fully shaved, I wonder if maybe he *is* a skinhead), but during his "Slither" shredding, he's lost in his own world, and the crowd boos him without restraint.

It's my turn to rock. I go out onstage, begin tuning up my air guitar, and then approach the microphone. "Can I get a little more guitar in the monitor, please?" I strum a few test chords, wave my thumb up in the air to indicate that I need just a little more guitar, and then give the "okay" signal. The song begins, and I feel I am off to a slow start. But there's a group of rowdy dudes in the very front of the crowd who are totally into it. One guy hops up on his friend's shoulders and lifts up his T-shirt to show me his tits, *Girls Gone Wild*—style. These are not the breasts I would have chosen to inspire my performance, but somehow they help. I pack a lot of moves into my sixty seconds of "Slither": front kicks, a split-leg jump kick, a foot on the monitor, my trademark look of shock and surprise ("Holy shit—I *rock*!"), a full windmill, and a half windmill, and I end the song feeling good. Not great, but good enough. My scores: 5.8, 5.9, 5.9, and 5.8.

"It smells like victory," I say to the documentary crew as I walk off, heading backstage to wait for the final results. Everyone's telling me I must have won. But I am not sure I really believe it. After a few minutes of tabulating, the scores are in.

"Ladies and gentleman," begins the emcee. "The 2005 New York City regional champion is: *Björn Türoque!*"

Here's the thing. I didn't dream this. I am not lying. It really happened.

I finally won.

But would you kill me if I said there was something missing?

I hang out with people backstage and try to bask in the glory, but there's no one from the press asking for an interview. There are no air groupies. No girls want me to autograph even a single breast. Lingus, ever the giver of shit, elbows up to me and says, "So, you know what C-Diddy said to me?"

"What did he say?" I ask, thinking maybe C-Diddy has finally come around to offer some honest respect for the Björn man.

"He said, 'I didn't realize Björn had to dress up like Wonder Woman to win.'"

A Pyrrhic victory is defined as one offset by terrible losses. I had been defeated so many times in the past—I had lost so much air. Now that I had won, was it worth it? Had I lost too many times to be able to enjoy winning? In previous showdowns, I went mano a mano with the best. Two of them went on to be crowned the *greatest air guitarists in the world*, but in New York in 2005, there were no C-Diddys, no Sonyk-Roks, *no Asians.* I was the best, sure, but compared to whom—a clown and a skinhead?

We do not err because truth is difficult to see. It is visible at a glance. We err because this is more comfortable.

—Aleksandr Solzhenitsyn

I knew the finals in LA would feel different. At least this time a late-night TV talk show host wasn't sending me, and I wasn't roving the country hoping eventually to emerge triumphant in a local competition. Finally my air would be pure: I'd be going as a regional champion.

As the regional winners were gradually announced during the weeks prior to the LA finals, I checked them out on the air guitar website, trying to determine what, if anything, I had to fear. The American South had never before been represented in the US competition, and now Charlie "American Breeder" Wilson and Daniel "Glitter" Alvarez from Austin would be there to show us some Southern discomfort. *My prediction: Skynyrd.*

My friend Matt, who owns the club in Denver (he hosted the regional again this year), called to tell me that Denver's champ,

Randy "Big Rig" Strecker, was pretty good, but not mind-blowing. Then there's plain old Rob Brown from Boston, who doesn't even have a stage name, and Andrew "William Ocean" Litz from Chicago, whose stage name I do admire. I had no advance word about their prowess, but none of them sound Asian—how good could they be?

My real fear came from LA. There would be numerous Air Alums competing in the regional bout (see pages 256–257).

LOS ANGELES, July 14, 2005. I arrive at Key Club, same joint as last year, and it feels nearly routine, as though I'm showing up for work. But I also know deep down that this will be the last time I show up for the job, at least in this country. I've announced my retirement before, but that is simply the way of the aging rocker. It's my third year competing, and I did *finally* win a regional championship. So if the night does not end with my sporting the gold medal around my neck, I will ignite a funeral pyre and immolate my air guitar, Hendrix-style.

I share high fives, man-hugs, and closed-fist "punch-ins" with my old nemeses. It's as if we're all in a band that gets together once a year for yet another final reunion tour. We've fought each other hard along the way, but we're like an air family—dysfunctional yet comforting. It's great to see so many people here together again. Key Club is buzzing with video cameras, headset-wearing staff, competitors, and air roadies. I'm upstairs in the VIP lounge, which is being used for press interviews and air guitar orientation. Like any air guitar competition, it's mayhem. I begin the evening's drinking with a cold Budweiser.

"Dude, that's an awesome shirt," says Clayton Sweeney.

"Thanks, man." I am wearing my vintage Journey concert T-shirt with the sleeves cut off. I tell him how the shirt was given to me by one of my fellow air guitarists in Denver last year. The two of us were hanging out downstairs after the competition when I noticed McNichols Arena[1] pictured on the back of his Journey shirt. I told the guy that the shirt was from my first concert *ever*, at which point he took it off and actually gave me *the shirt off his back.*

"Wow," says Sweeney. "That's pretty fuckin' awesome."

"Yup. It's the power of air guitar, man. Never underestimate it."

I wish Clayton Sweeney luck, do a few interviews with various news and media outlets, and then Aer Lingus arrives to review the rules with the rowdy bunch. I can't help but feel a little anxious due to the presence of a young girl in an incredibly short skirt, black knee-high boots, and a camouflage tank top that reads "Freedom Rocks." I know an exhibitionist when I see one, and I get that tingly feeling that although she's already wearing very little in the way of clothing, we'll be seeing a lot *more* of her. Which I am all for; I just worry that her supple tan thighs might bias this evening's judges.

---

[1]McNichols is the arena where the Denver Nuggets used to play basketball, and as a kid, I occasionally went to games there with my father. This stopped abruptly after my dad got in a verbal altercation with a pimply parking lot attendant who told us there were no more spaces available. My dad insisted there were, and then decided to plow forward anyway despite the attendant's warnings. The attendant was holding on to the driver's-side window, which, due to the freezing winter temperature, shattered when my dad hit the gas pedal. The poor kid got fired. I never went to a basketball game again, and I suspect this incident marked the beginning of my hatred for all sporting events.

SONG: "ON YOUR KNEES" by W.A.S.P.

The Airtight Messiah, *left*, had retired from competition but was now acting as a manager for this guy, Heavy Thundar, *right*. When he went to sign in, Thundar (who plays in a band called Holy Shit) was still unsure what song his manager had chosen for him. Upon being informed that the song was by W.A.S.P. (a band that didn't really start selling records until Tipper Gore complained about them), he was reportedly disappointed—not quite heavy enough, I suppose.

SONG: "ACE OF SPADES" by Motörhead

Psycho Dave would be avenging his bitter 2004 disappointment, and undoubtedly harbored residual anger stemming from that year's hapless judging. This year, Psycho Dave was hoping a wig, a Judas Priest "British Steel" T-shirt, and a hot chick that he had in tow would help him secure a victory. (The hot chick? That's Psycho Dave's cousin....)

SONG: "LITTLE FIGHTER" by White Lion

Krye Tuff edged me out of the LA title in 2003, only to be handily defeated by the Master, C-Diddy. And in 2004, Mr. Tuff—aka Gordon Hintz—suffered another defeat in his hometown run for state assembly in Oshkosh, Wisconsin, where his father was once mayor. Like Björn, Tuff would have the chip of defeat on his shoulder.

SONG: UNKNOWN—but there's a lot of soloing in it.

"Clayton Sweeney wishes to rock you" was all this guy's air bio said. Clayton Sweeney was just a mysterious dude with facial hair who wanted to be the greatest air guitarist in the world. There's nothing wrong with that. In 2004, he came in third place in the LA regional.

SONG: "THE BEAUTIFUL PEOPLE"
by Marilyn Manson

After winning in New York, here's what Björn told the press about the Rockness Monster: "I've heard the Rockness has been doing some serious training—and I don't wanna be a dick, but I did teach him everything he knows. Now the master needs to have his victory. The Rockness is just a boy—he has years ahead of him. I am getting old. I need to win this."

Look deep into the eyes of the Rockness. Do you see the Asian Fury? Björn does.

SONG: "CUM ON FEEL THE NOIZE" by Quiet Riot

I am told that the mime, *right*, drinking a Corona, did compete in 2004, but I don't remember him. Maybe because he is a mime.

"I do this for a living. But this isn't fun, this is a way of life." —Derek Generic, aka The Corona-Drinking Mime

SONG: "GIRL, YOU HAVE NO FAITH IN MEDICINE" by The White Stripes

Mother Rucker, 2004's Minneapolis champion, had finally recovered from his numerous air-related injuries. After a few months of physical therapy, Mother Rucker was back for more punishment.

Possibly due to the pain he still felt in his left ankle, Mother Rucker had become a heavy drinker and was prone to starting sentences with phrases like, "And another thing…"

SONG: "STAY WITH ME TONIGHT" by R&B/Soulmeister Jeffrey Osborne

When Power played air drums to Rush's "Tom Sawyer" in 2004, it was as if we were actually watching the band in action, only better: the drums were invisible and we didn't have to suffer the indignity of having to look at Geddy Lee.

Power's twin brother, Control, *left*, was now managing both his brother's and Psycho Dave's stagnant air guitar careers. Control asked repeatedly if he could manage Björn as well. Björn said no.

SONG: "SET ME FREE" by Sweet (If it ain't broke...)

Then there was me, Björn Türoque.

My friend Minji had made me another costume, which, though it did not call Wonder Woman to mind, did make me look like a Solid Gold dancer. The ensemble consisted of a small gold vinyl vest, tight gold see-through mesh pants with matching armbands, and a white headband with red flames.

I debated sticking with the old Wonder Woman garb, but was torn—Minji *had* put a lot of work into this one.

Lingus tells us that tonight's judges are Nina Gordon from Veruca Salt (who also judged in 2003); actor John Cho from the movie *Harold & Kumar Go to White Castle*; Matchbox Twenty's drummer, Paul Doucette; and Evanescence founder Ben Moody. We are all assured by Lingus that they will be a substantial improvement over the 2004 judiciary.

We are told to head to a small, crowded dressing room in the basement because some other event is happening in the club's Plush room. We'll hang out there until called onstage. Since I won't be competing during the first part of the evening, I spend this period drinking and tuning in to the psyches of the other competitors. Veterans Psycho Dave and the Rockness Monster sit on a banquette in the dressing room, discussing Psycho Dave's former boss, John Tesh. Psycho D quit working for The Tesh about three weeks ago.

Rockness: I love John Tesh.

Psycho Dave: If I were gay, I would want to have sex with him.

I start to wonder about Psycho Dave. It's not the first time I've heard him joke about wanting to have sex with a man.

Rockness: I'm not, and I do.

Psycho Dave: He is a musical genius. I should say in all honesty, having listened to a lot of his stuff, that much of it can only be described as genius. And I say that as a music fan.

Rockness: Yeah. Yanni is nothing compared to John Tesh. It's like John Tesh, then Pantera, then Black Sabbath [with each name, Rockness' hand, raised high in the air, gets successively lower] and then Yanni.

They are obviously joking, but Psycho Dave is serious to a degree—at least about liking The Tesh's music. Psycho Dave and I have talked at length about The Tesh, whom I find an endlessly amusing subject, particularly when I imagine him in his office, humming the *Entertainment Tonight* theme song, bossing Psycho Dave around. Whenever I make fun of The Tesh's perfect hair, beaming teeth, or cheesy music (favorite album title: *Sax by the Fire*), Psycho Dave comes to his defense by saying, "He's actually a really nice guy."

The evening gets rolling, and I watch and take notes from the sidelines. The first competitor onstage whom I recognize is Mother Rucker. He begins his song with his back to the audience (a classic move) to show off his jacket, into which he has sewn Christmas lights to form the letters *MR*. Tragically, his performance to "Girl, You Have No Faith in Medicine" is mostly a fiasco. It's like his air guitar is actually an *air* air guitar, as if, instead of playing guitar he is juggling or playing hot potato. Towards the end of the song he jumps into the air and then lands right on his knees. It looks incredibly painful, and I imagine it will only add to his litany of air guitar—related injuries. His scores are fairly abysmal, and I feel bad for the Mother Rucker.

Psycho Dave has the first really stellar performance of the night. He rocks "Ace of Spades" with every bit of intensity that he can muster, and he's pretty damn good. His scores are good too: two 5.8s, a 5.7, and a 5.9. Whether he makes it into the compulsory round or not, Psycho Dave has avenged last year's unjust defeat: he was scored fairly and can go home without having to verbally accost the judges.

Krye Tuff does "Little Fighter" by White Lion. KT avoided competing last year: he was entering the state assembly race of Oshkosh, Wisconsin, and didn't want to damage his chances of winning.[2] Now, back in the spotlight, he looks as psyched as Tony Iommi rocking Ozzfest with Black Sabbath in 2001. Though Krye Tuff's moves are solid, this is a case where song selection really costs him. The track is glam, to be sure, but it's kind of slow. Maybe it has one too many minor chords in the progression? I can't quite put my finger on why it doesn't attain critical mass. Nina Gordon, who had a hard-on for The Tuff back in 2003, gives him a 5.9, and his other marks—5.8, 5.7, and 5.5—are good, but he and I both know they're not enough for the stiff competition here tonight. I see him backstage, and he's a bit devastated. This on top of last year's political loss must be too much for one man to stomach. My heart goes out to The Tuff.

Then it happens. Cherry Lain, the hot chick with the camouflaged miniskirt and tank top—and the night's only female performer—takes the stage to play Hendrix's version of "The Star-Spangled Banner." She titillates the audience and most of the judges (at least the male ones) with her sexy moves: hair flips, sultry shoulder dips, back bends, and a jump into full splits on the floor. I find her idiotic but erotic. She must be a stripper in

[2]Sadly, considering the Republican election sweep of 2004, competing would likely have had little impact on Hintz's campaign. Maybe if more politicians dedicated themselves to peace through Airness as Krye Tuff does, we'd have less turmoil in the world.

real life, I think, as her performance looks so much like a classic striptease. It's a pale imitation of Sonyk-Rok's 2004 Catholic-schoolgirl-uniformed "Hot for Teacher," which made fun of gender stereotypes while successfully exploiting them; Cherry Lain's performance has all of the exploitation but none of the mock.

Cherry Lain's "Freedom Rocks" tank top also smells to me like political titsploitation—as if she thinks she is offering some kind of USO tribute to the troops. It reminds me of when the *Playboy* Bunnies get flown in by helicopter to entertain the soldiers in *Apocalypse Now*. Things start off fine, but the sex-starved men quickly become a riotous mob. They don't need their dicks teased by strippers; they need to get the hell out of Vietnam. Cherry isn't "supporting the troops"; she is trying to win an air guitar competition. Now, I'm not saying that I'm not susceptible to her sexual charms. She *is* hot; most everyone agrees. She gets great scores (a 5.6 from Nina Gordon, a 6.0, a 5.9, and a 6.666!) and will no doubt make it to the compulsory round.

Heavy Thundar wears leather pants and a tight black ladies' tank top, and has an authentic "I've spent several years in and out of rehab" vibe. He follows Cherry Lain, and ends his heartfelt performance of "On Your Knees" by yelling at judge Paul Doucette, "Your girlfriend smashed my motor home!"

Doucette, confused, answers, "I don't even have a girlfriend, dude."

"She did, man. She crashed into my motor home!" he shouts.

There's a momentary standoff until Thundar is escorted

offstage, sparing the audience a potential Psycho Dave–like psychotic episode.

Then the Rockness Monster is unleashed. He's wearing a T-shirt—the one with his cousin's face printed on it—and has all the nonchalance of a guy waiting for the bus as he stands onstage tuning his air guitar. In typical Rockness style, he begins slowly, just getting his bearings. But as soon as "The Beautiful People" truly gets rolling, Rockness injects himself with one thousand CCs of adrenaline. He is feral. Unleashed. A blur. His left shoe flies off. He keeps going. He twists. He flies. He rolls. He headbangs. He pauses. . . . He looks out into the crowd. He detonates.

He is . . . Asian Fury.

Three 6.0s and a 5.9 later, Rockness thanks the judges and walks offstage, quickly returning to the quiet, unassuming little dude he was when he arrived. I stand at the side of the stage, panicked.

Power spends the first thirty seconds of his song doing a striptease, removing his tennis outfit to reveal . . . *an even smaller* tennis outfit. He serves a couple of fierce overheads with an air racquet and then switches to air guitar in order to slice into the cheesy solo of "Stay With Me Tonight." It's campy, to say the least, but the judges—who award Power's performance with *three* 6.0s and a 5.8— think it works. I think it's funny, but know it won't fly in Finland— too much schlock, not enough rock. I'm half hoping he wins the next round so that I can face him instead of Rockness in the finals.

The final competitor of the round is a guy I first met a few days ago. I had just finished doing an interview for the documentary crew and was walking through their offices when I saw an older man entering with his son, who looked about fourteen.

"Hey, are you competing?" I asked the kid, thinking he's definitely the youngest competitor I've ever seen.

"Nah," he said, pointing to the older guy. "My dad's competing. I'm just hangin' out."

"That's cool," I said, and shook the dad's hand, thinking, *There's no way in hell my dad would ever compete in one of these, which is fine, as he would mortifyingly suck.* I suspect the kid's somewhat embarrassed for his dad. I know I would be. "So, are you kind of embarrassed about your dad competing?" I pried.

"Nah. I think it's cool," he says.

"Wow. Okay. Cool," I replied. "Good luck!"

Old Man Metal, as he is called, sports a gray wig and moustache, a black leather motorcycle hat (in the Rob Halford style), a Judas Priest T-shirt, and lots of chains. He hobbles onto the stage with the aid of a cane, but the moment Priest's "Riding on the Wind"[3] blasts over the PA, he is magically rejuvenated. Old Man Metal then tosses his cane aside and rocks as hard as Angus Young. He doesn't fare poorly either: 5.9, 6.0, 5.999, and 6.0.

During intermission, I meet Cherry Lain's Svengali and

---

[3] I appreciate it when someone's song choice offers a metareference to air guitar. This one is almost as clever as my usage of Air Supply's "Making Love Out of Nothing at All." Other good suggestions in this vein would be the theme song to TV's *The Greatest American Hero* or Phil Collins' "In the Air Tonight" (if only either had a guitar solo).

"manager," a guy who runs airguitar.com, a pathetic Web site dedicated to selling panties and calendars with pictures of strippers playing air guitar. I add it up and realize that this guy has entered Cherry Lain into the competition so that he can profit off her success, should she win. "Imagine the marketing opportunities!" he must be thinking. "Cherry Lain thongs will be bigger than Ugg boots!"[4]

But in the compulsory round, Cherry Lain's phoniness is exposed: she gyrates around trying to look sexy, still ripping off Sonyk-Rok's moves but entirely forgoing the air guitar. The compulsory song (Jet's "Are You Gonna Be My Girl") is irrelevant— eventually Cherry starts prancing about the stage like the exotic dancer she has revealed herself to be, and she is, to her embarrassment and my satisfaction, booed off the stage.

Psycho Dave, Power, and Old Man Metal each have their way with the song, but none of them knocks it out of the park. It's the Rockness Monster who manages to clean up, earning a perfect score of four 6.0s. "He was the only one that fucking tuned!" says judge Ben Moody. "He makes me embarrassed to actually play guitar."

With Rockness' victory, I am crushed. I will now face him in the national finals. I know I must give it my all, but I have never defeated an Asian. And it's his home turf. My odds are one in seven, but really odds don't matter. I know it's down to the Rockness and Björn.

---

[4]The idea of someone trying to make money off of air guitar is obviously ridiculous. Though Aer Lingus and I did once play an eight-minute air duet at a corporate party, and got paid four hundred dollars each. Lingus later told me that when he arrived home that night, he took off his clothes, stood naked on his bed, lathered himself in twenty-dollar bills, and shouted at his girlfriend, "See this? This is air guitar money, baby!" They are no longer together.

Here's how round one of the finals goes:

Rob Brown from Boston sucks.

Charlie "American Breeder" Wilson, from Asheville, North Carolina, in the middle of a cross-country medley that begins with ZZ Top's "La Grange," switches to "Free Bird," and ends with "Welcome to the Jungle," whips off his overalls and plays in his underwear and cowboy hat. Maybe "American Inbreeder" would have been a more apt name? Anyway, he sucks.

Daniel "Glitter" Alvarez uses a *lot* of glitter, but still sucks.

Then I am up.

My whole air guitar career has boiled down to this moment. I'm Eminem in *8 Mile*. I'm every hero of every golf or boxing or karate movie you've ever seen. I'm Gary Cooper in *High Noon*. In my mind, tumbleweeds are rolling across the stage and a brisk wind is rattling the curtains. Time stops.

And then . . . I give the finest fucking performance of my life. And I am not just saying that because it's my last competition and that's how it works in the movies. It really is spectacular. I start off by borrowing Magic Fingers' move from New York and pouring an entire beer on my head. Then I cue the music. Every move is precise, clean. I am so connected with the audience that it feels like we are two teenagers lying down and locking tongues in the flatbed of a pickup truck. My wah-wah pedal move is perfect, my pick slide dead-on. My back-to-the-audience reverse strum combined with butt wiggle is tremendous. When "Set Me Free" hits its final chord and cymbal crash, I hear a roar come over the crowd that sounds as if it's not for me but for someone godlike. Like the second encore of a Led Zeppelin reunion concert—complete with a reanimated John Bonham back from the dead on drums. Someone (presumably female) from the audience throws me a rose. I catch it and put it in my mouth, taking a bow.

"I could watch two hours of that," says Nina Gordon. Score: 6.0

"They keep telling us about a thing called Airness, and we didn't know what it was until now," says John Cho. Score: 6.0

"Erotic and flawless," adds Paul Doucette. Score: 6.0

"There's nothing I can add to that," says Ben Moody. Score: 6.0

I could die a happy man.

But it ain't over till the fat lady sings—or, in this case, till the skinny Asian airs.

Andrew "William Ocean" Litz, from Chicago, is next. He's wearing a jean jacket with cutoff sleeves, very short cutoff jean shorts, and a pink bandanna around his head. Make of that what you will. He plays "Juke Box Hero" by Foreigner. He ends with the evening's second exhibition of full splits (the first was Cherry Lain), and that alone is enough to get him three 5.9s.

During Randy "Big Rig" Strecker's performance, I run downstairs to change into outfit number two: the gold vest and gold mesh pants. It's a risk, I know. The judges may think I'm trying *too* hard, or they may be impressed. The audience may think I look ridiculous or like a rock star. I weigh the options carefully and decide, *What the fuck. This is my last shot.* I change quickly, and wrap myself in my cape to conceal the new threads.

I run back upstairs just in time to see Rockness go to work.

The Rockness Monster, in his third performance of the night, seems well aware of everything that's right about Jane's Addiction.[5] He's re-edited the opening of "Stop!" to announce, "Creado y regado de Los Angeles"—born and bred in Los Angeles—"the Rockness Monster!" As the song is introduced, Rockness with his back to the crowd, slips on his red tasseled armbands. First verse: He tosses his axe into the air (from whence it came) and catches it, moving at full tilt. . . . Then, just as the song's quarter-tempo bridge arrives, Rockness jumps off the drum riser and begins moving in slow motion. With the word "Go!" that leads into the solo, he quickly cranks back into full speed and finishes the action-packed sixty seconds by launching himself into the air over the audience. He lands as gracefully as a feather on the enthusiastically raised hands of the crowd, then surfs back onto the stage to receive unanimous 6.0 scores.

Fuck.

The top three air guitarists now proceed to the ultimate round of the torturously long night: the final compulsory song. William Ocean, Rockness, and I are invited back onstage to listen. It's the Scorpions' "Rock You Like a Hurricane," a song I know about as well as "Happy Birthday" or "Sweet Child O' Mine," which is to say I have rocked out to this song *a lot*. Because we've tied with perfect

---

[5]I've always thought Jane's Addiction made some of the best air guitar music ever. I spent hours in college drunk, alone and with friends, standing on top of coffee tables and beds playing along with songs like "Mountain Song," "Ain't No Right," and "Stop!" Jane's Addiction songs are like car chases, moving with raw, hyperfast intensity until they hit the edge of a cliff, then free-fall, the music slowed as if sinking in murky water. My junior year of college, I discovered that Jane's Addiction offered excellent musical accompaniment to sex. (Freshman year, with the aid of Hüsker Dü, I realized that guitar-heavy rock and punk were far superior to Van Morrison and Miles Davis, which, embarrassingly enough, I had employed for the task in years prior.) This is not a *hard and fast* rule, but if a song is good for getting things rolling in the sack, it's good for air shredding.

scores, a coin toss is necessary to determine who will go last—me or Rockness. Since he represents the home team, Rockness gets to pick heads or tails. He picks heads.

I wonder if you can guess who won the coin toss?

Here's how the story ends:

Total score (out of possible 24): 23.3

William Ocean performs with ignited sparklers in his shoes (Richard Reid–style).

Total score: 23.8

I, Björn Türoque, start off like a Category 5, but the winds quickly die down and I end up more like a Category 2.

Total score: 24

The Rockness Monster is going to Finland.

Epilogue

Where I am, I don't know, I'll never know, in the silence you don't know, you must go on, I can't go on, I'll go on.

—Samuel Beckett, *The Unnamable*

OULU, FINLAND August 29, 2005. "Air guitar is like instant Western meditation," says Tappo Launonen, whom I've nicknamed "The Guru." He sits at a handmade picnic table made of tree trunks, waxing philosophical. He tosses a ball to Devil, one of a family of wolves he is currently training for their starring roles in a Finnish action film.

Devil sinks his fangs into the ball. I recoil in fear.

We are deep in the forests of Finland, about one hundred and seventy-five kilometers east of Oulu. I have come seeking knowledge from the Guru himself, and Tappo (one of the competition's founding fathers) is living up to his reputation as the Yoda of air guitar.

"In the East, it takes time to develop that state of mind, but for us, everything moves so fast. Through air guitar, we can acquire a Zen state."

I nod my head in agreement. It's best to agree with any large Finn holding two adult wolves at bay.

Tappo and I discuss the past, present, and future of air guitar. "Zac Monro has the true spirit of air guitar," Tappo continues. "He has such an aura. All air guitarists have an aura, of course, and this is how I see them perform." A wolf pup hops into Tappo's capacious lap. I am hanging on every word.

"And I think Björn Türoque is like Zac Monro—he has this quality. It is really the purest form of air guitar." I think he may be saying all this in order to make me feel better about my eighth-place finish in the world championship a few nights ago, but then his eyes close and he seems to enter a kind of autoinduced trance. "But C-Diddy . . . he changed air guitar, maybe forever. It is now a performance art. This is not a bad thing; I think it's good for air guitar—it makes it something new." He pauses. The wind has picked up, and I can now see Tappo's breath as he sits, contemplative, speaking slowly and quietly among the wolves. "I miss the Magnet. Zac was the best. . . . He really was the best."

You see, I was all set to let the Rockness Monster go to Finland alone to defend freedom and attempt to secure America's rightful place in the annals of air for the third year in a row. I was ready to go to Jane Air's friend's wedding outside of Boston the weekend of the world finals. Then a friend of mine e-mailed me to ask if I wanted to write a story about the world competition for a British newspaper. How could I say no?

Jane Air was not happy.

But I had to go to Finland for *absolutely the last time, I promise*, in order to attend a funeral—Björn's. (Considering the amount of drinking involved, it was more of a wake, really.) I didn't go expecting to win. It wasn't about winning at that point. I realized that going to Finland one last time offered something I desperately needed: closure.

I start off at High Altitude Camp, where we are provided with an in-depth history of the world championships, choreography training, and a grueling outdoor *air-obic* warm-up. The camp, located on the banks of a malodorous brown body of water known locally as the Asshole River, looks like something out of a slasher movie, complete with bunk beds and a gnarled, macabre-looking tree in the campground's center.

No slashing occurs, but we do attend a lecture by the world's first air guitar PhD candidate: University of Salford grad student Amanda Griffiths, who details the subtle differences between the world stage (song clips are only sixty seconds, people take it rather seriously) and the British regional competitions (songs are up to three minutes, participants are as drunk as humanly possible).[1]

"You've gotta have commitment and believe in what you do,

---

[1] The University of Salford is in England, near the center of Manchester (which happens to be the birthplace of a ton of great bands, including Joy Division and the Stone Roses—if you haven't seen *24 Hour Party People*, do so immediately). Salford is the first university in the world to offer a PhD in air guitar, and Griffiths is thus far its exclusive candidate. Griffiths had read online about the legend of Björn Türoque, and contacted me several months prior to the world championships to exchange thoughts on air guitar. Claiming that we both were equally obsessed with the art form she even suggested that perhaps Björn was the American version of *her*. When I heard she would be here in Oulu, I was worried she would be a complete loser, but after a few beers one night in the Hotel Cumulus bar, I realized her PhD is not a publicity stunt—she gets it. Griffiths is fanatical about air guitar for all the right reasons: the music, the drinking, the performance, and the camaraderie. What will she do with a PhD in air guitar? That remains to be seen. . . .

don't you?" explains Griffiths. She goes on to describe the UK finals (unsanctioned by the AGWC), which have been dominated for the past three years by a legendary air guitarist known as Satan Whoppercock, who embarked on his most recent winning performance by emerging onstage from an eight-foot homemade phallus.

That night, twelve or so air guitar enthusiasts, including myself, from as far away as Japan, Denmark, New Zealand, and the United Arab Emirates, sing songs by the fire, pass around a bottle of whiskey, and sweat together in the traditional Finnish sauna. We wrap up the night by eating grilled sausages in a specially designated sausage hut and playing my favorite musical drinking game, in which one person comes up with a word and everyone takes turns singing a lyric with that word in it. Obviously one's capacity both to think up lyrics as well as to sing them deteriorates rapidly after downing a bottle of whiskey. And like any drinking game, that's the point. The Finns are surprisingly good at the game, knowing far more American pop songs with the word "air" in them than I do.

I awake with a blazing hangover, which takes the entire day to recover from. In that evening's dark-horse round, I narrowly squeeze into the finals by playing an old standby, "California Über Alles," and tie for fourth place with a local Finn, Eero Ojala (which might be either his real or his stage name, I'll never know). Later in the evening, one of the judges, the Finnish world champ of 1999, tells me that my performance looked "too rehearsed," which is why she gave me the 5.3 that nearly knocked me out of the running. Maybe it was my still-throbbing head and alcohol-induced nausea that accounted for my perceived stiffness, or maybe I'm just sick of trying.

After the qualifiers, I muster the energy to host the greatest evening of Aireoke I have ever witnessed. Nobody shits in a pizza box, but it's still spectacular. By evening's end, the entire room has become a sweat-drenched international Aireoke all-star jam session.

Here is a partial list of the evening's song highlights, chosen by air guitar fans from around the world:

"Kickstart My Heart," Mötley Crüe

"Enter Sandman," Metallica

"No One Knows," Queens of the Stone Age

"1969," the Stooges

"50Ft Queenie," PJ Harvey

"Jump," Van Halen

"War Pigs," Black Sabbath

"Symphony of Destruction," Megadeth

"Last Nite," The Strokes

"Fuck Her Gently," Tenacious D

"Cherry Pie," Warrant

"Dueling Banjos," *Deliverance*

"The Final Countdown," Europe

"Walk," Pantera

"Paradise City," Guns N' Roses

"Good Times Bad Times," Led Zeppelin

"You Shook Me All Night Long," AC/DC

"Killing in the Name," Rage Against the Machine

The next day, we head to the press conference to draw numbers for the evening's world final. I remind Marika, the producer of the competition, how I was screwed in 2003, when, despite winning the qualifying round, I had to go first in the finals.

"Yes. Yes. We've changed dat dis year," she says, remembering how I protested in 2003 about this unimaginably unfair oversight on their part. "Dis year we have numbers in a bucket, and everyone will pick der number to find out de order."

"Okay, great. That seems fair," I say.

Of course, minutes later, I pick number one from the bucket anyway. *Number fucking one!* Then I buckle over, laughing.

From that moment on, I know it's over. It's a relief, actually.

"In honor of de tenth anniversary of de air guitar championships," explains Marika after everyone's order has been determined, "de final round will be different this year. De top ten air guitarists of de night will advance to de compulsory round and each pick a number onstage. De number dey pick will correspond to one of de ten years of air guitar championships, and de air guitarist will play de compulsory song from dat year. Dis year's compulsory song," she announces, "will be Green Day, 'American Idiot.' "

So one person would get "American Idiot"; another would get last year's Hives track, "Walk Idiot Walk"; another would get 2003's "Get Your Hands Off My Woman," by The Darkness; and so on. There are some total duds in the mix too, like the lugubrious "Smoke on the

Water" and an obscure Guns N' Roses track from the *Use Your Illusion II* album, the ridiculously titled "Locomotive (Complicity)."

The competition is held in an enormous converted slaughterhouse, with 2,500 Finns in attendance. As in 2003—when over five thousand Finns turned up not for air guitar but to see Hanoi Rocks and Pikku G—most of the audience is there to see the most unpronounceable *humppa*[2] band ever, called Eläkeläiset.

Before the show, the mood is frenzied. Electric. My fellow competitors and I enjoy a group warm-up outside, and I am reminded of the preshow yoga led by Zac Monro in 2003, and though he is not in attendance tonight, his spirit lives on. There really is something absurdly inspiring about a bunch of people in outlandish getups standing in a circle stretching their calves, thighs, and shoulders, preparing to face off in an air guitar competition.

Backstage we help one another get dressed, and pass around a bottle of whiskey. I am shocked at how similar my outfit is to that of the Australian champ, Darrin "Jimmy Dangles" Smith. I tell Dangles repeatedly (I tend to repeat myself when drunk) that he is the spitting image of Jesus—or, at least, the guy who plays Jesus in *Jesus Christ Superstar*, the greatest rock opera film ever made besides *Tommy*. Coincidentally, Dangles tells me he is heading to India to do Christian missionary work after the competition in Oulu.

I am the first competitor on the enormous stage, and though my performance is rock solid, my scores are dismal. It's not just me, though, and I don't think it's because I was the first up—I sense a

[2] *Humppa* is an onomatopoetic word describing the Germanic-sounding accordion music this band of drunken Finns favors. Their songs praise drinking, dancing, and *humppa*.

distinct wave of anti-American sentiment when Sonyk-Rok, last year's champ who is here defending her title, is also given a low score. Granted, it seems to me that her heart isn't in it. Rockness Monster, who puts on a show just as good as the one he did in LA, is scored so low that he isn't even in the top ten, barring him from the final round. Is it a coincidence that "American Idiot" is the compulsory song of 2005? Has the United States' international arrogance and disastrous foreign policy of the past few years finally caught up to her? Have we marred the peace-through-air-guitar mission?

I take over backstage as Executive Whiskey-Bottle Master and proceed to polish off a large percentage of its dark, soothing liquid. The audience, meanwhile, keeps cheering, "Humppa! Humppa!" hoping to get the air guitar segment of the evening over with as quickly as possible.

I'm in tenth place going into the second round, and my luck continues its descent into hell when, of course, I draw the horrific train wreck known as Guns N' Roses' "Locomotive (Complicity)" for my compulsory song. Nearly blind with drunkenness at this point, I have no idea what I am doing onstage. Somehow I pull ahead two slots to secure an eighth-place overall standing. My satisfaction at having finally beaten the Rockness (who finished eleventh overall) is overshadowed by my grief when Team USA gets shut out of even the bronze medal.

The winner is a Dutch guy known as The Destroyer, who dresses as a robot with silver face makeup and does a mechanized air-guitar-meets-performance-art medley of two Daft Punk songs. I analyze his performance as signifying the death of rock and roll, conquered by computers and synthetic music. When I explain this to Destroyer, he has no idea what I am talking about, but nods politely as he holds his prize—the $2,500 handmade Plexiglas Flying Finn guitar.

The group rendition of "Rockin' in the Free World" is spectacular. Flames shoot high into the air, avalanches of confetti drop from the ceiling, and the spirit of world peace is palpable.

Later that night, stumbling through a crowded bar at the after-party, Björn runs into a girl he recognizes. It's one of the members of his Finnish groupie triumvirate of 2003—the cute shy one. Björn is completely shocked to run into her. She says her friend, the gap-toothed girl who danced on his thigh, is also in the bar, and then she phones their other friend who is only blocks away, to join the Björn/groupie reunion.

The girls have hardly aged a bit in two years; in fact, they might just be of legal age now (sixteen in Finland). Björn and the girls share a round of drinks and watch some horrible Finnish hip-hop band play (there is probably no genre of music worse than Finnish hip-hop); he continually repeats how happy he is to see them; and then, abruptly, they all tell him they have to go meet their boyfriends. His disappointment is pronounced. Björn's fantasy of finally reuniting with these blond angels and taking all three of them back to his hotel in true rock star style is shattered. Björn's mojo has left the building.

The air guitar cabal heads back to the basement of Hotel Cumulus, and we stay up until five or six in the morning drinking beer from our honor bars, dancing to MTV—the only source of music—and playing a lot of air guitar. A British guy and I find two small ironing boards, atop which we spontaneously decide to go surfing. After about five seconds, his disintegrates into pieces beneath him and he comes crashing to the floor, to cheers all around.

I wake up sometime around four in the afternoon. I look down at Björn, who slept next to the window on the floor of the hotel room. He is blue and lifeless. His eyes are open, and his hands are clutching an empty whiskey bottle. He smells like puke.

According to the Finnish coroner, Björn died just like Hendrix, Jim Morrison, John Bonham, Stumpy Joe, and Bon Scott—drunkenly choking on his own vomit in the middle of the night. It was the way he would have wanted to go: like a rock star.

I say good-bye to everyone who's still around the hotel, and get into a car with Alexandra, the director of the documentary, who is *still* videotaping my every move. We head south to Tampere, Finland's third-largest city, to visit the luthier of the Flying Finn guitar, Matti Nevalainen. Perhaps mistaking me for the winner of the competition, Matti has me sign one of his guitar bodies, which he hangs on his "wall of fame" among others signed by guitar legends from bands such as Whitesnake, Molly Hatchet, and Roomful of Blues. There's also one signed by C-Diddy. Then we plug in one of his custom guitars with a Lucite top mounted onto real snakeskin. Matti cranks up the amp to eleven, and the small store is engulfed in rock. I am pleasantly reminded that I am actually more skilled on the "there guitar" than I am on the air guitar.

Tampere is a perfectly pleasant town, boasting "the world's

highest gravel ridge," but that's not quite reason enough to stay there. So Alexandra and I head back north to meet up with Tappo, the aforementioned Yoda of air guitar.

Driving through Finland is fairly simple: there are not a lot of cars on the road, but one must keep an eye peeled for the occasional giant moose dashing onto the highway. Fortunately we don't spot any moose, though we do see a family of reindeer grazing in the forest just twenty or so feet from the road.

"*Päivää*,[3] Rudolph!" I shout out the window.

"We spend the day with Tappo, his elfin-looking friend with an unpronounceable name,[4] and his young assistant, as well as the unexpectedly friendly family of wolves. Tappo tells me that although he is no longer directly involved with the competition, he is still proud after ten years that he helped get it started. I thank him for being partially responsible for bringing me all the way to Finland—a country I would never have thought I had any reason to see—twice. I also let him know that both trips provided me with some of the best moments of my life. He understands. He is the Guru.

"When I am standing there in the audience, and the 'Rockin' in the Free World' is playing, and everyone is there with their air guitar," he tells me of the competition's finale two nights ago, "I close my eyes and I feel the music, and it is just me with my air guitar. I feel a little bit of wetness in my eyes, you know? It is quite beautiful, this thing."

---

[3]That's Suomeski, or Finnish, for "hello."

[4]Reijo Jääskeläinen

When Tappo and his friends launched the Air Guitar World Championships in Oulu ten years ago, they had no idea how many lives they would touch. Tappo freely admits that it began as a joke—but behind the joke, there really was a dream of peace through air guitar. Some would find it absurd. Others would embrace it. Some, like myself, would discover their own true calling. But when air guitarists from around the globe are all onstage playing together, it's as if we are in one giant band, as if we're actually creating the music. The sound moves through us. In this brief, transcendent moment when we come together, all the ills of the world have been vanquished. We have achieved their dream.

Tappo's wolf training work is done for the day. The wind has picked up, and we are all hungry. Alexandra and I squeeze into our tiny European rental car and follow Tappo through a rainy deluge back to Oulu. We meet for a final evening's meal at Matala, one of Oulu's best restaurants, according to the Guru. I start with the milk-fed veal carpaccio with artichokes, which is as tender as one would hope razor-thin slices of young calf could be. For an entrée, I know I have no choice but to order the traditional Finnish reindeer fillet with lingonberry sauce. I feel slightly guilty eating Rudolph, but I must say, he is rather delicious.

I look out the window of Matala and notice that the rain has finally stopped. As Alexandra, Tappo, and I sit finishing our wine and reindeer, I wonder if I'll ever return to Oulu. Now that Björn is dead, will I ever compete again? Has air guitar truly saved my life, as Zac "The Magnet" Monro once declared it could? As competitive air guitar continues to become more popular, will it—as the Finns truly believe it can—usher in an era of world peace?

Who knows?

Until then, we'll just have to keep on rockin' in what's left of the free world.

.

*Björn Türoque's Ten Greatest Competitive
Air Guitar Songs of All Time*

Rock critics are big into list making. I'm no rock critic, though;
I'm an air guitarist. I can only speak from years of personal experience in my quest for competitive air guitar glory as to what makes
a track truly roadworthy. When assembling this list, I selected
songs I felt could best lead a performer to the holy land of Airness.
They may not all have the best two-and-a-half-minute-long solos,
but they have drama. I know people will write me angry letters that
I left out some preposterous Yngwie Malmsteen fugue, or that I am
just some pussy who doesn't know shit about rock and roll—and I
encourage you to express yourself as you see fit.[1] As you'll note in
Appendix C, correspondence regarding such matters can get quite
heated, and I look forward to reading your angry diatribes. But
until you've logged as many air miles as I have, you'll just have to
take my advice and pull out your air guitar and give these a rip.

Note: It's up to you to determine the best sixty seconds of each of
these songs and, if need be, cut and paste. Medleys are encour-
aged. Good luck.

---

[1]Björn can be reached at rockstar@aireoke.com.

1. "Ace of Spades," Motörhead. The title track of their 1980 album, "Ace of Spades" is as good as rock gets. It's hard, fast, and vicious. Lemmy's voice sounds as though he eats glass-shard omelets for breakfast—he's the Tom Waits of speed metal. If you can get your hands to move as rapidly as Fast Eddie Clarke's, you're set. As for the lyrics, I can't think of a better metaphor than gambling for the high-stakes world of competitive air guitar.

2. "Set Me Free," Sweet. My performance to this song not only broke my own personal losing streak, but was also enough to convince the most adamantly anti–air guitar person I've ever met that doing sound for an air guitar competition was not, as he first believed, the nadir of his thirty-year career in rock. If you don't own Sweet's *Desolation Boulevard*, you are not worthy.

3. "Kickstart My Heart," Mötley Crüe. I originally had Metallica's "Master of Puppets" in this slot, but the Crüe had two umlauts more than Metallica, and sometimes it comes down to umlauts. From the opening, where the guitar's retuning sounds like a motorcycle accelerating and switching gears, to the bridge—a quiet, self-reflective moment where Vince Neil talks about how the Crüe is "still kickin' ass" after all these years—to the solo, which sounds as though it's processed through a dying gorilla, this is an air guitarist's wet dream. The best part: get the audience to sing along with the *whoa*s and the *yeah*s, and the number of the beast is imminent: 6.0, 6.0, 6.0.

4. "Crazy Train," Ozzy Osbourne. As two-time world champion air guitarist Zac Monro once told me, "Air guitar is like a speeding locomotive:

you've no idea where it's heading." Ozzy seems to know exactly where he's heading in this song—off the rails with a mad quickness. *Guitar World* magazine readers declared Randy Rhoads' "Crazy Train" guitar solo the ninth-best guitar solo of all time, making it the fourth-best *air guitar* song of all time according to Björn Türoque. There's logic in there somewhere. Added bonus: the lyrics are about world peace. Seriously—look 'em up.

5. **"California Über Alles," Dead Kennedys.** The DKs' first single has staccato stops, sudden tempo shifts, a bridge with a mounting crescendo, and a military march at the end. One could probably write a PhD dissertation on the lyrics alone. There's no solo, but who cares—there's almost *too much* to work with already in this three-minute-and-one-second hardcore punk masterpiece. Oh, and the singer's first name is Jello, the bassist's name is Klaus Flouride, and I need not mention the song title's (nongratuitous) umlaut.

6. **"The Mole," The Bags.** This song is about masturbation (at least, it is to me), which is, come to think of it, a much better metaphor than gambling for air guitar (see #1). "The Mole" moves at breakneck speed, allowing you to cram multifarious moves into your sixty seconds, and the guitar's distorted tone is so sharp and crisp that it will slice through the souls of the judges (presuming they have souls, which, if they are judging an air guitar competition, cannot be counted on—especially if they work for a music management company).

7. **Van Halen: where to begin?** As noted earlier in the book, "Eruption" is a competition cliché, but it provides an excellent training ground to get your fingers warmed up and nimble. "Hot for Teacher," "Yankee Rose" (a David Lee Roth solo effort with Steve Vai on guitar), "Ice Cream Man" (for an acoustic to electric changeover), and "Unchained": any of the above should be considered worthy of inspiring airisimilitude. If air keyboard competitions ever take off, "Jump" is the obvious choice.

8. **"You Shook Me All Night Long," AC/DC.** Angus' melodic, perfect solo on this track lasts exactly thirty seconds, giving you another thirty to prove your mettle. It's such a crowd-pleaser that even Celine Dion performed a live cover of the song. (Best to stick with the original for competition, though.)

9. **"Led Medley (Björn Türoque Special Edition)," Led Zeppelin.** These are the songs, in order, that I edited down to make my lick-o-licious Led Medley: "Good Times Bad Times," "The Ocean," "Heartbreaker," "Living Loving Maid (She's Just a Woman)," "Whole Lotta Love," "Kashmir," "Stairway to Heaven," "In the Evening," and "The Ocean" again, because the ending is like a totally different song. Pretty much any Led Zeppelin track could be used in competition, except for "D'Yer Mak'er," which is basically reggae—a genre totally off-limits for air guitar.

10. **"Get Your Hands Off My Woman," The Darkness.** Justin Hawkins, lead shrieker of The Darkness, once said, "I find the process of air guitaring rather silly." If he hadn't said this, I would have put this song higher. It is, however, the only song on the top-ten list written in the last fifteen years.

Andy McCoy & Angela McCoy
Hanoi Rocks Guitarist/Air Guitar Judge: Oulu, 2003

A reality television show about Andy and Angela titled *The McCoys Show* ran in Finland in 2003, with approximately one million viewers (or 20 percent of the population of Finland) tuning in for each episode. Today, Hanoi Rocks continues touring, playing numerous shows throughout Europe and Japan.

Zac "The Magnet" Monro
World Champion 2001, 2002

"I wander the streets of London lonely as a crowd, and I think to myself that life is a circus: everyone wants to be the ringmaster and wear the big hat, but we are all just clowns here, walking down the street looking longingly at hot-looking acrobat chicks in leotards, with lots of makeup, and feathers coming out of their asses.

"I'm very happy with where air guitar is right now, though I wish the UK would get its act together and set up a world-sanctioned national championship rather than the cabaret that takes place every year."

David "C-Diddy" Jung
2003 New York, Los Angeles, World Champion; 2004 Third Place, World Championships

Retired from competitive air guitar and living in Los Angeles, C-Diddy is pursuing his thespian quest to be a guest star on *Friends*—which stopped airing in 2004. The PUDS Scooper business (www.pudsscooper.com), his family's pooper-scooper manufacturing company, has grown considerably in the past few years, and C-Diddy continues his war to clean up the streets of America. C-Diddy and his wife, Kim, plan to have kids soon—airs to the throne, no doubt.

Rory "Air-Do-Well" O'Flaherty
2003 New York Competitor, Unranked

Air-Do-Well lives in New York City and deejays at the monthly Aireoke party where he has been known to leap from the DJ booth for impromptu performances. Air-Do-Well retired from competition in 2004, though rumors of a future comeback are "rife on the circuit," so he claims.

Dan "The Airtight Messiah" Kapelovitz
2003 Los Angeles Competitor, Unranked

The Airtight Messiah, aka Dan Kapelovitz, still acts as the figurehead of The Partridge Family Temple, "an unpop-culture-worshipping, psychedelic sex cult" (www.PartridgeFamilyTemple.com), and produces the "mind-expanding television program" *The Three Geniuses* (www.3geniuses.com).

Gordon "Krye Tuff" Hintz
2003 Los Angeles Champion

Krye Tuff is currently an instructor in the political science department at the University of Wisconsin–Oshkosh, where he teaches American government. He also remains a local government consultant with Public Administration Associates, LLC. He'll continue running for the Wisconsin State Assembly until he wins.

Tuff performed with an air band at the First Presbyterian Church talent show in May of '05, and reportedly blew some minds. "I saw Def Leppard this summer, and during 'Photograph' I went off and these girls were throwing money at me. I think about the 'perfect minute' all the time and get busted at intersections playing in my car."

Lance "The Shred" Kasten
2003, 2004, 2006 New York Competitor, Unranked

Lance "The Geritol Shredmaster," as he now calls himself, gave the New York City regional another go in 2006 with a fiery rendition of Green Day's "Jesus of Suburbia," which his sixteen-year-old daughter picked out for him. Unfortunately the judges weren't feeling it. The Shred waits for the day when his daughters can take up the air guitar torch that burns so deeply within him.

MiRi "Sonyk-Rok" Park
2004 New York, Los Angeles, and Disputed World Champion;
2005 Seventh Place, World Championships

Since herniating a disc in her lower back in January of 2006, MiRi "Sonyk-Rok" Park has been playing her air guitar *unplugged*. As an American Studies graduate student at Columbia University she is writing her thesis on the history of B-boying in New York City, and will graduate in the spring of 2007. Herniated disc or not, Sonyk-Rok is never seen without her air guitar.

Fatima "Rockness Monster" Hoang
2005 Los Angeles and U.S. Champion; Eleventh Place, World Championships

After his tragic eleventh-place finish at the 2005 World Championships, the Rockness Monster spent several weeks in a recovery program at an undisclosed location. He now teaches ceramics at Glendale Community College.

He still carries his axe and is a regular on the Aireoke and competitive circuits.

"Psycho" Dave Roberts
2004 Los Angeles Competitor, Unranked; 2005 Los Angeles Runner-Up

"Psycho" Dave Roberts is a graduate student at the University of Miami, studying broadcast journalism. Does he miss working for The Tesh? "I learned a lot working for Tesh. And, after all, it was while working for him that I discovered air guitar, so that's really great. Tesh gets made fun of a lot, and there were a lot of times when he'd yell at me, and a couple of those times it was for something that was genuinely my fault. But I should say, though, that he really pushed me to be my best, and a lot of my drive was not just because I didn't want to get yelled at, but because I wanted to show him that I was someone he could count on. I hope that he saw me as someone he could count on, because thankfully he didn't fire me.

"I am still doing air guitar and I'm still loving rock and roll with the same fire and passion as I did when I first discovered it. As far as the love life goes . . . I love all of you. And yes, I'm still available . . . TO ROCK! (And ladies, my e-mail address is psychodave@psychodaverocks.com.)"

Michael "Mother" Rucker
2004 Minneapolis Champion

Michael "Mother" Rucker was last spotted touring the rat-infested bars and fluorescent-drenched DMVs of the Pacific Northwest. A worried admirer observed, "Mother has gone somewhere dark, and I don't know if he'll return unscathed." While pledging his eternal bachelorhood ("until Angelina Jolie comes around"), MR continues to wed himself to the love of "the rock" and sexiness of "the roll." His injuries are healing nicely.

Ambrose "Magic Fingers" Martos
2005 New York Runner-Up

Ambrose Martos spent 2006 on a one-year tour as a "principal clown" with Cirque du Soleil.

Andrew "William Ocean" Litz
2005 Chicago Champion; 2006 New York Champion

2005's Sparkler-footed Chicago champ William Ocean moved to the Big Apple in 2006 in order to compete against more worthy opponents. There, he narrowly defeated "Couch Potato" for the 2006 New York championship by leaping into the air and landing on his back—stealthily crushing a beer can in the process.

Michael "The Destroyer" Heffels
2005 World Champion

"It's funny how people suddenly take this thing for serious when you're the world champion," Heffels wrote from Amsterdam. "You figure the Dutch don't grow world champions on trees." The Destroyer spent 2006 traveling the world doing roughly two air guitar gigs and workshops each month in places like Finland, France, Great Britain, and Japan. Destroyer also experimented with the new "Virtual Air Guitar" at Helsinki's Heureka Science Center: "The idea is cool, you put on some orange gloves (which are read by a camera) and then you move your hands around your virtual guitar. The left hand makes chords (lower to higher notes) and the right hand plays the rhythm. You also have a foot switch you can use to play in the 'solo mode.' It's all MIDI and very slow to respond, so it sounds shitty and is hard to play. Often things come out randomized. But like I said, the idea is good, it just needs some more development."

Amanda "Kiki" Griffiths
Air Guitar PhD Student

Since a fiery exchange following the Oulu competition in 2005 (where Kiki was a judge), lines of communication between Björn and the world's only Air Guitar PhD student have been tragically severed. One can only assume that a lucrative professorship in the field awaits her upon completion of her PhD.

Cedric "Aer Lingus" Devitt
U.S. Air Guitar Partner

In 2003, Aer Lingus retired from professional competition to start the U.S. Air Guitar Championships with co-commissioner T. Ruckspin. It's been almost nothing but air ever since. If you ever want to catch up with him you'll find him backstage drinking with other air guitarists, exchanging war stories about the golden years of air guitar. In his spare time, Lingus works for an interactive ad agency making pop-up banners.

Kriston "DJ Teddy Ruckspin" Rucker
U.S. Air Guitar Partner

Teddy Ruckspin comes up with names for companies and products. "Need a name for a new toothpaste? A mega-mall with indoor skydiving? I'm your guy."

Though he was instrumental in bringing competitive air guitar to the United States, Ruckspin chooses to work strictly *behind the scenes* and prefers to focus on developing future world champions. "I am a scary judge of air guitar talent," he says. "The U.S. Air Guitar Championships are reaching more cities every year and we hope that it will soon be widely recognized as our unofficial national pastime. If there's one thing that America deserves to dominate, it's air guitar."

Ruckspin was last seen smuggling a cheeseburger out of a hotel suite in Austin, Texas, drunkenly shouting, "How ya like me now? Oh yeah, now you're all my best buddies, right? Now I got a cheeseburger in my hand! You aren't my real friends. You're fucking transparent."

Alexandra "The Airess" Lipsitz
Director, *Air Guitar Nation*

In 2006, The Airess celebrated the U.S. premiere of her award-winning documentary, *Air Guitar Nation*, by kickin it old-school in her Ratt hat, partying down with her air guitar posse, and doing some mean shredding of her own. If there's air guitar happening, the Airess will be there to capture it on camera.

Björn Türoque & Dan Crane
Perennial Second Place Air Guitarist/Author

This is the last known photo of Björn and Dan. They were researching air groupies in a hot tub somewhere in Los Angeles.

E-mails from Deranged Air Guitarists

(Special thanks to US Air Guitar for some of these)

1/25/2003

I want an air guitar stick. Please explain to me how I can get one. It's really important. If you have one lying around I could use, please mail it to me as soon as possible.

Thanks

Mark
Orlando, FL

9/24/2004

Dear AIR guitarists and supporters:

You people make me sick to my stomach, literally. I saw the Mika or whatever the hell her name is on Conan Show and I seriously wanted to throw up. I thought this world was going to hell in a handbasket for music wise as it was, but you people (and your STUPID air guitar s#*T) made it even worse. You put the most horrible label on music, and you are the biggest disgrace I've ever seen to society. One phrase for you people: GET A LIFE! For God's sake, get hobbies, get lifes. Or here's a pointer: get a REAL guitar! You are losers that don't understand how to cherish and show your appreciation to rock and roll and/or other music. I mean for God's sake, when that oriental "champion" girl was on Conan O'Brian show, he said something along the lines of "just make sure not to break your F string" and she started laughing like she agreed. Then he was like "well you can't because there is no F string on your guitar . . . or is there?" and she looked confused. Does that stupid cheap woman not know the F*#King string names on the guitar?! What kind of world is this coming to where people have INTERNATIONAL competitions of who plays the best AIR guitar?! My 3 year old BROTHER could play air guitar. This is a disgrace, and I know many people that I've talked to that feel the exact same way. You people deserve a slap across the face. Disgusting losers . . .

Sincerely,

a disgusted resident of Michigan, USA

(The same guy follows up with another e-mail a few months later.)

1/7/05

Why is God's name would you have a AIR GUITAR competition? You think that crap takes talent? It's people like you that are making the music industry go to complete crap. The only thing people get famous for anymore is if they have a 'cool' or 'attractive' image to sell. People don't make music anymore because they LOVE it, they do it in today's society because it's "cool" and it makes great money. This is complete crap, and I feel so bad for musical legends who have to see something that they started go to such CRAP. I wonder how Jimmy Page, or Eric Clapton, or Paul McCartney think of this . . . This is complete crap, and you people need lives, and stop selling talentless industry junk.

7/15/05

Björn,

Great job last night. Genuine airness. Rockness Monster was great, but in that last round, you got jobbed. The combination of the hometown fans and peer pressure on the judges gave them no choice. Okay, they had a choice, but an unpopular one. Sorry you had to be the bridesmaid this time around but take solace in knowing that you were the best in the house.

Eric

8/1/05

Hello,

I've practiced actual guitar playing and studied music seriously for the past 10 years. I've performed the music of Frank Zappa, Steve Vai, Joe Satriani and other "impossibles" many, many times; my mind and fingers are each "rockstars" in their own right. I've also been taking dance lessons for the past couple years (ballet, jazz, tap and hip-hop) to improve my body dexterity and stage presence. Now, I want to—as the real deep and mystic people say—"transcend" the guitar altogether by playing no guitar at all.

My question: Where can I find some quality DVD tutorials to guide and improve my air guitar skills?

Andrew Gregor
www.AndrewGregor.com
guitarist.performer.transcriber

9/29/05

Hello Björn,

My name is Charlie and I am an undergrad student at Harvard. I am writing you because I discovered professional air guitar through the internet this summer and instantly became obsessed. In fact, I was so moved by it all that a friend and I wrote a one-act musical about air guitar for a student playwright festival on campus this fall.

The musical is called "Finding Their Guitar" and tells the story of a boy destined to be a rock star. Unfortunately, he is born with a rare degenerative disease that causes weakness in his arms, so he cannot hold a guitar. When he thinks all is lost, a guru appears and teaches him about the art of air guitar. The guitarist agrees to follow the path to airness and the musical ends with his championship competition performance. This musical is a heartwarming story of overcoming adversity and is a lesson about life as much as it is about air guitar. It's a comedy by the way it takes the subject matter so seriously, and I feel it is very much in the spirit of air guitar and in accord with the outreach you do.

We would be honored if you could make it to the performance, but understand that the life of a rockstar is a busy one, so we do not expect your attendance. If you get a chance, please write me back and let me know if you want more info—I could even send you a copy of the script if you are interested. Also, do you know how to contact C-Ditty (sic)? You and he were our greatest artistic influences, and I would love to be able to reach him as well.

Thank you for your time, and I look forward to hearing from you.

Air thee well,

Charlie

12/8/05

Dear Björn Türoque,

Last night I had a dream that we were both competing in an air guitar competition. You truly were on top of your game, playing air guitar with your teeth again and with hot ice packs in your sleeves. At the end of the night, we were tied. In order to break a tie, the judges called for an "air-off." We had to play to the same song at the same time! I don't know who won, but it was a blast!

Mike

Air Kisses

Björn and Dan would like to thank the following people without whom a) our air guitars would not exist, and b) this book would have been ridiculously impossible:

Zoë "Jane Air" Wolff whose help and support was infinite.

Alex "The Airess" Lipsitz for always keeping the camera rolling, Cedric "Aer Lingus" Devitt, and Kriston "Teddy Ruckspin" Rucker for rightly believing that air guitar would be the next American pastime.

Matt "Jairy Maguire" McGowan who convinced me it was a good idea to write a book about an invisible art form. Sean "Ninja Master" McDonald, Larissa "Doolbot" Dooley, and Ben "Les Paul" Gibson for making the book an *actual* book.

The Magical Elves: Jane "Hot Lips" Lipsitz, Dan "Aircut" Cutforth, Bri "Fire Woman" Dellinger, Jackie "Air Supplier of Desire" Robbins, Michael "Mother Rucker" Rucker, and Tim "Devil May Air" Sullivan, as well as Anna "The Barbairian" Barber for keeping the air circulating.

Pauline "MacGuffin" O'Connor, Dave "6 Feet Over" Jargowsky, Jon "I Hate Air Guitar" Huck, Minji "Kimchee Power" Kim, Marika "Finnair" Lambert, Ralph "Rufus Sewer" Martin, Rory "Air-Do-Well" O'Flaherty, Adam "Sunshine Superman" Higginbotham, Vanessa "Lil' Wanderer" Mobley, Dale "The Bedazzler" Hrabi, Jane "Airbus" Bussmann, Hugh "The Airy Freak" Rodman, Sean "Awesomely Fine" Gottlieb, Josh "Air Brunch" Liberson, Eve "Fresh Air" Abrams, Amy "Grin N' Air It" Barrett, Jonathan "Lethal Weapon" Lethem, Morgan "Moog" Harting, "Airoline" Harting, Danielle "Duchess of Stratosphere" Dispaltro, Yoktan "Airsatz" Haddad, Charlie "Southpaw Shooter" Amter, Seth "The Edumacator" Meyers, Amanda "Kiki" Griffiths, Ethan "Power" Gold, Katrina "F-Stop" Dickson, Rahav "Snap" Segev, and Susannah "The Viking Valkyrie" Sayler for advice, wisdom, outfits, photos, drinks, and keeping me afloat.

The air guitarists: Zac "The Magnet" Monro, David "C-Diddy" Jung, Fatima "Rockness Monster" Hoang, MiRi "Sonyk-Rok" Park, Gordon "Krye Tuff" Hintz, Dan "The Airtight Messiah" Kapelovitz, David "Psycho Dave" Roberts, Jay "Jammin J-Bone" Rostosky, and everyone else who never stopped rocking.

The family: Nancy "Rocket Chick" Conrad, Mike "Major Menace" Crane, Janice "Super Nana" Lubbin, Seymour "Grandmaster Snack" Fortner, and Jeff "Snackboy" Crane for giving me air.

And Friedrich "The Nihilist" Nietzsche—thanks for nothin'.

Dan Crane writes about music, food, and culture for the *New York Times*, *Slate*, and the *Los Angeles Times*. He also plays in a faux French rock and roll band called Nous Non Plus.

Björn Türoque has participated in numerous air guitar competitions throughout the world. Since joining the circuit, he and his air guitar have appeared on CNN, VH1, *Last Call with Carson Daly*, *Fox & Friends*, in a *Bill & Ted's Excellent Adventure* special edition DVD, and in a Japanese girl band's music video. He's lectured on the subject at the Experience Music Project museum in Seattle, and is the founder of Aireoke: when air guitar meets karaoke. His heroes are guitarist Jimmy Page, sculptor Richard Serra, and philosopher Friedrich Nietzsche. Björn retired from official competition in 2005.